India and the Pandemic

India and the Pandemic

The First Year

Essays from *The India Forum*

Orient BlackSwan

INDIA AND THE PANDEMIC: THE FIRST YEAR

ORIENT BLACKSWAN PRIVATE LIMITED

Registered Office
3-6-752 Himayatnagar, Hyderabad 500 029, Telangana, India
e-mail: centraloffice@orientblackswan.com

Other Offices
Bengaluru, Chennai, Guwahati, Hyderabad, Kolkata, Mumbai, New Delhi, Noida, Patna, Visakhapatnam

First published by Orient Blackswan Private Limited 2021

ISBN 978-93-5442-009-2

032782

Typeset in
Adobe Jenson Pro 11/13
by Shine Graphics, Delhi 110 094

Printed in India at
Akash Press, New Delhi

Published by
Orient Blackswan Private Limited
3-6-752 Himayatnagar, Hyderabad 500 029, Telangana, India
e-mail: info@orientblackswan.com

Contents

Abbreviations *ix*
Tables and Figures *xiii*
Acknowledgements *xvii*

Introduction 1
Faizi Ahmad, C. J. Kuncheria and *C. Rammanohar Reddy*

Section I—Early Stages of Covid-19 in India

1. Covid-19 in India: The Chronicle of a Pandemic Foretold 25
Thomas Abraham

2. Coping with the Coronavirus Pandemic: Are Indians Safe? 32
K. Sujatha Rao

Section II—Dealing with Pandemics in India's History

3. Covid-19 and the Spectres of Colonialism 45
Pratik Chakrabarti

4. Manufacturing Epidemics: Pathogens, Poverty and Public Health Crises in India 54
Sheetal Chhabria

5. 'The Government Will Come to Its Senses': Calcutta's Workers and the Plague of 1898 66
Prerna Agarwal

6. Past and Present: Can India Beat Corona the Way it Beat Smallpox? 73
Harish Naraindas

Section III—Covid-19: The Initial Impact

7. India's Tryst with Covid-19 93
Vikram Patel

8. The Twin Crises of Covid-19 and How to Resolve Them 101
Ananda Lal Roy and *Maitreesh Ghatak*

Section IV—The Law, the Judiciary and Covid-19

9. Exodus Constitutionalism: Mass Migration in Covid-19 Lockdown Times 113
Upendra Baxi

10. Gendering the Pandemic in the Prison 130
Pratiksha Baxi and *Navsharan Singh*

11. Migrant Workers, the Lockdown and the Judiciary 145
Harsh Mander

Section V—The Lockdown and After

12. India's Lockdown 157
Debraj Ray, S. Subramanian and *Lore Vandewalle*

13. Hunger Grows as India's Lockdown Kills Jobs: Results of a Survey from 12 States 171
Rahul Lahoti, Amit Basole, Rosa Abraham, Surbhi Kesar and *Paaritosh Nath*

14. How Many Casual Workers in the Cities Have Sought To Go Home? 182
Nomaan Majid

15. The Gig Economy in the Pandemic: Outsourcing Risk, Privatising Gain? 193
Gayatri Nair

Section VI—Impact on the Economy

16. Understanding India's Economic Slowdown: Need for Concerted Action 205
R. Nagaraj

17. The Unequal Effects of the Covid-19 Crisis on the Labour Market 243
Radhicka Kapoor

18. States' Loss of Fiscal Autonomy in a Centralised Federal System 255
M. Govinda Rao

19. Knowns and Unknowns in the Covid-19–triggered Global Economic Crisis 263
C. P. Chandrasekhar

Section VII—Impact on Society

20. Psychosocial Challenges in the Midst of the Coronavirus 275
Honey Oberoi Vahali

21. A Novel Virus, a New Racial Slur 284
Naorem Pushparani Chanu and *Gorky Chakraborty*

Section VIII—The Future

22. Extreme Events in Nature: An Ecological History of the Present 295
Ramprasad Sengupta

23. Four Future Scenarios, or, What's Different about the Covid-19 Crisis? 311
Itty Abraham

24. Seven Lessons for the Future: For the World after Covid-19 320
Prem Chandavarkar

Notes on the Contributors 333

Abbreviations

ACT-UP	AIDS Coalition to Unleash Power
APU	Azim Premji University
BoP	Balance of payments
BPO	Business process outsourcing
CARES	Coronavirus Aid, Relief and Economic Security
CDC	Centres for Disease Control and Prevention
CES	Consumer expenditure survey
CMIE	Centre for Monitoring Indian Economy
CPI	Consumer price index
CrPC	Criminal Procedure Code
CSE	Centre for Sustainable Employment
CSO	Central Statistical Office
DMA	Disaster Management Act
DPIIT	Department of Promotion for Industry and Internal Trade
DUET	Decentralised urban employment and training
ECB	External commercial borrowing
EDB	Ease of Doing Business
EUS	Employment and Unemployment Survey
FDI	Foreign direct investment
FPI	Foreign portfolio investment
GDP	Gross domestic product
GST	Goods and Services Tax
HPC	High Power Committee
IBC	Insolvency and Bankruptcy Code
ICMR	Indian Council of Medical Research
ICU	Intensive care unit
IDP	Internally displaced person
IEC	Information, Education and Communication
ILFS	Infrastructure Leasing and Financial Services

ILO	International Labour Organisation
IMA	Indian Medical Association
IMF	International Monetary Fund
IOM	International Organisation for Migration
IPBES	Intergovernmental Science Policy Platform on Biodiversity and Ecosystem Services
IPL	Indian Premier League
MERS-CoV	Middle East respiratory syndrome coronavirus
MGNREGA	Mahatma Gandhi National Rural Employment Guarantee Act
MGNREGS	Mahatma Gandhi National Rural Employment Guarantee Scheme
MSME	Micro, small and medium enterprise
NAS	National Accounts Statistics
NBA	News Broadcasters Association
NCRB	National Crime Records Bureau
NCW	National Commission of Women
NDA	National Democratic Alliance
NFSS	National Food Security Scheme
NMW	National minimum wage
NPA	Non-performing asset
NRC	National Register of Citizens
NREGS	National Rural Employment Guarantee Scheme
NSO	National Statistical Office
NSS	National Sample Survey
NSSO	National Sample Survey Organisation
OBC	Other Backward Castes
OCI	Overseas Citizens
OECD	Organisation for Economic Cooperation and Development
ONGC	Oil and Natural Gas Corporation
OPEC	Organisation for Petroleum Exporting Countries
PCR	Polymerase Chain Reaction
PCS	Private corporate sector
PDS	Public distribution system
PIL	Public interest litigation
PLFS	Periodic Labour Force Survey

PPE	Personal protective equipment
PPP	Public–private partnership
QE	Quantitative easing
R&D	Research and development
RBI	Reserve Bank of India
RT-PCR	Reverse transcription polymerase chain reaction
RWS	Regular wage salaried
SAARC	South Asian Association for Regional Cooperation
SAL	Social action litigation
SARS-CoV-2	Severe acute respiratory syndrome coronavirus 2
SC	Scheduled Castes
SHO	Station house officer
ST	Scheduled Tribes
SWAN	Stranded Workers Action Network
UAPA	Unlawful Activities (Prevention) Act
UNCTAD	United Nations Conference on Trade and Development
UNHCR	United Nations High Commissioner for Refugees
UPS	Usual Principal Status
UPSS	Usual Principal + Subsidiary Status
UTP	Undertrial prisoners
VAT	Value-added tax
WHO	World Health Organisation

Tables and Figures

Tables

I.1 Growth 2020 and Covid-19: Asian Economies 11

10.1 Age of Women in Pandemic-struck Prisons, June 2020 131

14.1 Size and Distribution of the Workforce (UPS), 2017–18 184
14.2 Accommodation Arrangements of Casual Workers (Percentage Distribution), 2018 185
14.3 Distribution of Accommodation Arrangements of Casual Workers by Period of Stay, 2018 186
14.4 Distribution of Adverse Accommodation Arrangements of Casual Workers by Duration, 2018 187
14.5 Size of Select Casual Labour Categories, 2017–18 188
14.6 All Urban Workers with Adverse Accommodation Contracts, 2017–18 189

16.1 Total Employment, Labour Force, Unemployment Rates, 2004–05 to 2017–18 218
16.2 Agriculture and Rural Wages (Year-on-year Wage Growth in %), 2014–18 219
16.3 India's GDP by Items of Final Demand (%), 2011–12 to 2017–18 223

17.1A Average Monthly Wage/Salary Earnings for RWS Workers in Current Weekly Status (Rs), 2018–19 245
17.1B Average Earnings Per Day by Casual Labour Engaged in Works Other than Public Works (Rs), 2018–19 245

17.1C Average Gross Earnings during the Last 30 Days from Self-employment Work in Current Weekly Status (Rs), 2018–19 245
17.2 Distribution of Workers by Educational Qualifications within Each Category of Employment (%), 2018–19 246
17.3 Distribution of Workers across Sectors by Educational Qualifications, 2018–19 248
17.4 Sectoral Breakdown of Employment by Employment Category (%), 2018–19 249

Figures

13.1 State-wise Distribution of Respondents, 2020 173
13.2 Work Activity Status of Respondents Prior to Lockdown, 2020 174
13.3 Loss of Employment for those who were Working in February 2020 175
13.4 Employment Loss by Work Activity Status in February 2020 176
13.5 Impact on Households, 2020 177
13.6 Reach of Relief Measures, 2020 178

16.1 Annual GDP Growth Rate (%), 2012–13 to 2019–20 212
16.2 Inflation Rate (%) and Oil Price ($/Barrel), 2012–13 to 2018–19 214
16.3 Saving and Investment Ratios (% of GDP), 2005–06 to 2017–18 214
16.4 Trade Ratios, 2011–12 to 2017–18 215
16.5 Share of Manufacturing and Industry in GDP, 2013 and 2018 216
16.6 RBI Capacity Utilisation Index, 2008–09 to 2019–20 217
16.7 Value of Stalled Projects as a Percentage of Total Projects under Implementation, 2012–19 217
16.8 Poverty Rates in India (% of Population), 1993–94 to 2017–18 221

16.9 Bank NPAs as a Percentage of Gross Advances, 2006–07 to 2017–18 225
16.10 R&D Expenditure as a Percentage of GDP, India and China, 1996–2018 233

22.1 Total World-wide Number of Natural Disaster Events Recorded, 1970–2019 296
22.2 Milankovitch Cycles 301

Acknowledgements

The essays in this volume were written at a difficult time for the authors. All of them were struggling with the lockdown and dealing with different aspects of Covid-19. Yet, they responded immediately to requests for essays from *The India Forum*, a publication that was barely a year old, and produced high-quality analysis.

The authors were all equally prompt in agreeing to have their pieces published in this volume, and very quickly made the corrections and revisions as needed to be done.

Our gratitude, therefore, to the authors who with their essays have given this collection a breadth and depth that we are sure readers will appreciate.

Equally deserving of our gratitude are the publishers, Orient BlackSwan, who saw the value of this volume, and agreed to our proposal. At Orient BlackSwan, Nilanjana Majumdar and Insiya Poonawala shepherded the publication process with the highest level of professionalism, and to them a special thank you. Insiya is any author's dream editor. Where it is often the author who keeps making demands of the editor to complete the editing process, here it was the other way around and we were kept on our toes. So it is thanks to her that this was done in time.

We hope the readers of this volume will find the essays here rich in analysis and insight.

C. Rammanohar Reddy
Editor, *The India Forum*
Hyderabad, 5 January 2021

Introduction

Faizi Ahmad, C. J. Kuncheria and C. Rammanohar Reddy

In early January 2020, when news reports first started appearing outside China about a new virus that was causing a 'pneumonia-like' illness among the people of Wuhan, *The New York Times* reported, 'There is no evidence that the new virus is readily spread by humans, which would make it particularly dangerous, and it has not been tied to any deaths' (Wee and McNeil, Jr 2020).

It did not take long for humanity to realise that this was a particularly dangerous virus. The scale of the upheaval in the world since has been immense; no part of the world has been left untouched, and no aspect of human life unaffected. By end 2020, over 1.5 million people had died worldwide; the global economy had contracted the deepest since the Second World War; and the gains over the decades in poverty eradication, health and wellbeing may have been erased.

Even a year after the severe acute respiratory syndrome coronavirus 2 (SARS-CoV-2) was identified, there continues to be a struggle to fully understand how the virus spreads; the impact that the novel coronavirus (Covid-19) disease has on human beings; and the medium- and long-term social and economic consequences of the pandemic.

No society can claim to have got the better of the virus in its first year of spread. Some countries were indeed less affected than the others (the countries on the African continent stood out in this regard). Some, for both locational and specific reasons, did do better than the others (New Zealand, which is relatively isolated, also enjoyed a determined and caring administration, for example). Early successes were soon overtaken by a 'second wave' of infections, which even in countries like Germany, that had reasonably dealt with the early onslaught, threatened to overwhelm health systems and people alike, and push them into yet another cycle of lockdowns and shutdowns of the economy (Eberle et al. 2020).

The world on the whole has to prepare itself for a long-drawn-out process before it settles down to 'living' with Covid-19 with a measure of normalcy, even if this is going to be a 'new' normal.

Has Covid-19 been a cataclysm for human civilisation then? Large as the disruption has been to all aspects of society, it is yet useful to put things in perspective. The influenza pandemic of 1918–20 also swept the world. It infected about 500 million people—a little under a third of the world's population at the time—and killed an estimated 40–50 million, perhaps more (Taubenberger and Morens 2006). Covid-19 has not yet run its course, but there is optimism grounded in reasonable certainty that we will not experience human fatalities anything like what the world did a century ago with the Spanish influenza. By November 2020, SARS-CoV-2 had infected 67 million people (less than 10 per cent of the world's population of 7.8 billion) and had taken the lives of more than 1.5 million. Tragic as the human cost has been, over 45 million people have been cured so far. Both were novel viruses and for both there was no immunity, but the smaller scale of destruction this time indicates vast improvements over the past century in public health, increases in nutrition, and also the ability of governments to respond to the situation.

The world recovered from the 1918–20 pandemic, and there is no reason why it cannot recover from the 2020 pandemic. The question is: what will the recovery be like? The world learnt little from the 1918–20 pandemic; the colonial powers and the new economies of North America embarked on a wild growth spree, which ended in the Depression of the 1930s that also laid the foundations for the cataclysm that was the Second World War.

Scholars and historians of disasters are relentless in pointing out that there is little that is 'natural' about 'natural disasters'. A massive earthquake, as the one witnessed in Kathmandu in 2015, does not reveal the devastating power locked in tectonic plates, but rather the years of corruption and unplanned development that have rendered cities in fragile terrains vulnerable to destruction. The awesome gale forces of a hurricane lay bare the decades of racialised division of urban amenities and of post-disaster relief in cities, as did Katrina in New Orleans in 2005. The floods that destroy homes, land and livelihoods in north Bihar with yearly regularity speak to the continued reliance on blind technocratic solutions to control rivers, rather than to the furies of the South Asian monsoons. Political ideologies and ruling ideas push towards certain solutions while foreclosing others. It has been pointed out that during the 1918–20 influenza pandemic, 'colonialism's link with commerce and the compulsion to keep trade channels open did provide an excuse to look away from pandemic outbreaks'. Also, 'colonial powers would invest heavily in upgrading public health infrastructure in their own backyards but provide endless excuses to avoid doing the same in their colonies' (Tumbe 2020: 188).

In like manner, Covid-19 puts in plain sight the years of neglect in investing in public health and welfare nets. The spectacle of the United States flailing in its response to the crisis, and progressing to the top of the mortality chart, is an example of how privatised and expensive healthcare are ill-suited to wellbeing. The disparities within states in India in dealing with Covid-19 further illustrate the point. Kerala, with its investments in public healthcare and other social welfare measures, has been able to keep its mortality rates low (even as its famed 'model' in containing the spread has worn at the edges during the course of the year). States that have for years neglected public health have struggled to contain the virus, and the spread of its contagion into wider society.

The coronavirus might be agnostic towards its human hosts, but the paths taken by Covid-19 and its aftermaths are clearly marked out in advance.

By end 2020, a handful of research laboratories and pharmaceutical companies had announced that humanity had won the race to discover a vaccine to immunise the world's populations. Where normally vaccines take years to develop, the concerted global effort—helped somewhat by the prior (and unfortunately) abandoned early-2000s work on SARS vaccines—led to the development and successful trials of a few vaccines. There remained uncertainties about how successful the vaccines would be and, even if they were, what proportion of the population would willingly have itself vaccinated.

The spectre of 'vaccine nationalism' of richer countries hoarding vaccines, and poorer countries unable to afford the enormous costs of vaccinating entire populations, continues to hang over us. Canada, for instance, has stockpiled enough doses to vaccinate its population almost five times over (*BBC* 2020b), while in India, the high quoted price of the developed vaccines could overwhelm the country's budget, and will almost certainly lead to unequal access.[1] A proposal to quickly and cheaply produce generic vaccines, co-sponsored by India and South Africa, by suspending intellectual property rights for any vaccine, has been opposed in the World Trade Organisation by countries including the US and Britain (Prabhala, Jayadev and Baker 2020).

It is clear that societies cannot rely on vaccination as an immediate tool to control the pandemic, and will have to continue using public health measures to deal with the disease. Physical distancing, reduced mobility, staggered reopening of factories and workplaces, and even more lockdowns—all look likely to continue as features in our lives in the second year of the virus.

The eruption one after another of a series of zoonotic diseases since the early 2000s—SARS, H1N1, Ebola, the Middle East respiratory syndrome coronavirus (MERS-CoV), and now SARS-CoV-2—has signalled the need to shift to a different kind of social and economic life. The improvements in air and water quality during the lockdowns in different countries in mid-2020 also indicated what was being lost by high levels of environmentally degrading economic activity. Yet, as the lockdowns were lifted and economies worked to recover lost jobs, the importance of reconsidering our way of life was quickly forgotten. It does seem doubtful whether human societies will learn from the first year of Covid-19 to organise a more conflict-free interaction with wildlife and nature.

II

How did India fare in coping with Covid-19 in the first year of the pandemic?

In the early days, when almost nothing was known about the virus, there was much speculation that India would come out without experiencing the worst of Covid-19. A supposed in-built immunity and the high summer temperatures on the subcontinent would all help the country escape relatively unaffected. These unverified expectations led not only to a neglect of early precautionary measures like the contact tracing (and not just screening) of travellers returning from abroad, but also to the expression of plainly unscientific opinions on containing the virus.

In the event, India has felt the full brunt of Covid-19. The bald figures are that, as of 7 December 2020, 9.70 million Indians were infected by Covid-19 infections, of whom 1,40,974 have died.[2] India registered the second largest number of cases (after the US) and the third highest number of deaths (after the US and Brazil). Given the size of India's population, this scale of infections and deaths should have been expected.

In relative terms—by cases per million population or deaths per million population—India fares much better than what the absolute numbers suggest. Helped by an age structure that weighs in favour of the young (who are known to mainly suffer only mild infections), it has a relatively low case-fatality rate. Yet, it must be noted that there is scepticism about the reported numbers, and legerdemain about what constitutes a 'Covid-19 death'; and we might never exactly know the toll from the disease (Babu 2020; Biswas 2020b; Pulla 2020; Shewade and Parameswaran 2020).

From September 2020 onwards, the number of new infections in India started to drop. Where earlier there were fears that the number would stay around 1,00,000 everyday, they fell to around 20,000 by early December. It would appear that the country had put the worst behind it, absent a 'second wave' in 2021.[3]

Looking back, it is not so much India's inability to prevent the large number of infections in 2020 that should be cause for regret as to how the country coped with the pandemic. There was an absence of community and a lack of humanity in how both the state and society responded to Covid-19. Collectively, the people were wrenched through an enormous amount of suffering which the country, when it looks back later at the events of 2020, will not be proud of.

Much of public discourse orchestrated by the state seemed at times to be more about creating the impression that India was doing very well, than of actually dealing with the pandemic. Clear the fog of propaganda about how well the country did, and there does not seem much to defend in the first year of Covid-19.

On the part of the government, initially there was a reluctance to deal with the approaching pandemic with any serious urgency, distracted as the central political leadership seemed with other events. Then when it was apparent that the pandemic was beginning to spread uncontrollably in the metros, on the evening of 24 March, the central government imposed a three-week national lockdown with just four hours' notice. There was no prior announcement and there seemed to have been no planning, unlike in other countries such as South Africa, which did give some warning and had carried out as much planning as was possible in an emergency situation.[4] The lockdown in India lasted for a total of nine weeks (25 March to 1 May, and was then extended partially or fully in different parts of the country until 31 May). The Indian lockdown was considered the most severe in the world,[5] but one does not need the counter-factual to acknowledge that it failed to control the spread of the virus.

When the lockdown was finally lifted, infections and deaths started to rise sharply, with India in a few months becoming the country with the second largest number of infections. It also turned out that neither the central nor the state governments had used the lockdown to strengthen public health facilities on an emergency footing to cope with the spurt in infections that was to follow, though that was one of the unstated justifications for the lockdown. The 'life over livelihood' argument had failed, with both lives and livelihoods lost to the pandemic and the lockdown.

Even more egregious was the enormous centralisation of the whole process, despite health being a joint responsibility of the central and state governments, and despite the reality that it was the states which would have to implement any control measures. The colonial-era Epidemic Diseases Act of 1897, enacted to deal with the Bombay plague, was wielded like a sledgehammer; and the powers under the National Disaster Management Act of 2005 were read as giving the Centre overriding authority over the states. State governments were barely consulted while framing rules. A series of notifications, clarifications and amendments on the dos and don'ts began to flow with worrying regularity from the central home ministry, which, rather than the health ministry, took the lead in dealing with Covid-19.

States were saddled with the responsibilities and costs of dealing with disease surveillance, quarantine, emergency healthcare and welfare during the lockdown, but little came by way of economic support from the Centre. The national lockdown was ill-suited, both from an epidemiological and economic point of view, for a diverse country as India. In hindsight, the lockdown only created dangerous incubation spots in the cities, and as workers scrambled to the safety of their homes with the relaxation of lockdown, they became unwitting carriers of the virus into small towns and villages (Gettleman et al. 2020). And finally, when the lockdown began to weigh down dangerously on the economy and wearily on people's morale, the Centre simply receded, passing on the responsibility to the states to cope with the aftermath, including in the poorly provisioned hinterland.

While one-party China appeared to have controlled the spread of the virus after it locked down the province of Hubei, democratic India with a more severe shutdown of an entire country did not achieve the same success.

It is not, however, the failure to control Covid-19 that stands out in the aftermath of the lockdown. It is the unimaginable devastation wreaked on the urban poor that will define those nine weeks. With a sudden and complete closure of all economic activities, the urban workers, who in any case were leading a precarious existence, found themselves—literally—on the streets. The urban economy in India runs on migrant workers. Yet, an insensitive state refused to provide any immediate relief. These workers then had no choice but to go home. With all train and bus services at a halt for the first four weeks of the lockdown, the migrant workers and their families began to take the long journey back on foot, in what should be called India's Great Trudge Home.

It was a human tragedy that had not been witnessed since Partition. At the very least, 5 million workers and their families in cities all over the country headed back to the North East, Uttar Pradesh, Bihar, Odisha, Chhattisgarh and elsewhere. Men, women and children walked hundreds of kilometres in the blazing summer sun. It was a sight on the roads that should have caused collective shame. It did not.

Barring a few exceptions, the media chose not to highlight this human tragedy. The lockdown had stifled all democratic political activities; so political parties too were largely silent. If the central government was callous, state governments were insensitive. Sometimes the workers were not allowed to cross state borders; sometimes the police harassed them for walking on the highways; sometimes they were forced to set up temporary shelters outside towns and cities, and on at least one occasion they were sprayed with disinfectant (Rashid 2020). Those who managed to reach their homes were herded into makeshift quarantine centres lacking basic amenities, and quite often they were left to fend for themselves as they contracted the illness and spread it to their families.

We may never know how many died during this ordeal, not of the disease but of the events surrounding it. No state agency cared to monitor their movement. We do know that many died in accidents. Some died when the trucks in which they were packed to the edges overturned; some collapsed on the roads; and in one instance, a group of workers sleeping on what they thought were silent railway tracks were crushed to death by a train (Banerjee and Mahale 2020). Some died silently on railway platforms and roadsides as hunger and physical exhaustion overtook them.

Yet, neither then nor later did the political leadership express regret, other than posting the occasional social media message, over this tragedy that had been wrought by the sudden imposition of a nation-wide blanket lockdown. It was left to concerned citizens working with civil society organisations to organise relief by way of food, transport assistance and, in some cases, even shelter. If the callousness of the state towards the migrant workers was unforgivable, it is just as damning that within a few months the episode and its fallout seem to have disappeared from public memory. The central government belatedly announced in late May—two months after the lockdown was imposed and the Great Trudge Home had begun—that the returning migrants would be eligible to free grain for two months and could be enrolled in an expanded Mahatma Gandhi

National Rural Employment Guarantee Scheme (MGNREGS) (*Hindustan Times* 2020).

Another section of society that suffered immensely during the lockdown and thereafter was India's school-going children. With schools closed, first during the lockdown ahead of the summer break and then until end 2020, and children unable to physically attend class, 'online education' became a major part of the lives of Indians of all classes. Yet, with the country unprepared, with teachers untrained, with online education systems made up on the go, and with most children without either adequate computer facilities at home or reliable internet connectivity, it was more than 'a lost year' for them. Strangely, beyond preparing material for digital distribution, neither the central nor state governments seemed to be worried about how to help children navigate this most difficult of years. As always, in India's divided society, it was the children of the rural poor who suffered the most (Bera 2020).

The larger economy collapsed during the height of the lockdown. As subsequent official (provisional) estimates showed, the economy contracted by 23.9 per cent in the April–June quarter of the fiscal year 2020–21 (covering the peak of the lockdown), and by 7.5 per cent during July–September, both with respect to the corresponding quarters in 2019–20. The Indian contraction was the steepest in the world, a natural outcome of the most severe lockdown. The human cost of this lockdown was shown up in the first instance by a sharp surge in unemployment rates which, according to independent agencies, climbed to 23.5 and 21.7 per cent in April and May 2020, respectively (Centre for Monitoring Indian Economy 2020). The full effects of this body blow to people's livelihoods and wellbeing is yet to be reckoned with, especially as it came on the heels of an economic downturn that had already reversed several of the improvements in health and nutrition of the past decades.

Over the course of the year, the central government announced a series of relief measures for the poor, for agriculture, and for small and large businesses. These were in the form of additional spending, temporary direct and indirect tax concessions, credit guarantees, liquidity enhancements and also bank finance. Yet, the size of additional government spending was small given the circumstances.

According to the International Monetary Fund's (IMF) analysis, India's direct stimulus spending until September 2020 amounted to only 1.8 per cent of the gross domestic product (GDP), while 'below the line' aid (that is, off-budget support like waivers, credit guarantees, etc.) was equivalent to 5.2 per cent of GDP, amounting to a total of 7 per cent of GDP (Lokeshwarri 2020).

Despite suggestions to the central government to expand spending, if necessary by monetisation of the deficit as well, there was a strange refusal to do so. It appeared that even in the midst of the biggest ever economic contraction in decades, the government found it more important to stick to fiscal orthodoxy and not widen the fiscal deficit. There was instead a pooling of old and new programmes, adding new ones with off-budget funding and packaging it as a fresh attempt at self-reliance: 'Atmanirbhar Bharat'.

The other consequence of the refusal to open the purse-strings was a debilitating impact on state governments, which found their revenues collapsing even as they were expected to share a larger part of the burden of spending on health services. Indeed, all of 2020 saw a continuing struggle between the states and the Centre, with the latter pleading for what were their statutory dues [compensation for a decline in the Goods and Services Tax (GST) collections], as well as additional funds. Yet, this was met with a stubborn refusal to do so.

It was a mark of the times that in the midst of the lockdown and during the limping recovery thereafter, India's wealthy saw their assets increase manifold, and oligopolies strengthened their grip on the Indian economy. According to one reliable estimate, even as the Indian economy shrunk and rendered millions unemployed, the wealth of the industrial tycoon Gautam Adani more than doubled to $32 billion, while that of the bigger tycoon, Mukesh Ambani, grew by a more 'modest' quarter to $75 billion (*The Economist* 2020). A handful of India's biggest companies received large amounts of foreign investment; they were awarded lucrative contracts in infrastructure; and they came to straddle virtually all sectors of the economy. It was as if a weakened economy was available for the picking by the richest firms in the country. Another reflection of the times was that the stock market, after suffering slumps in the early days of the lockdown, recovered by the end of the year to cross previous peaks. It was found that India's top 100 billionaires had been able to preserve their wealth during the year and 'fewer billionaires had seen an erosion of their wealth than in 2019' (*Forbes India* 2020). All this in an economy that was still in a recession and where the poor in rural and urban India had seen loss of work and a decline in consumption (as revealed in a number of field surveys conducted by civil society organisations, one of which is reported in this volume).

When the curtains of propaganda and media management were drawn, it was clear that India had done poorly when compared to other countries in the neighbourhood and in Asia. A compilation by a former chief economic advisor to the Government of India is striking (see Table I.1). As of mid-October 2020, India suffered the highest number of Covid-19 deaths per million population in a select group of Asian countries, and was slated to show the largest degree of contraction in 2020. There could not be a stronger rebuttal of the misplaced sense of confidence among official circles in the country about India's record in dealing with Covid-19, and mitigating its impact on the economy.

Table I.1: Growth 2020 and Covid-19: Asian Economies

Country	*GDP Growth 2020 (at Constant Prices, in %)*	*Covid-19 Deaths Per Million Population*
Bangladesh	3.8	34.0
China	1.9	3.0
Vietnam	1.6	0.4
Nepal	0.0	25.0
Pakistan	–0.4	30.0
Indonesia	–1.5	46.0
Sri Lanka	–4.6	0.6
Afghanistan	–5.0	38.0
Malaysia	–6.0	6.0
Thailand	–7.1	0.8
India	–10.3	83.0

Source: From IMF and Worldometer, 18 October 2020, as tweeted by @kaushikcbasu, 19 October 2020, available at https://twitter.com/kaushikcbasu/status/1318023864992075776?s=20 (accessed 1 December 2020).

A crisis should have brought Indian society together, and its institutions should have combined to deal with Covid-19 and its after-effects. But the opposite happened. There was little sign of either community or togetherness. Instead, all the cleavages were out in the open, and more were added.

The Centre seemed to work to further strain the spirit of federalism in its relations with the states. The courts seemed oblivious to the suffering of the people, especially the migrants. It took an urgent appeal from senior lawyers and jurists before the Supreme Court belatedly ordered relief to the migrants in late May, by which time most of them had reached home (Rajagopal 2020).

In the realm of politics and governance, it was almost as if the Executive was using the pandemic to dilute democratic practice in the country. Parliament saw only a brief and further shortened Monsoon session in the middle of 2020, and the Winter session was cancelled altogether citing Covid-19. This was in contrast to elsewhere in the world, where parliaments did their best to function normally (Venkataramakrishnan 2020). With Parliament not in session, important ordinances were passed in the fields of agriculture and industrial labour, and later rushed through the legislature without proper scrutiny. The dilution and abuse of democratic practice was so widespread and deep that one respected international study identified India as the democracy with the most number of 'concerns about democracy developments' during the pandemic (IDEA International 2020). India had already been identified in the same study as a country that was already 'backsliding' in democratic practice on the eve of the pandemic.

In urban India, in the early days, fearful communities ostracised those who had been infected and did little to support the quarantined. In colonies and apartment complexes, the middle class and wealthy shut out the rest of the world, asked domestic help not to come to work and refused to pay them salaries. The elderly and the disabled who lived alone were denied the services of their paid caregivers and were left to fend for themselves. India's service sector workers who kept the urban economy ticking asked why they had to suffer because of 'a disease brought from outside by the rich' (*BBC* 2020a; Nidheesh

2020). Indeed, there were even reports in the early days of Covid-19 of health workers who were asked by landlords to vacate their homes (Chaudhuri 2020).

The most striking manifestation of a sharpening of the divide came in the form of the frenzy built up by the media, and tacitly encouraged by the state, over an early case of the spread of the virus in a congregation of the Tablighi Jamaat in Delhi in March 2020 which had participants from different parts of the world. This was portrayed in the media as an example of 'Muslims' spreading the virus, leading to virulent anti-Muslim hysteria across social media. Government spokespersons too started handing out data on the Tablighi infections, claiming that nationally infections had spiked because of the congregation (*Outlook* 2020). This forced the World Health Organisation (WHO) to caution against the 'religious-profiling' of Covid-19 victims (*Down to Earth* 2020). In spite of such warnings, many of the members of the congregation were arrested, ostensibly for spreading the infection and violating visa rules. It was months before high courts struck down the arrests with harsh indictments of the authorities (Thapar and Wahidi 2020).

The darker side of India on display during 2020 should not blind us to the tremendous commitment demonstrated by doctors, nurses, public health staff of local governments and the paramedical staff. As in other countries, the healthcare workers were the ones who cared for the sick in hospitals, often at great personal cost and for low wages (Baru and Zafar 2020; Khasne et al. 2020). A number of civil society organisations—small and large—demonstrated extraordinary sensitivity to support the migrant workers during their exodus, providing income support, offering temporary shelter and arranging for their travel home, with little regard for exposure to the virus (Participatory Research in India 2020). It seemed that it was left to the healthcare workers and isolated citizens' groups to try and step in and repair the damage caused by state and society at large.

III

Some of these issues and more were covered in *The India Forum*, which from March 2020 onwards has been publishing a stream of essays related to the pandemic. The collection in this volume is a selection of the essays that were published in the first year of Covid-19 in India.

The chapters are presented here as they were published in *The India Forum*, without any major revision. They should be seen as an evolution of our understanding of a new phenomenon as it spread and intensified across the country.

In Section I ('Early Stages of Covid-19 in India'), Thomas Abraham and K. Sujatha Rao grapple with the question of whether the country could have been better prepared for the spread of the virus. Abraham argues that by mid-February, there were Indian Council of Medical Research (ICMR) studies showing that irrespective of the screening of travellers, the virus was going to travel across the country rapidly (Chapter 1). Yet, little was done and valuable time lost before the imposition of the nation-wide lockdown on 25 March. In an early piece written before the lockdown of late March, Rao warned of the consequences of not carrying out a series of actions, including accelerated testing (Chapter 2). She also highlighted the importance of cooperation between the Centre and the states. As would be the case, neither happened, with serious consequences for the control of the disease.

Section II ('Dealing with Pandemics in India's History') offers past experiences of epidemics in South Asia and how they reconstituted both state and society. The 1897 plague outbreak in Bombay, Pratik Chakrabarti argues, set the stage for the colonial state to amass emergency powers, and use them to reorder urban spaces and control the movement of suspicious bodies (Chapter 3). Chakrabarti shows how public health emergencies lead to episodes of greater governmental control and surveillance over subjects and citizens.

Past epidemics, including the plague, have been invoked by many commentators in trying to understand Covid-19. Sheetal Chhabria's chapter, also set temporally in the 1897 Bombay plague epidemic, interrogates this genre of writing (Chapter 4). She asks what lessons could be drawn for the present if we view the plague not as a pathogenic episode, but as the consequence of poverty, and the under-provisioning of health and sanitation during colonial rule. Prerna

Agarwal's chapter on the experiences of Calcutta under the 1898 plague argues that the pandemic changed how labour could negotiate with both the state and with factory and mill owners (Chapter 5). This coming of age of labour presaged the waves of labour movements in the city in the twentieth century. And finally, Harish Naraindas explores the almost impossible story of the global effort to eradicate smallpox in India in the second half of the twentieth century (Chapter 6). He argues that in India, where the disease was endemic, the collaboration of vaccinators with local communities made the mission a collective—and successful—resistance against the 'pox'. Taken together, the section both provides historical precedents as well as complicates our understanding of past epidemics to think more deeply about our present moment.

Section III ('Covid-19: The Initial Impact') has two important chapters written during the early stages of the spread of the pandemic. Both deal with the issues of health and livelihoods; both deny that there is a trade-off between health and the economy/livelihoods. Vikram Patel presciently warned, among other things, of the devastating impact the lockdown was going to have on the health of the people who suffered from ill-health before the lockdown and needed to but could not get care, and those who lost their livelihoods (Chapter 7). Ananda Lal Roy and Maitreesh Ghatak offered a detailed set of options for short- and long-term interventions in both public health and the economy, seeing the two as connected rather than separate (Chapter 8).

As the lockdown began hammering the lives of the poor and the migrants, there were expectations that the judiciary would intervene to uphold the rights of citizens and direct the state to provide support. Three chapters address different aspects of this issue in Section IV ('The Law, the Judiciary and Covid-19'). Upendra Baxi made the argument that constitutionalism seemed to have deserted the courts, especially in the matter of protecting the rights of the workers who were forced to take to the streets (Chapter 9). Pratiksha Baxi and Navsharan Singh make a case for the release of all women prisoners during the pandemic (Chapter 10). Harsh Mander's piece recounts the story of one of the first petitions, filed in April 2020, seeking the

Supreme Court's intervention to provide relief to migrant workers (Chapter 11).

Section V ('The Lockdown and After') focuses on the crises that emerged during the extended shutdown: in jobs, livelihoods and hunger. Debraj Ray, S. Subramanian and Lore Vandewalle argue against a policy that ignored the devastation caused to livelihoods (Chapter 12). A quantification of the impact on jobs and consumption among the migrant workers is to be found in the analysis by the researchers at Azim Premji University, led by Amit Basole, who worked with civil society organisations to survey a sample of 5,000 workers in April–May 2020 (Chapter 13). The big question is how many workers could have and did take the Great Trudge Home? Nomaan Majid makes a careful and conservative estimate by studying National Sample Survey (NSS) data on the urban informal sector workforce that would have found itself vulnerable (Chapter 14). In a case study of one industry, Gayatri Nair writes of the unique vulnerabilities of the workers in India's gig economy during the pandemic (Chapter 15).

The macroeconomy is the subject of the four chapters in Section VI ('Impact on the Economy'). In the first chapter of the section, R. Nagaraj updates his essay that was published on the eve of the pandemic. His argument is that the economy was in a poor state even before the pandemic hit. Revisiting the analysis, Nagaraj offers a suite of measures to pull the economy out of the quagmire it now finds itself in (Chapter 16). Turning to specifics, Radhicka Kapoor analyses the Periodic Labour Force Survey (PLFS) data for 2018–19 to identify the sections of the workforce that would most experience the dislocations caused by the pandemic and the lockdown (Chapter 17). M. Govinda Rao analyses a unique set of issues: the violation of the spirit of federalism in a series of economic policy decisions taken by the Centre on the mobilisation of resources to deal with Covid-19 (Chapter 18). In an essay written during the early stages of the pandemic, C. P. Chandrasekhar discusses the very unique challenges faced by the global economy (Chapter 19).

While much of the public discourse was, naturally, about public health and the economy, there were many social disruptions that could not be ignored. Section VII ('Impact on Society') discusses two of them. Honey Oberoi Vahali explores what could have happened to people when they were confined to their homes for weeks on end during the lockdown (Chapter 20). Naorem Pushparani Chanu and Gorky Chakraborty recount the racial profiling of, and attacks on, citizens from the North East because of their Mongoloid phenotype (Chapter 21).

Finally, Section VIII ('The Future') has three chapters that examine different aspects of the future as well as the past. Ramprasad Sengupta gives a brief overview of the several human–nature conflicts throughout the history of *Homo sapiens*, conflicts that have become even more aggressive and are leading to the emergence of zoonotic viruses with growing frequency (Chapter 22). Itty Abraham looks to the future and extracts strands of meaning from the predictions and speculations of four groups of thinkers: the pro-state progressive optimists, end-of-globalisation pessimists, disaster capitalism pessimists, and techno-optimists (Chapter 23). Finally, Prem Chandavarkar asks what lessons we can draw from the Covid-19 pandemic, and if we can build a more humane society that lives in greater harmony with nature (Chapter 24).

Vast as the area covered by this collection is, it is not exhaustive. Important spheres have not been covered. Two deserve mention: what the pandemic—the lockdown and then the continued closure of schools—did to the lives of children; and the impact on women during the lockdown and in households where the man had lost his job. Domestic violence did see a spurt, and this ugly phenomenon needs careful study if we are to respond to it effectively. In the years ahead, there will doubtless be many studies that explore what SARS-CoV-2 did to children and women.

This collection of 24 essays offers rich insights into the impact of the pandemic and the response of state and society. These are, of course, not final analyses. But written in the middle of the first year of the pandemic, this volume, one of the first of its kind, offers what we could call 'a real-time window' into the impact of SARS-CoV-2 on India in the year it arrived and then spread in the country.

Notes

1. Pfizer's vaccine costs $37, the two-shot Oxford vaccine is $3 a dose, much higher than the 50 cents that the respected virologist Gagandeep Kang has said an ideal vaccine ought to cost for mass use (Biswas 2020a; *The Wire* 2020).
2. Figures for India as per the Worldometer real-time statistics, collected from https://www.worldometers.info/coronavirus/#countries (accessed 7 December 2020).
3. There has been much discussion about the reliability of India's numbers. There is a general feeling outside the government that the official numbers are far fewer than the real numbers, the result of misclassification, poor reporting and collection mechanisms, low levels of testing, or the occasional reliance on antigen tests, rather than the more reliable reverse transcription polymerase chain reaction (RT-PCR) tests. There have been accusations as well of the occasional deliberate suppression of the numbers in some states, but this has not been established.
4. The government of South Africa gave the country four days' notice: the lockdown was announced on Monday, 23 March 2020, and took effect on the midnight of Thursday, 26 March (Burke 2020).
5. See 'COVID-19: Government Response Stringency Index', *Our World in Data*, available at https://ourworldindata.org/grapher/covid-stringency-index?tab=chart&stackMode=absolute&time=2020-01-22..latest&country=~IND&region=World (accessed 20 December 2020).

References

'Attempt to Murder Charge against Man who Attended Tablighi Event "Abuse of Law": Allahabad HC'. 2020a. *The Wire*, 5 December. Available at https://thewire.in/law/allahabad-high-court-tablighi-jamaat-attempt-murder-abuse-of-law-power (accessed 8 December 2020).

'Corona Cases Spiked Due to Tablighi Jamaat: Health Ministry'. 2020. *Outlook*, 1 April. Available at https://www.outlookindia.com/newsscroll/corona-cases-spiked-due-to-tablighi-jamaat-health-ministry/1787861 (accessed 8 December 2020).

'Coronavirus: How India's Lockdown Sparked a Debate over Maids'. 2020a. *BBC*, 5 May. Available at https://www.bbc.com/news/world-asia-india-52529922 (accessed 8 December 2020).

'Forbes India Rich List 2020'. 2020. *Forbes India*. Available at https://www.forbesindia.com/lists/india-rich-list-2020/1877/all (accessed 8 December 2020).

'Free Food Grain Supply for 8 Crore Migrants for Next 2 Months: Nirmala Sitharaman'. 2020. *Hindustan Times*, 14 May. Available at https://www.hindustantimes.com/india-news/free-food-grain-supply-for-8-crore-migrants-for-next-2-months-nirmala-sitharaman/story-bqRuwxF4dACid5EcDoQYmK.html (accessed 20 December 2020).

'India's Super-rich are Getting Much Richer'. 2020. *The Economist*, 5 December. Available at https://www.economist.com/asia/2020/12/05/indias-super-rich-are-getting-much-richer (accessed 8 December 2020).

'Pfizer Vaccine's Price may be Throwing off Indian Government, Report Says'. 2020b. *The Wire*, 14 December. Available at https://science.thewire.in/health/pfizer-vaccines-price-may-be-throwing-off-indian-government-report-says/ (accessed 20 December 2020).

'Refrain from Religious Profiling of COVID-19 Cases: WHO in Context of Tabligh'. 2020. *Down to Earth*, 7 April. Available at https://www.downtoearth.org.in/news/health/refrain-from-religious-profiling-of-covid-19-cases-who-in-context-of-tabligh-70262 (accessed 8 December 2020).

'Rich Countries Hoarding Covid Vaccines, Says People's Vaccine Alliance'. 2020b. *BBC*, 9 December. Available at https://www.bbc.com/news/health-55229894 (accessed 20 December 2020).

Babu, Giridhara R. 2020. 'The Challenges in Counting the Dead'. *The Hindu*, 14 August. Available at https://www.thehindu.com/opinion/lead/the-challenges-in-counting-the-dead/article32347217.ece (accessed 8 December 2020).

Banerjee, Shoumojit and Ajeet Mahale. 2020. '16 Migrant Workers Run over by Goods Train near Aurangabad in Maharashtra'. *The Hindu*, 8 May. Available at https://www.thehindu.com/news/national/other-states/16-migrant-workers-run-over-by-goods-train-near-aurangabad-in-maharashtra/article31531352.ece (accessed 20 December 2020).

Baru, Rama V., and Seemi Zafar. 2020. 'Low Wages, Poor PPE: Contractual Healthcare Workers Face the Worst of the Pandemic'. *The Wire*, 20 May. Available at https://thewire.in/rights/health-workers-safety (accessed 19 December 2020).

Bera, Sayantan. 2020. 'How Rural Schooling is Going into the Dark'. *Mint*, 16 December Available at https://www.livemint.com/education/news/how-rural-schooling-is-going-into-the-dark-11608044666364.html (accessed 19 December 2020).

Biswas, Soutik. 2020a. 'India Coronavirus: How Do You Vaccinate a Billion People?'. *BBC*, 26 November. Available at https://www.bbc.com/news/world-asia-india-55048925 (accessed 8 December 2020).

Biswas, Soutik. 2020b. 'India Coronavirus: How a Group of Volunteers "Exposed" Hidden Covid-19 Deaths'. *BBC*, 20 November. Available at https://www.bbc.co.uk/news/world-asia-india-54985981 (accessed 8 December 2020).

Burke, Jason. 2020. 'South Africa to go into 21-day Lockdown on Thursday Night'. *The Guardian*, 23 March. Available at https://www.theguardian.com/world/2020/mar/23/south-africa-to-go-into-21-day-lockdown-on-thursday-night (accessed 8 December 2020).

Centre for Monitoring Indian Economy. 2020. 'Unemployment Rate in India'. Available at https://unemploymentinindia.cmie.com (accessed 8 December 2020).

Chaudhuri, Prasun. 2020. 'The Frontline Corona Soldiers'. *The Telegraph*, 31 December. Available at https://www.telegraphindia.com/culture/people/coronavirus-2020-the-frontline-corona-soldiers/cid/1801738 (accessed 31 December 2020).

Eberle, Lukas, Markus Feldenkirchen, Milena Hassenkamp, Martin Knobbe, Veit Medick, Marcel Rosenbach, Lydia Rosenfelder and Gerald Traufetter. 2020. 'Germany is Faring Poorly in the Second Wave of the Coronavirus'. *Spiegel International*, 11 December. Available at https://www.spiegel.de/international/germany/germany-is-faring-poorly-in-the-second-wave-of-the-coronavirus-a-afc634db-9220-496b-8aca-fd19f2e0962f (accessed 20 December 2020).

Gettleman, Jeffrey, Suhasini Raj, Sameer Yasir and Karan Deep Singh. 2020. 'The Virus Trains: How Lockdown Chaos Spread Covid-19 across India'. *New York Times*, 15 December. Available at https://www.nytimes.com/2020/12/15/world/asia/india-coronavirus-shramik-specials.html (accessed 19 December 2020).

IDEA International. 2020. 'Taking Stock of Global Democratic Trends before and during the COVID-19 Pandemic'. The Global State of Democracy, special brief, December. Available at https://www.idea.int/sites/default/files/publications/global-democratic-trends-before-and-during-covid-19-pandemic.pdf (accessed 19 December 2020).

Khasne R. W., B. S. Dhakulkar, H. C. Mahajan and A. P. Kulkarni. 2020. 'Burnout among Healthcare Workers during COVID-19 Pandemic in India: Results of a Questionnaire-based Survey'. *Indian Journal of Critical Care Medicine* 24 (8): 664–71. Available at https://pubmed.ncbi.nlm.nih.gov/33024372/ (accessed 8 December 2020).

Lokeshwarri, S. K. 2020. 'What's Influencing the Size of India's Covid-19 Relief Stimulus?'. *Business Line*, 24 November. Available at https://www.thehindubusinessline.com/data-stories/data-focus/whats-influencing-the-size-of-indias-covid-19-relief-stimulus/article33171458.ece (accessed 7 December 2020).

Nidheesh, M. K. 2000. 'A Rich Man's Disease, a Poor Man's Burden, and the Toll it's Taking on Self-esteem'. *Mint*, 24 March. Available at https://www.livemint.com/news/india/a-rich-man-s-disease-a-poor-man-s-burden-and-the-toll-it-s-taking-on-self-esteem-11584993132052.html (accessed 8 December 2020).

Participatory Research in India. 2020. 'Response of Indian Civil Society towards Covid-19'. Research paper, July. Available at https://www.pria.org/knowledge_resource/1594293825_Response%20of%20CSO%20towards%20covid19.pdf (accessed 8 December 2020).

Prabhala, Achal, Arjun Jayadev and Dean Baker. 2020. 'Want Vaccines Fast? Suspend Intellectual Property Rights'. *New York Times*, 7 December. Available at https://www.nytimes.com/2020/12/07/opinion/covid-vaccines-patents.html (accessed 20 December 2020).

Pulla, Priyanka. 2020. 'What Counts as a Covid-19 Death?'. *BMJ* 370. Available at https://www.bmj.com/content/370/bmj.m2859 (accessed 8 December 2020).

Rajagopal, Krishnadas. 2020. 'Supreme Court Orders Centre and States to Immediately Provide Transport, Food and Shelter Free of Cost to Stranded Migrant Workers'. *The Hindu*, 26 May. Available at https://www.thehindu.com/news/national/supreme-court-takes-suo-motu-cognisance-of-migrant-workers-issue/article31679389.ece (accessed 8 December 2020).

Rashid, Omar. 2020. 'Coronavirus: In Bareilly, Migrants Returning Home Sprayed with "Disinfectant"'. *The Hindu*, 30 March. Available at https://www.thehindu.com/news/national/other-states/coronavirus-in-bareilly-migrants-forced-to-take-bath-in-the-open-with-sanitiser/article31204430.ece (accessed 20 December 2020).

Shewade, Hemant Deepak and Giridara Gopal Parameswaran. 2020. 'COVID-19 Deaths may be Higher than Reported'. *The Hindu*, 10 August. Available at https://www.thehindu.com/opinion/op-ed/covid-19-deaths-are-not-as-low-as-reported/article32310814.ece (accessed 8 December 2020).

Taubenberger, Jeffrey K., and David M. Morens. 2006. '1981 Influenza: The Mother of All Pandemics'. *Emerging Infectious Diseases* 12 (1): 15–22. Available at https://www.ncbi.nlm.nih.gov/pmc/articles/PMC3291398/ (accessed 8 December 2020).

Thapar, Arushi and Zaid Wahidi. 2020. 'Bombay HC's Tolerance Lesson on Tablighis'. *Article14*, 22 August. Available at https://www.article-14.

com/post/bombay-high-court-s-tolerance-lesson-on-tablighi-jamaat (accessed 8 December 2020).

Tumbe, Chinmay. 2020. *The Age of Pandemics 1817–1920: How They Shaped India and the World*. New Delhi: HarperCollins.

Venkataramakrishnan, Rohan. 2020. 'If India has Handled Covid-19 So Well, Why has the Centre Cancelled Parliament's Winter Session?'. *Scroll.in*, 17 December. Available at https://scroll.in/article/981462/if-india-has-handled-covid-19-so-well-why-has-the-centre-canceled-parliaments-winter-session (accessed 19 December 2020).

Wee, Sui-lee and Donald G. McNeil, Jr. 2020. 'China Identifies Virus Causing Pneumonialike Symptoms'. *New York Times*, 8 January. Available at https://www.nytimes.com/2020/01/08/health/china-pneumonia-outbreak-virus.html (accessed 7 December 2020).

Section I

Early Stages of Covid-19 in India

1

Covid-19 in India

*The Chronicle of a Pandemic Foretold**

Thomas Abraham

On 23 January 2020, the city of Wuhan in central China imposed public health measures of a stringency the world had not seen in recent times, to stamp out the new coronavirus disease, Covid-19. Roads in and out of the city were blocked; trains and flights were cancelled. In the days that followed, as the virus continued to spread unabated, restrictions became progressively more stringent. The city's 11 million people were more or less confined to their homes. As the ripples of infection spread wider, similar restrictions were imposed on other cities in China.

India watched this drama unfold in real time and was given plenty of warning about how quickly the virus could spread, and the enormous impact it could have on hospitals, doctors, nurses and healthcare workers. The first infection in India was detected as early as 30 January.

The initial epidemiological studies from Wuhan indicated that that around 80 per cent of those infected had mild symptoms. The real issue would be with the 20 per cent who required hospitalisation and intensive care, of which half would require respiratory support through ventilators and other oxygenating devices. Wuhan had to construct two 1,000-bed hospitals exclusively to care for coronavirus patients from the city.

Simple modelling at the end of January or February, when the basic parameters of Covid-19 were well known, would have indicated

* First published in *The India Forum*, 3 April 2020.

that if the disease took hold, India would need to be ready for a wave of patients requiring intensive care. This would have required identifying beds and identifying and training personnel to deal with critically ill patients without getting infected themselves. It would have involved ensuring there were enough gloves, masks and other protective equipment for frontline healthcare workers. It would have meant ensuring there was enough capacity in the country to test for the disease as numbers surged.

When there were warnings from January about the nature of this virus and the experience of China, how did it happen that India was forced to resort, in end-March, to a hastily thought out 21-day nationwide lockdown? Why could not the country begin preparing for a possible lockdown from earlier? Why could not the public have been taken into confidence and prepared for what was to come? Why were economic safety nets not put in place for the vulnerable?

Except in a few states, none of these early warnings appears to have been taken seriously until around the second half of March, by when six weeks if not more of valuable preparation time were lost. Thus, on 22 March, when case numbers were climbing sharply, Cabinet Secretary Rajiv Gauba was still urging state chief secretaries to immediately identify hospitals to be set aside for treatment of Covid-19 cases (Ministry of Health and Family Welfare 2020a). Two days later, this was followed up by another letter to the states:

> [Y]ou will appreciate at this stage the highest priority needs to be accorded to establishing medical facilities such as hospitals, clinical labs, isolation ward and expanding and upgrading existing facilities to combat the challenge posed by COVID-19. These facilities need to be well equipped with ventilators, PPE [personal protective equipment], masks and drugs to treat the patients. There is also a need to create adequate isolation facilities to prevent further infections. The medical, paramedical and sanitation staff needs to be trained to attend the affected persons. (Ministry of Health and Family Welfare 2020b)

These letters are remarkable both for their timing as well as the assumptions they made. In terms of timing, letters like this, asking states to start planning hospital capacity, should have gone out in early February, when it was clear the disease was spreading internationally.

Once case numbers had started rising, and infected people had started popping up in most states, as they had by March, the time for planning was over. The time for action had begun.

The assumptions the Cabinet Secretary's letter made in terms of 'establishing medical facilities' were unrealistic, given the historically underfunded Indian public health infrastructure. How were 'hospitals, clinical labs and isolation wards' to be established at the drop of a hat? How were these facilities to be 'well equipped with ventilators, PPE, masks and drugs' when at the best of time government hospitals are chronically short of equipment?

A Reuters news report cited a study by Invest India, the government's investment promotion agency, that the country would require 3.8 crore masks, compared to the 91 lakh available at the end of March with manufacturers (Kalra and Ghoshal 2020). With businesses locked down and supply chains disrupted, it is late in the day to only now be thinking about procuring masks and other equipment for an epidemic that is beginning to take off.

Ventilators are crucial to keep alive those whose lungs have been damaged by the virus. The Centre for Disease Dynamics, Economics and Policy at Johns Hopkins University, as reported in the *Mint*, estimated that India had between 30,000 and 50,000 ventilators available, but demand was likely to surge to around 10 lakh by July as patient numbers rose (Seethalakshmi and Nandan 2020). With a global shortage of ventilators, meeting this number could clearly be a challenge.

Similarly, the Cabinet Secretary asking that 'medical, paramedical and sanitation staff be trained' to handle these patient numbers was unrealistic given the unfilled vacancies of medical staff at every level in many states.

A False Sense of Security

It will be a task for the future to reconstruct when the government woke up to the full magnitude of the epidemic that could hit the country. The prime minister's 'Janata Curfew' on 22 March, followed by a nationwide lockdown for 21 days from 25 March, were signs of a realisation that the epidemic was about to explode, and the only way to slow it down and buy time to prepare was through this lockdown. The economic and social cost of the lockdown will be immense, particularly on those who depend on a daily wage to feed themselves.

The extent to which the lockdown slows down the speed of the epidemic remains to be seen. If we are lucky, the lockdown would have given the epidemic a few more weeks of time to ward off its full fury. The tragedy of workers without jobs trudging along empty highways and under the scorching sun for hundreds of kilometres to try and get back to their villages will be one of the defining images of this pandemic, and an illustration of the haste and lack of preparedness that went into the decision.

The government has stoutly maintained that it has been on the ball from day one and was fully prepared to tackle the disease. On 28 March, the Press Information Bureau responded to criticism that the lockdown had been poorly planned. It described the government's response from January onwards as 'pre-emptive, pro-active and graded'. It also provided a timeline to demonstrate the speed with which it introduced screening of travellers from China and elsewhere.

It is true that India responded quickly and began screening travellers from China on 18 January. This was an essential first step to take. Those bringing the virus into the country had to be isolated and prevented from spreading it further. International airports across the country began screening travellers, largely by asking them to fill in self-declaration forms. Those who said they had fever were screened and sent to hospitals. Travellers with no symptoms were only required to get in touch with health authorities if they developed symptoms.

This form of screening probably gave a false sense of security. Some states like Kerala took airport screening and follow-up of suspected cases seriously and started detecting travellers with the virus. Other states were more lax, and fewer cases were detected. The relatively small number of cases detected and the large numbers of travellers screened allowed the government to say that the country had been successful in keeping the disease at bay.

But the government must also have been aware that travel restrictions were not going to keep the epidemic out of India.

A modelling study in February by a team of scientists at the Indian Council of Medical Research (ICMR), that included the head of epidemiology Dr Raman Gangakhedkar, showed that even under a best-case scenario, where all travellers with symptoms were identified at airports and isolated, the restrictions would not keep the disease out of the country (Mandal et al. 2020).

This was because a certain proportion of those infected by the virus, up to half by some estimates, are either pre-symptomatic or asymptomatic. Despite not presenting symptoms, they are capable of passing on the disease to others. Since airport screening was focused on symptoms, a good proportion of infected but asymptomatic people would have passed the screening process.

Also, once they left the airport, the follow-up of travellers who might be carrying the disease was far from perfect. The Cabinet Secretary, in a letter on 26 March to state chief secretaries, pointed out that not all of the 15 lakh passengers screened at airports were followed up by state governments for surveillance (Ministry of Health and Family Welfare 2020b). In other words, airport screening was a process that at the best of time, bought a little extra time to prepare for a full-scale explosion of disease across the country. It was not an indication that Covid-19 had been kept out of India.

Faulty Protocols

The false sense of security that airport screening provided was backed up by low reported figures of Covid-19 cases in India. These reported figures could have been low because of the testing guidelines from the ICMR. The protocols that were in place until mid-March only required travellers from Covid-19 affected countries to be tested if they exhibited symptoms within a 14-day period of home quarantine. Those who did not develop symptoms were given an all-clear.

Data from patients in Wuhan showed that 99 per cent of infected patients would develop symptoms in 14 days, and there would still be 1 per cent who would slip through and go on to infect others. Testing could have plugged this gap. Similarly, while contacts of those who tested positive were also placed in home quarantine, they too were only tested if they exhibited symptoms within 14 days. A small percentage of infected cases might not have exhibited symptoms. Wider testing would have prevented them from spreading the virus wider.

The ICMR's testing protocol did not even require all suspect Covid-19 cases to be tested. The ICMR [and the World Health Organisation (WHO)] definition of a suspect Covid-19 case included anyone with severe acute respiratory illness which could not be satisfactorily explained by any alternate diagnoses. Logically, these cases should have been tested to get an indication of how far the disease was spreading.

ICMR scientists who appeared at daily press briefings repeatedly defended this restrictive testing regime on the grounds that it was more than enough to detect possible cases. This was despite the evidence that countries such as Singapore and South Korea, which had widened testing, had greater success in stopping the spread than the United Kingdom and the United States, which like India did not rigorously test suspect cases.

It was only on 20 March that the guidelines were broadened to test all hospitalised patients with severe respiratory illness, as well as asymptomatic contacts of confirmed Covid-19 patients. For the first time, healthcare workers were also included if they developed symptoms. There was no explanation from ICMR on why the guidelines were expanded, after all this while being described as being more than adequate. Reading between the lines, it was clear that there was a shortage of testing capacity, both in terms of laboratories that were authorised to test as well as in supplies of probes for the tests, which had to be imported. It was only in the middle of March that more labs in universities and research institutions as well as private testing firms were roped in. This could have been done significantly earlier. More cases might have been detected and isolated to slow the spread of the disease. More extensive testing might have meant that the current lockdown would not have been necessary.

The logic of the 21-day lockdown is to slow the rate at which this virus transmits, and buy more time to prepare the health system for an influx of severely ill patients. It will not stop the virus from transmitting. Wuhan went into lockdown in January. It is still seeing a trickle of new cases, even though each day brings fewer cases than the previous. The lockdown is only now being relaxed and businesses are just beginning to reopen.

In India, the numbers are still rising steadily, and different epidemiological models estimate two to three months of rising numbers before the figures begin to plateau and eventually fall. The human cost in terms of illness and death is likely to be large. India could not have avoided this epidemic. The question is whether better preparation of the health system, as well as the public at large could have helped to reduce the toll this disease will take.

References

Kalra, Aditya and Devjyot Ghoshal. 2020. 'India Needs at least 38 Million Masks to Fight Coronavirus: Agency Document'. *Reuters*, 28 March. Available at https://www.reuters.com/article/us-health-coronavirus-india-equipment/india-needs-at-least-38-million-masks-to-fight-coronavirus-agency-document-idUSKBN21F0HO (accessed 16 November 2020).

Mandal, Sandip, Tarun Bhatnagar, Nimalan Arinaminpathy, Anup Agarwal, Amartya Chowdhury, Manoj Murhekar, Raman R. Gangakhedkar and Swarup Sarkar. 2020. 'Prudent Public Health Intervention Strategies to Control the Coronavirus Disease 2019 Transmission in India: A Mathematical Model-based Approach'. *Indian Journal of Medical Research* 151 (2): 190–99.

Ministry of Health and Family Welfare. 2020a. Letter from Cabinet Secretary Rajiv Gauba to State Chief Secretaries, 24 March. Available at https://www.mohfw.gov.in/pdf/doletter24032020.pdf (accessed 16 November 2020).

———. 2020b. Letter from Cabinet Secretary Rajiv Gauba to State Chief Secretaries, 26 March. Available at https://www.mohfw.gov.in/pdf/ChiefSecretary26032020.pdf (accessed 16 November 2020).

Seethalakshmi S., and Rahul Nandan. 2020. 'Local Ventilators Need of the Hour to Prepare for COVID-19'. *Mint*, 28 March. Available at https://www.livemint.com/news/india/local-ventilators-need-of-the-hour-to-prepare-for-covid-19-11585332113169.html (accessed 16 November 2020).

2

Coping with the Coronavirus Pandemic

*Are Indians Safe?**

K. Sujatha Rao

The recent decades have shown how lethal viruses can be. Be it HIV that resulted in 32 million deaths during 1988–2015, or the spate of epidemics witnessed since 2003—Swine Flu, SARS, MERS, Ebola, ZIKA, H1N1, and now the novel coronavirus or Covid-19—viral outbreaks have resulted in enormous individual suffering and economic loss. The speed with which the coronavirus is spreading has stunned the world. Within three months, it has infected over 1,98,000 people (confirmed cases) and left 7,948 dead in over 150 countries (as of 17 March 2020). This reminds us of the 1918 flu pandemic that killed 33 million people across the world within a year.

The impact on the global economy and movement of people has already been disruptive. Following the devastation caused by the massive dislocation in international business, first due to China's reduced trade with the rest of the world and now because of the shutdowns in much of North America and western Europe, the economic fallout is likely to be severe. Some commentators are already talking of a contraction in the gross domestic product (GDP) on the same scale as happened during the 1930s Great Depression (Gopinath 2020). Such an outcome should not be surprising. Sierra Leone and Liberia saw their GDP in 2015 erode by double-digit rates during the Ebola crisis (World Bank 2016).

* First published in *The India Forum*, 26 March 2020.

India's Response

India detected its first case of coronavirus in Kerala on 30 January. This was a student from Wuhan, the epicentre of the epidemic in China. Up until the first week of March, the number of active cases in India was less than 40. On 4 March, there was a wave of 22 cases detected, followed by another on 10 March with 15 cases, and a third wave on 17 March with 23 cases. As of 18 March, there were an estimated 161 cases, of which over 80 per cent were in six states: Maharashtra, Kerala, Haryana, Delhi, Uttar Pradesh and Karnataka.

With the national political leadership first preoccupied with the Delhi state assembly elections and then by the visit of US President Donald Trump, the month of February was wasted. In contrast, Taiwan had already imposed active airport screening and had launched a massive Information, Education and Communication (IEC) campaign on preventive measures. Singapore and South Korea sealed their borders and took up active testing of all those with a history of travel to the affected areas, as also their contacts. While these early measures helped Singapore and Taiwan stop the virus in its tracks, India lost valuable time.

Barring some exchanges of letters and advisories at the bureaucratic level, the political decision-making required to handle the unfolding epidemic started only in mid-March. This was in the wake of over 14 states and union territories reporting positive cases and the rapid increase in the number of infected cases in Italy, South Korea and Iran. India suspended most visas including those of Overseas Citizens (OCI) until 15 April, extended an entry ban on all those coming from not just the initially listed seven countries—China, South Korea, Iran, Italy, Spain, France and Germany—but also from all of Europe and some countries of the Middle East too. Several entry points by land were also closed.

Half a dozen states have ordered the shutting down of all social activities—schools, colleges, malls, cinema houses, pubs, restaurants, conferences—including paring down the number of invitees to weddings and postponing the cricket Indian Premier League (IPL). However, while such social distancing lockdowns are useful, inconsistencies are inevitable. So while social gatherings are to be restricted to no more than 50 persons, the daily commute of lakhs of people on urban public transport systems is allowed.

This is an extraordinary time. India has never before faced such a national emergency where significant parts of social and economic life have been halted across vast swathes of the country, including in the political capital of Delhi and the financial capital of Mumbai.

The prime minister has exhorted people to eschew unnecessary travel, adhere to common-sense precautions in personal hygiene like washing hands with soap and sneezing into a handkerchief, and staying at home if unwell. He has had one video meeting with leaders of the South Asian Association for Regional Cooperation (SAARC) countries for fighting this battle together.

While all this is impressive and appears adequate, given the modest number of cases India has so far reported, what is incomprehensible is the near absence of collective decision-making and a spirit of 'cooperative federalism' between the Centre and the states.

The control of infectious diseases is a concurrent subject in the Constitution, and yet there has been no face-to-face dialogue between the Union and state governments at the highest political level about the enforcement of control measures. Neither the prime minister nor the Union health minister has called the chief ministers or the state health ministers for any meetings to mobilise the political leadership needed to contain the spread of this infection that knows neither politics nor geographic boundaries.

This is starkly different from the approach taken by the central government in 2009 when it was faced with the H1N1 epidemic. The then Union health minister, who was also a senior Congress leader, personally spoke to every chief minister and had face-to-face meetings with state health ministers and health secretaries to review the action taken and to be taken. Clearly, while the crisis is now being 'managed' bureaucratically, with the Cabinet Secretary reviewing the situation with the state government officials, the much-needed political leadership is tardy. The lockdown efforts are uneven, as they are being decided at the state level and do not fit into any consistent pattern. Time will tell if the uncoordinated action we are now witnessing will have any impact on the trajectory of the epidemic in India.

What Do These Measures Mean and Are They Enough?

The intensive enforcement of the classical measures of protection of public health has one objective: containment and reducing transmission. India is at the early stage of the epidemic with a 'window of opportunity' to prevent the spread of the infection into the community. Thus, efforts are needed to contain the spread by disrupting transmission. Such containment is done by screening persons who might have been in contact with the source of the infection. Screening helps identify people who have symptoms of infection such as a cough and fever. Throat and nasal swabs are sent for a Polymerase Chain Reaction (PCR) test to one of the 54 laboratories set up for the purpose. All positive samples go to the National Institute of Virology, Pune, for a confirmatory test. If confirmed, the individual is admitted to the hospital for treatment or quarantined and isolated.

Identification of an infected person leads to what is known as 'contact tracing'. This entails tracking the movement of the individual over the previous three days, sanitising the places visited and testing all those who had come in contact with the infected person. The purpose of this laborious process is to '[f]ind, isolate, test, and treat every case, to break the chains of transmission' (World Health Organisation 2020).

The efficacy of contact tracing as a strategy depends on thoroughness, diligence and speed, as demonstrated by Kerala. If poorly implemented, it can also raise concerns, as in the case of the first reported death in India from coronavirus. The history of this patient indicated travel from Karnataka to Hyderabad in Telangana, and back to Karnataka, where he died. Did Telangana go through the rigour of contact tracing of the people he came in contact with while at Hyderabad, and sanitising the three hospitals he visited in the city? If not, the possibility of new infections emerging cannot be ruled out. Time will tell.

Contact tracing is an effective methodology but needs diligence and well-trained human resources. The question that nags all is what will happen if the infection were to spread to the backward districts of say Bihar, Chhattisgarh or Jharkhand—states that have weak public health systems and limited public health personnel resources.

Contact tracing and testing are strong public health strategies that were found to be extremely valuable in India's efforts to reduce HIV infections as well as to eradicate polio. An effective public health response is one that quickly detects, tests and treats the infected. As the Director General of WHO said, 'You can't fight a virus if you don't know where it is ... Every case we find and treat limits the expansion of the disease' (World Health Organisation 2020).

It is the slow response of Government of India to this vital element of an effective strategy that is causing widespread concern. The testing rate of India is abysmally low, at five tests per million against over 4,000 for South Korea. The 56 testing sites across India that the government has notified are far too few. In Andhra Pradesh, for instance, there are two sites located at the two extreme ends of the state—Visakhapatnam and Tirupati. How do people access them?

To test or not test is a tricky issue and not entirely value-free. India's policy so far has been restrictive. Testing is confined to individuals with a travel history of coming from infected countries or to those who have been in contact with such persons. Based on such a restrictive policy and adding test results of 500 randomly selected persons suffering from pneumonia but with no travel history, the authorities claim that the epidemic in India is currently limited to clusters and has not entered the community. The attendant risk of missing infections, deliberate under-reporting or, as reported in a section of the media, denying testing to even those with symptoms and a history of travel to or from an infected country, has not been factored in. There are, therefore, questions about the reliability of the government's figures on the number of infections in the country.

The importance of stepping up testing cannot be over-emphasised. Successful strategies are based on solid evidence. Testing is the only source of such evidence. Information that can help determine the nature, characteristics and the epidemiology of the virus is vital to plot its trajectory and model its future pathways, all for taking pre-emptive action. Containing the virus does not mean locking up all people in their homes. It means a nearly accurate identification of the probable areas and persons the virus is likely to visit and then securing them.

Modelling will help come up with policy responses and aid in taking tough decisions that are critical for low-resource settings, as is the case in India. If the fatality rate among the elderly is 16 per cent and among 10-year-olds less than 0.2 per cent, why shut down schools? If those with co-morbidities like diabetes or hypertension are more vulnerable, why stop the healthy young from going to parks? The answers to these questions will facilitate a careful calibration of strategies so that the elderly and those with co-morbidities can be targeted for prevention and treatment.

Another public health action required for reducing transmission is information dissemination for behavioural change. Unlike HIV, the coronavirus does not lodge in the blood stream, or like multi-drug resistant tuberculosis, get transmitted through the air. The virus causes an upper respiratory infection. Since touching our faces with our hands is a common practice, prevention lies in frequent washing of hands with soap, not touching surfaces that may be contaminated and immediately thereafter touching our eyes, nose or mouth—the entry points to our lungs. As the virus gets transmitted through droplets via an unprotected cough, it is essential to ensure coughing into one's sleeve or a handkerchief.

These are simple behavioural changes, yet difficult to internalise. For instance, a Harvard University study showed how despite their best efforts in a few selected district hospitals of Uttar Pradesh, the behavioural change required of nurses to wear gloves and wash their hands before and after touching a patient was only half-successful. Repeated exhortations and monitoring are critical to induce change.

Crafting a Right Response

The nature of responses and the theory of change is, however, based on the availability of the right kind of information and knowledge, and the current state of understanding of the causality of infection, mode of transmission and impact. It is for this reason that aggressive information dissemination is at the core of guiding and regulating behaviour at the level of society, communities, individuals, caregivers and patients.

At this stage, information dissemination is the most effective social vaccine at hand. This means that all media channels must be mandated to provide critical information at regular intervals, frontline workers are suitably trained, hospitals and public spaces are provided with posters, handouts and audio clips, social media channels are utilised extensively, and call centres are established. In other words, as stated by the WHO:

> Every person must know the signs and symptoms and how to protect themselves and others. Every health worker should be able to recognize this disease, provide care and know what to do with their patients. Every health facility should be ready to cope with large numbers of patients, and ensure the safety of staff and patients. (World Health Organisation 2020)

The right information is also necessary to ensure that people are not misled and exploited by persons claiming cures and magic remedies or promoting therapies that have no scientific basis. For example, yoga, pranayama, good nutrition and ayurvedic therapies like cow-dung application or cow-urine intake may be good for one's wellbeing and promoting immunity, but to claim that they can cure a coronavirus infection is not just wrong but misleading.

The government and our scientists should have clarified these issues more rigorously rather than getting intimidated by the lobbies of traditional medicine that seem to have proximity to political power. Scientists should instead be asking for analysis based on science and evidence.

An emerging concern is the sustainability of the measures related to social distancing that are being undertaken in India and elsewhere, locking out all social and economic activity. Undoubtedly social distancing is an effective strategy. But questions of equity and sustainability arise. After all, for how long can schools, colleges, markets and economic activity be shut down? What about the mental stress that such social isolation measures may create, not to mention the loss in incomes and the attendant stress at the family level, particularly among those sections of population that live on daily earnings? These are important questions to ask while formulating a strategy.

While containing the infection and enhancing health security are vital, in the absence of an attendant welfare policy, the burden of the risk is disproportionately being borne by the poor. The loss of incomes, loss of mid-day meals at schools, loss of an academic year due to postponement of exams, or the loss of future jobs with the lockdown of industrial and economic activity in an already slowing economy can create a survival and existential crisis for millions of people. Can policies on rescheduling of repayment of loans, short-term income support, take-home rations, etc., be instituted till the crisis blows over?

The Way Forward

The coronavirus in its present avatar is new and no country really knows how to handle it. Each country is learning and sharing its experience. It is believed that India has a window of another two weeks to contain the infection. As of now, going by the number of the infected, the steps taken by the government appear to be effective. But the government now needs to shift its focus from international travellers to domestic preparedness, to expanding testing, and scale up information dissemination to people and caregivers as swiftly as possible.

With no vaccine or standardised therapy available, formulating treatment protocols can be complicated. It is because of the vast range of unknowables around the coronavirus that the response has been more or less confined to the government alone—state laboratories and public hospitals. That has served us well so far as the number of infected has been manageable until now. However, it is necessary to have a Plan-B as well for the 'in case' and 'what if' scenarios.

A Plan-B is necessary as a sudden spike in caseloads can overwhelm the public health system. It takes a while for the private sector to recalibrate and adjust to cope with new caseloads that require higher standards of sanitation and infection control measures, respiratory support systems and, more importantly, personnel trained in intensive care. The adequacy of intensive care units (ICUs) and general beds to accommodate a much higher number of patients needing hospitalisation is a serious issue. India has barely 20 per cent of the ICU beds that South Korea has, and overall, less than one hospital per 1,000 of the population. Even these facilities are inequitably distributed, with the northern states having far fewer beds, hospitals, personnel and ICUs. And it is in the northern states of Uttar Pradesh and Haryana that we are seeing a growing number of positive cases. The private sector is also weak in these states. It is such a scenario that makes enforcing prevention rigorously the best bet: 'Not testing alone. Not contact tracing alone. Not quarantine alone. Not social distancing alone. Do it all' (World Health Organisation 2020).

It is important to quickly bring on board biostatisticians and epidemiologists, particularly those with the experience of having handled SARS and H1N1, to analyse the experiences of other countries, apply those analytical tools to the Indian context, and make the quantitative projections necessary for formulating policy in this ever-changing scenario. There is no copy and paste approach possible, or mere imitation. What is needed is hard-nosed evidence and reason to guide action as the social and economic consequences can be very severe.

Policies need to be tempered keeping the social cost in mind. They must not be seen as asserting state authority over individual freedom, as was the case when the British enacted the Epidemic Diseases Act of 1897—the law being invoked now to contain coronavirus—to enforce public health measures in India during the plague in the late nineteenth century. They were well-meaning in intent but were perceived by the local populations to be an arrogant abuse of power as they found their homes, families and traditions uprooted and disrupted.

What we need are balance and transparency where people are engaged, involved and made participants in the process to tackle the virus and prevent it from taking over our lives.

References

Gopinath, Gita. 2020. 'The Great Lockdown: The Worst Economic Contraction since the Great Depression'. *IMFBlog*, 14 April. Available at https://blogs.imf.org/2020/04/14/the-great-lockdown-worst-economic-downturn-since-the-great-depression/ (accessed 16 November 2020).

World Bank. 2016. 'Impact of West Africa Ebola Crisis: 2014–15 Update'. Available at https://www.worldbank.org/en/topic/macroeconomics/

publication/2014-2015-west-africa-ebola-crisis-impact-update (accessed 16 November 2020).

World Health Organisation. 2020. 'WHO Director-General's Opening Remarks at the Media Briefing on COVID-19', 13 March. Available at https://www.who.int/director-general/speeches/detail/who-director-general-s-opening-remarks-at-the-mission-briefing-on-covid-19---13-march-2020 (accessed 13 November 2020).

Section II

Dealing with Pandemics in India's History

3

Covid-19 and the Spectres of Colonialism*

Pratik Chakrabarti

The Covid-19 pandemic has brought about unique challenges for governments and public health authorities across the world. It has also provided them with exceptional legal and judicial powers to restrict and control people's lives and livelihoods. But while the virus may be new, the modes of its control and prevention are not. Key aspects of the outbreak of Covid-19 and the measures to control it have historical and colonial legacies. Although the lockdown and the restrictions on public life in India appear unprecedented, they reproduce measures that colonial governments and public health officials had used to segregate, isolate and confine people during epidemics.

These measures include the legal provisions used for control, the development of experimental vaccines, the tracing of the asymptomatic carriers, the asymmetrical social and economic consequences, and the violation of basic human rights, particularly those of the poor and marginalised communities. Historically, governments have sought to deal with large-scale epidemic outbreaks through isolation and vaccination, both of which are at play in dealing with Covid-19. The extraordinary powers assumed by governments to undertake this twin task raise questions of ethics, human rights and the use of state powers over the lives and bodies of its citizens.

The historical instances of pandemic control in South Asia are vital to revisit. They illustrate the precedents of how political and social power operates in such times. In times of crisis, governments,

* First published in *The India Forum*, 10 July 2020.

health officials and privileged citizens keep returning to certain familiar patterns of self-preservation, which often add to the suffering of the most vulnerable.

Colonialism provided the first model of using scientific means of pandemic control for the large scale and often coercive regulation of people's lives and livelihoods. This model has been useful for postcolonial states in the current crisis. In imposing the strict restrictions of the lockdown for Covid-19, the Indian government invoked the very same Epidemic Diseases Act, originally passed by the British government during the plague outbreaks of 1897. This was a unique act, designed specifically to control an epidemic outbreak, giving special powers to the state, which is partly why it has appeared relevant for Covid-19.

The Colonial Mould

The outbreak of the plague epidemic in Bombay in 1897 fundamentally changed the relationship between the colonial state and its subjects. This was the first instance when the state acquired special legal and judicial powers for an apparently humanitarian cause: to prevent the spread of the epidemic. To do so, it specifically targeted the poor and the migrant workers, seen as the carriers of the disease, restricting their movements, demolishing their homes, and subjecting their bodies to medical experiments. This became the model for subsequent governments to use disease or epidemics to justify authoritarian measures, all the way into the current pandemic.

The Epidemic Diseases Act gave the colonial government the right to inspect and isolate anyone suspected of being infected with plague, in public places, trains, ships and inside their homes. It simultaneously protected the state or government officials from any legal action while acting under the act. Prior to this, the colonial government had in 1895 introduced the Pilgrim Ships Act to control the movement of Haj pilgrims from South Asia on health grounds. This gave local authorities in India new powers to board the pilgrim ships at any time to carry out inspections and apprehend any passenger in the name of disease prevention. The two acts combined to provide the colonial authorities almost unrestricted power to restrict the movements of the poor, migrant workers and Muslim pilgrims.

The Epidemic Diseases Act was used in large parts of the plague-affected localities of Bombay and Pune, in demolishing dwellings, and clearing so-called 'vagrants', beggars and migrant labourers. These measures continued to be the mainstay of the colonial state's anti-plague campaign well into the first part of the twentieth century. The government used the acts to prohibit immigration from India, particularly from the infected areas, for the suspension of railway travel to certain areas, and the obstructing of the Mecca pilgrimage. After the plagues ceased, the Epidemic Diseases Act was employed rarely, perhaps because there were few such sudden pandemic outbreaks.

Vaccination by Trials

The Bombay plague provided the opportunity to public health officials and scientists for the production and the large-scale experimentation of vaccines in the colonies. Just a decade before the outbreak, the French microbiologist Louis Pasteur had created the first attenuated vaccine for the rabies virus. This created the possibility that all viral and bacterial diseases could be prevented by similarly developed vaccines.

When plague broke out in the 1890s, bacteriologists Alexandre Yersin and Shibasaburo Kitasato had independently announced the isolation of the plague bacillus in Paris and in Hong Kong, respectively. With the outbreak of the plague, scientists developed competing vaccines, similar to the present-day global rush to produce vaccines for Covid-19 and to conduct human trials. In India, the Russian-Jewish scientist Waldemar Haffkine prepared his own plague vaccines in a small lab in Bombay.

Bombay, with its vast and diverse population and confined spaces such as jails, hospitals and slums, became the ideal site for experimenting with these vaccines. During the outbreak, colonial medical officials experimentally injected residents with at least six different types of vaccines. European bacteriologists such as A. Lustig, Yersin and Paul-Louis Simond saw Bombay as the perfect laboratory for their vaccines and visited the city to observe the experiments.

The authorities carefully selected groups of communities as samples for the experiment with the respective vaccines. These vaccinations were not designed to introduce any immunity against plague among the population, but were carried out as 'trials' (Chakrabarti 2012: 49–55). There is no evidence that any kind of consent was ever sought for these experiments. While the colonial government did not introduce any legal protection for those being vaccinated, even experimentally, it introduced laws to enforce vaccination.

These colonial measures were part of a trend in the nineteenth century where governments across the world assumed greater legal powers to conduct large-scale vaccination. Smallpox vaccinations were made compulsory in various parts of the world. Beginning in 1853 in the UK, it was soon applied in the colonies. The outbreaks of smallpox in 1865 in Calcutta, in 1876 in Bombay and in 1884 in Madras led the provincial governments to introduce compulsory vaccination acts in these Presidencies.

The coercive nature of vaccination has left a strong legacy of anti-vaccination campaigns and protests. Throughout Europe and North America, opponents regarded vaccination as threats to their health as well as an invasion of their rights. They formed anti-vaccination leagues, demanded that the government abolish compulsory vaccination, rioted, forged vaccination certificates, staged boycotts and hid sick children. In India, the persistence of the arm-to-arm method, in which children, often belonging to the lower castes, were used as carriers of the lymph for vaccination, was a matter of fierce public debate and resistance.

The debates have been on whether rights of individuals are greater than those of the welfare of the larger collective. As and when vaccines, prophylactics or drugs become available for Covid-19, there will be questions of how these can be made acceptable and accessible to large sections of the population. Historically, mass vaccinations and drug trials, particularly of those at early stages of their development, are as beset with the abuse of human rights as with the exercise of state power. Gaps in legal provision ensured that human subjects in colonial India had little control over their bodies in the pandemic state.

These trends continue into the postcolonial state, with state governments and public health authorities recommending the use of unproven hydroxychloroquine (Singh 2020) as a prophylactic against Covid-19 for slum dwellers (*BMJ Opinion* 2020), police (*Indian Express* 2020) and other frontline health workers (*News18* 2020), including those in present-day Mumbai. The recent controversy on the ICMR's rush to produce a vaccine for Covid-19 by Independence Day on 15 August, which has been deemed unfeasible by many experts, highlights that vaccine production timetables have deeply political mandates (Mukunth 2020). With the decision to cut out some of the unnecessary 'red tape', questions of the safety and efficacy of the vaccine, whenever it is available, will remain important.

Symptoms of the Asymptomatic Carrier

Identifying asymptomatic carriers, individuals who do not show any symptoms yet carry the pathogens in their bodies and are capable of infecting others, is a significant part of any preventive strategy for Covid-19. When millions of Indians might never be tested for the virus or its antibodies, how will we establish who is an asymptomatic carrier? In the absence of scientific proof, the question often is: who *appears* to be symptomatic?

Prejudices about class, gender and caste address this question. In India, the scientific idea of 'asymptomatic carrier' is introducing new forms of 'untouchability'. Upper caste and class Indians are seeking to distance themselves from the poor, Muslims and lower castes, whom they perceive as the carriers of the virus (Ghose 2020). There have been reports in India of migrant workers being sprayed with chemical disinfectants, of several of them restricted from returning to their homes while facing starvation due to lack of work, and of international travellers and visitors being assaulted by vigilantes.

The idea of the asymptomatic carrier was proposed by Robert Koch in 1902, when he suggested that healthy individuals, who show no signs of a disease, could carry within them germs with which others may be infected. Long before the discovery of asymptomatic carriers, certain communities in South Asia had historically been seen as likely carriers of disease. Koch's scientific thesis provided seeming validity to these entrenched layers of cultural, social, caste, racial and nationalist prejudice.

This has contributed to government actions against individuals or groups perceived as disease carriers and towards upper caste communities segregating themselves even further from the lower castes and the poor. In colonial India, the British widely regarded poor and working-class Indians as carriers of multiple diseases. As with the poor residents of Bombay in the time of plague, in times of the coronavirus, some groups continue to be presumed infected before proven.

The scientism of the so-called 'carrier-state' theory has become a tool to legitimise major and often prejudicial global and colonial immigration control and segregation policies. Twinning quarantine and immigration, authorities often identified certain groups as potential 'carriers' of diseases, and Jews, Irish, Mexicans, Haj pilgrims from South Asia and the Chinese were at various times in the past subject to rigorous medical checks or to lengthy quarantine at immigration points, and even barred from entering specific countries. To do so, authorities sometimes used existing legal provisions or created new ones.

The incidence of quarantine against Ebola during its outbreak in western Africa in 2014–15 and the restrictions imposed in the US on travel from that region shows how the question of the asymptomatic carrier and quarantine remain. In a notable case, Kaci Hickox, an American nurse treating Ebola patients in Sierra Leone, was quarantined on her return (ACLU New Jersey 2017). Research showed that the very low risk of Ebola transmission from asymptomatic individuals and that quarantines of asymptomatic individuals with potential Ebola exposure were unnecessary (ACLU, n.d.). In the ensuing legal case, the court declared that the quarantine of Hickox was not necessary since the evidence supported that asymptomatic persons were not infectious.

Conclusions

The resurrection of the Epidemic Diseases Act for Covid-19 reflects colonial modes of drastic governmental action, which has once again exposed the most vulnerable communities to greater health and economic risks. The strict lockdown measures for Covid-19 need to be seen alongside the general disinvestment in public health and the poor medical facilities available for the vast majority of the population. It is usually easier to establish quarantine measures than to build preventative healthcare. While the colonial government introduced strict quarantine, it did not invest similarly in public health.

In contemporary India as well, the lockdown is accompanied by an acute shortage of doctors, nurses, hospital beds and other medical infrastructure. In these lockdowns, in the millions of poor people suffering without food, income, shelter and adequate healthcare, colonialism is finding new forms of expression. As we deal with the current outbreak, we are also faced with the question of what Covid-19 will leave behind.

While on the one hand there is the possibility of more such outbreaks taking place, on the other there is also the prospect of greater social and political control of our lives becoming the norm. While we prepare ourselves for and take precautions against similar such outbreaks in the future, we need to simultaneously raise questions of liberty and freedom associated with such provisions. The colonial past provides important lessons on how pandemic outbreaks have not only caused huge mortalities, but have also sanctioned extreme governmental powers.

In the case of Covid-19, the impetus for such control has come not just from the Indian state. Society itself has sought to be governed at a much wider and deeper level. Several of the strong governmental actions enjoy support from large sections of the population. Among certain sections, the popularity of the government has reportedly soared because of the drastic lockdown measures it has taken (Gettleman and Yasir 2020). Bill Gates praised the Indian government's strong and 'proactive' actions against the outbreak, even as numerous migrant workers were stranded without food, money, or any means of travelling or earning their livelihood (*English Jagran* 2020).

What *is* the humanitarian position here; imposing more restrictions on people's lives or alternatively allowing them to make their choices? We are clearly seeking more governance or, more precisely, stronger state intervention than ever before. Is that choice, both in India and elsewhere, being made by certain sections of the society at the expense of others? For India, Covid-19 might imply that certain populations will be faced with long-term and stricter regimes of social control and exclusion, while their labour is extracted from a distance. Covid-19 has made the return of the spectre of colonialism more real.

References

'Fear, Politics, and Ebola', n.d. American Civil Liberties Union (ACLU). Available at https://www.aclu.org/issues/privacy-technology/medical-and-genetic-privacy/fear-politics-and-ebola (accessed 15 November 2020).

'Hydroxychloroquine to be Given to Health Workers Treating Covid-19 Patients, Says Maharashtra Govt'. 2020. *News18*, 29 April. Available at https://www.news18.com/news/india/hydroxychloroquine-to-be-given-to-health-workers-treating-covid-19-patients-says-maharashtra-govt-2597393.html (accessed 15 November 2020).

'Kaci Hickox's Settlement with Christie Administration Creates Quarantine "Bill of Rights"'. 2017. ACLU New Jersey, 27 July. Available at https://www.aclu-nj.org/news/2017/07/27/victory-detained-nurses-ebola-suit-secures-due-process (accessed 15 November 2020).

'Mumbai, Rajasthan Advise Hydroxychloroquine for Police, Doubts Over It Persist'. 2020. *Indian Express*, 14 April. Available at https://indianexpress.com/article/coronavirus/mumbai-rajasthan-coronavirus-covid-19-hydroxychloroquine-6361434/ (accessed 15 November 2020).

'Rolling Out Mass Hydroxychloroquine Prophylaxis for Covid-19 in India's Slums Risks Eroding Public Trust'. 2020. *BMJ Opinion*, 1 May. Available at https://blogs.bmj.com/bmj/2020/05/01/rolling-out-mass-hydroxychloroquine-prophylaxis-for-covid-19-in-indias-slums-risks-public-trust/ (accessed 15 November 2020).

'"We Commend Your Leadership": Bill Gates Praises PM Modi's Proactive Approach in Fighting COVID-19'. 2020. *English Jagran*, 22 April. Available at https://english.jagran.com/india/we-commend-your-leadership-bill-gates-praises-pm-modis-proactive-approach-in-fighting-covid19-10011017 (accessed 15 November 2020).

Chakrabarti, Pratik. 2012. *Bacteriology in British India: Laboratory Medicine and the Tropics*. Rochester: Rochester University Press.

Gettleman, Jeffrey and Sameer Yasir. 2020. 'Modi's Popularity Soars as India Weathers the Pandemic'. *New York Times*, 16 May. Available at https://www.nytimes.com/2020/05/16/world/asia/coronavirus-modi-india.html (accessed 15 November 2020).

Ghose, Sagarika. 2020. 'Covid-19 has Exposed Middle Class Paranoia and India's Class Faultlines'. *Times of India*, 14 June. Available at https://timesofindia.indiatimes.com/blogs/bloody-mary/covid-19-has-exposed-middle-class-paranoia-and-indias-class-faultlines/ (accessed 15 November 2020).

India. 1897. 'The Epidemic Diseases Act, 1897'. Available at https://www.indiacode.nic.in/bitstream/123456789/7799/1/a1897-03_epidemic_diseases_act%2c_1897.pdf (accessed 15 November 2020).

Mukunth, Vasudevan. 2020. 'ICMR's Rush to Produce "Indian Vaccine" for COVID-19 Suggests Politics is Driving Science'. *The Wire*, 3 July. Available at https://thewire.in/health/icmr-balram-bhargava-covaxin-clinical-trials-bharat-biotech-politics (accessed 15 November 2020).

Singh, Tanmay. 2020. 'Why the Health Ministry's Hydroxychloroquine Recommendation Is Not Legal'. *Science, The Wire*, 2 June. Available at https://science.thewire.in/health/covid-19-india-health-ministry-hydroxy chloroquine-recommendation-illegal/ (accessed 15 November 2020).

4

Manufacturing Epidemics

*Pathogens, Poverty and Public Health Crises in India**

Sheetal Chhabria

In February 1897, six months after the first case of bubonic plague was found in colonial Bombay, a thousand people were fleeing the city each day, spreading the disease throughout colonial India. Residents in central Bombay locked themselves up in their flats, afraid that plague officers would come knocking. Children were rounded up in ambulances if they seemed ill, often against the will of their relatives. By 1921, the plague would kill 10 million people throughout India.

But plague was not colonial India's only problem—cholera, smallpox, malaria, tuberculosis, vague 'fevers', and plain old starvation were constant sources of death. Between 1896 and 1921, malaria may have killed 20 million people, twice as many as the plague did in the same period (Kumar et al. 1983). Some 12–20 million people perished in India during the influenza pandemic of 1918 (Mills 1986). Throughout the history of British India, 23–35 million people died of cholera epidemics, and already by 1900 over 30 million people had died of famine-related causes (Davis 2002). All of these numbers are quite likely to be underestimates than overestimates due to the difficulty in gaining accurate figures and the politically motivated disinclination to report.

Surprising, then, that it was the bubonic plague which was declared *the* crisis to deal with in colonial Bombay. Then, as now, only

---

* First published in *The India Forum*, 8 May 2020.

one out of a handful of deadly afflictions—the one that most directly threatened commerce, trade and the accumulation of capital—was identified as a 'crisis'. The plague would be the Bombay government's priority for the following two decades. Once capital and labour started to flee the city in the plague's wake, the government undertook unprecedented efforts to bring them back in. The wheels of commerce had to be made to turn once again.

Ever since Covid-19 has interrupted life in India, media references to both the plague of 1896 and the influenza pandemic of 1918 have become commonplace. India's lockdown has produced disturbing scenes reminiscent of an earlier era: masses of migrants returning home on foot, a growing crisis of hunger alongside the cruel irony of godowns overflowing with 70 million tonnes of food surpluses (Sen, Rajan and Banerjee 2020), arbitrary powers usurped by police patrols across the country, and even the revival of plague-era laws like the Epidemic Diseases Act of 1897.

In both the nineteenth century and in the present, the eventfulness of the chosen crisis displaces attention away from longstanding structural vectors of inequality and mortality. The force of the market, ideologically and materially, determines which events can be narrated as a crisis and which cannot, just as it determined the government's priorities in managing it. When history seems to be repeating itself, it is perhaps only natural to look to the past. But some of the lessons on offer are misguided.

For example, some argue that the key takeaway from the plague of 1896 is that lockdowns, while inconvenient, are essential to controlling contagion (Verma 2020). They forget that lockdowns are measures of last resort undertaken when public health infrastructures are wanting because they are at capacity. Others write (Koshy 2020) that past epidemics teach us that we ought to be patient—'trust history, this will pass'—since microbes and humans have long shaped each other in human history, an argument that shades into social Darwinism.

But by far, the worst line of argumentation is a very subtle one that places diseases and epidemics outside of 'the economy' (Mitchell 2010). Such an argument assumes that diseases are simply products of nature, devoid of human imprint. As such, diseases interfere with an individual's ability to earn a living or a society's ability to pursue economic growth. Since Covid-19 has struck, far too many will be 'pushed into poverty' (Sen, Rajan and Banerjee 2020), and the best we can do is to mitigate their hunger and pain with relief until we can return to 'normal'. In this argument, poverty is a result of disease.

Instead, the colonial past might offer different lessons. Primarily we learn that poverty is not just a result but also a *causal condition* for much neglected endemic and epidemic diseases to thrive. Together, poverty, hunger and illness are *the common results* of a political and economic system biased towards the more privileged in society. Therefore, sporadic crisis episodes like the plague, the flu pandemic, and even Covid-19 burst onto a scene already ravaged by quieter and steadier crises of cholera, malaria, hunger and gruelling poverty.

If we return to the history of pandemics with this broader understanding, what more can we learn about our present predicament?

Pathogens Need Poverty

The first lesson of the health crises of a century ago is that most illnesses struggle to act alone. To produce mass mortality, pathogens require the compromised economic conditions that thrive along commercial networks. In other words, pathogens feed on chronic deprivation (Polu 2012).

Colonial India's mortality rates from communicable illnesses such as cholera were much higher compared with most of the world. For instance, in Britain, only 150,000 people died of cholera in the entire nineteenth century, a mere fraction of India's cholera deaths. Over the following century too, India maintained a global lead in disease mortality, due to a callous disregard for working-class lives and the systematic neglect of public health that was just as remarkable in the colonial era as it is now. How can we explain this?

Historians have found a key factor that accounts for India's disproportionately high rates of disease mortality: the simultaneity of illness with hunger. Both cholera and influenza thrived when prolonged bouts of hunger compromised the body's defences, leading to large discrepancies in mortality between hungry and sated populations. About cholera epidemics in the nineteenth century,

David Arnold writes that mortality doubled or tripled when cholera coincided with famine. Their 'lethal synchronization' (Arnold 1986) caused the highest recorded number of cholera deaths in Madras in 1866 and 1877, and in Bombay in 1877. Cholera mortality declined in the early 1900s but once again saw an upsurge during the Bengal famine and Partition in the 1940s. Similarly about the 1918 flu pandemic, Mike Davis (2010) finds famine and disease 'exquisitely synchronized'. The resultant grain hoarding by traders meant inaccessible prices for India's labourers. India's mortality rate, especially in Bombay's environs, made an especially large portion of global flu deaths.

If hunger was a predisposing condition to disease mortality, then sadly, hunger was not hard to produce. The colonial government's gradual erosion of the rights of smaller cultivators and the promotion of cash crops spelled for many the loss of access to livelihood and to food crops. As a result, there were regional famines in colonial India in every decade of the nineteenth century. While famines were said to be a result of 'natural conditions' like drought, it was in fact the changing social systems of ownership and control that alienated cultivators from basic entitlements like food.

To cope, several cultivators fled for the cities, even as they maintained connections in the villages. This protection strategy gave them some safety. They could flee the city during periods of downturn following speculative business cycles, like at the end of Bombay's cotton-led boom in the 1860s. When the famines in the 1870s killed some 10 million people in the countryside, they turned back to the city for relief.

But famished migrants got very little relief from a callous government eager to motivate cultivators towards industriousness rather than dependency on the state. Business owners refused to hire these 'unskilled' labour or invest in training them. Relief camps were governed by constant calculations: 'what is the bare minimum amount of grain *we* have to give to keep *them* alive but still motivated to work?'

Thus, as the government and its allies were busy debating whether and what they owed workers and famished migrants, India's working classes struggled to eat. In a climate of several endemic diseases, before antibiotics or the understanding of how pathogens work, compromised individuals became carriers who threatened the health of even the well-fed.

Thus, related to the first historical lesson that pathogens require compromised economic conditions, conditions created by the increase in commercial opportunities for some, is the fact that the poverty of one person produces disease in many. As a result, famines throughout the late 1800s coincided with repeated endemic outbreaks in colonial India.

Corrupting Public Health

The second lesson of colonial-era health crises is that moneyed classes opposed public health investments that benefited the population as a whole. As a result of that pattern continuing after Independence, India remains one of the worst places in the world to get sick (United Nations Development Programme, n.d.). It continues to produce an outsized number of deaths per disease outbreak, with illnesses that have all but disappeared from the 'developed' world regularly wiping out tens of thousands of inhabitants a year.

By the late nineteenth century, worldwide medical advances helped identify germs, rather than miasma or bad air, as the cause of most illnesses. But in colonial India, the belief in miasma and other discredited explanations for epidemics continued. While preventative public health measures like water management were starting to take hold in other parts of the world, in India 'public health' narrowly connoted post-outbreak disease management rather than anticipatory population-level planning.

Historical commonsense suggests that the colonial regime's low public health expenditures were a result of its self-interestedness. Wanting primarily to defend its colony, the colonial regime invested selectively, sanitising areas crucial to colonial rule, like military cantonments, but elsewhere encouraged Indians to look after their own wellbeing. Disproportionately low investments in sewage, drainage and water supply lines meant that colonial India did not obtain the public works that all but stopped water-related illnesses like malaria or cholera in what would become the developed world.

After all, British *colonial* rule was an external force meant to extract and exploit, not invest in a sustainable future.

But if we ask exactly why the colonial state failed to invest, it reveals a much more insidious story of how power works. In 1885, a year in which cholera killed many inhabitants, the *British Medical Journal* reported:

> Bombay, far from being a poor city, is perhaps the richest in India; and it is notorious that its wealthy inhabitants, being the most litigious people in the East, spend yearly in the law-courts, mostly in frivolous suits, enormous sums of money, which would be better spent in cleansing the city, where they live and prematurely die.

This complaint would become part of a longer pattern of volleying blame between the colonial regime and the Indian elite for exactly who should bear the burden of developing the country. But in that tussle, both sides won by deferring and displacing expenditures. The poorest of Indians lost.

Take, for instance, the difference in cholera rates between the cities of Bombay and Calcutta in the late nineteenth century. Capital city Calcutta, with its large population of colonial officials, constructed water supply and sewage systems, causing cholera rates to drop between 1870 and 1900 (Arnold 1986). By contrast, in Bombay, when municipal commissioner Arthur Crawford proposed an extensive drainage system, he was forced to resign when landholders protested against the proposed tax to cover the expenditures (Lewis and Harris 2013). As a result, Bombay's cholera rates remained higher than Calcutta's. Rather than share in the burden of building a public goods regime that might have mitigated some of the underlying causes of epidemics, the wealthy avoided such investments, be it housing for their labourers, fair compensation for work, or sources of clean water.

In sum, Indian aristocrats, landlords, financiers and industrialists did much to determine state agendas, colonial or otherwise. They blocked public health when it would cost them. But there could be one exception to this pattern. If the occasion of a crisis could be made lucrative, even the moneyed classes could take interest in 'the health of their city'.

The plague of 1896 was that exception. When plague arrived in Bombay in 1896, the panic in one of India's leading commercial hubs severely threatened the economy of the colony. The city came to a grinding halt. Factories and businesses voluntarily shuttered. Fixed costs or investments made in industrial production sat idle. Some 300,000 migrants left Bombay in 1897, making even rent-seeking a frustrating endeavour, given the dearth of the labouring and indebted classes.

To restore commerce, the city had to be cleansed of contagion. In 1898, the City of Bombay Improvement Trust was formed to restore the 'sanitary credit' of the city. Even though rural mortality was higher, focusing on the city showed how the Trust was more eager to address the 'crisis' of stalled commerce rather than public health. Over the next three decades, the Trust corrupted the meaning of 'public purpose'. Guided by the discredited miasma theory of contagion, it acquired properties so as to widen thoroughfares and 'let light and air in'. The Trust spent public money to overcompensate landlords who produced hypothetical building plans to claim higher compensation on the grounds their plots *could* have fetched higher sums (Chhabria 2019).

The city's capitalists and officials thus repurposed an institution formed to deal with a public health disaster into one that made the rich even richer, even as they failed to address Bombay's housing and sanitation problems. As a result, once the flu pandemic arrived alongside a drought in 1918, it spread especially through the city's 'slums' where the poorest were forced to contend with both illness and hunger all at once. By the 1920s, the health of the city meant anything but the health of its poorest residents.

Manufactured Epidemics

Using this historical analysis, we learn that the production of widespread poverty, the resultant malnourishment and hunger, and the neglect of public health investments *together* form the conditions under which India's real public health disaster is created time and time again.

Back in 1897, just before Bombay's Improvement Trust was formed, the *British Medical Journal* wrote that 'habitual and not spasmodic sanitation is the only real safeguard against epidemic disease'. In colonial India this would have required public investment and future-oriented planning. Even in the decades after Independence, advocacy for such planning has had to swim upstream against the interests of the propertied classes who could (and did) force the privatisation of public health (Krishnan 2015).

Our current Covid-19 crisis is not a singular event. It is one effect of a decades-long process that has produced impoverishment, hunger and ill-health, all at once (Gopalan 2020). Just as in the health crises of a century ago, illnesses do not act alone. To produce mass mortality, pathogens require mass poverty. As we have also seen, there is no solving of health crises when moneyed classes oppose public health investments that benefit the population as a whole. Not just in India but across the world, historically racialised, minoritised, neglected and impoverished communities disproportionately bear the burden of disease, including Covid-19 (*The Guardian* 2020). Mass hunger will certainly be the result of a poorly designed lockdown in India, but that so many were so close to the brink of starvation reveals just how deep the structural vectors of inequality and mortality already were.

We need to tackle the underlying structural inequities that breathe life into every natural disaster. Ultimately, pathogens are not outside of the world of commerce we have created. They are its effects. It takes human effort to make pathogens work. Cholera and malaria thrive where public water works are neglected. Influenza thrives under conditions of starvation. Malnourishment is the perfect breeding ground for a whole host of illnesses. To produce malnourishment, one has to neglect or mystify decades-long agricultural crises, farmers' demands, and the basic right to food and health. To be so very vulnerable to viral illness like Covid-19, one has to tether pharmaceutical industries to endless profit rather than public welfare (Davis 2020).

Decades of disinvestment and neglect mean that even after Independence, India's disease burden continues to be disproportionately high, even absent Covid-19. Just as in the colonial period, India's underdevelopment is manufactured, a product of neglect and failure to take seriously the need for genuine public goods and the need to discipline the self-interestedness of private interests. For-profit medical entrepreneurship (Krishnan 2015) is celebrated as a national achievement and has produced worse health outcomes than in well-funded public institutions driven by democratically scrutable metrics.

India has the largest number of undernourished people in the world (*The Hindu* 2015). Malnourishment is India's 'silent emergency', with higher child malnourishment rates than in sub-Saharan Africa and five times as much as in China (World Bank 2013). Tuberculosis claims the highest number of lives in India (Singh and Kumar 2019). One-fifth of maternal deaths and one-quarter of child deaths in the world occurs in India (Balarajan, Selvaraj and Subramanian 2011). Amongst children under five, India has the highest mortality rates worldwide (*Economic Times* 2019). India spends less than 1.5 per cent of its GDP on health, one of the lowest in the world even amongst developing countries (Chandna 2019).

If we have learned anything from the past or the present, it should be that only well-funded public health systems, where public purpose is not corrupted by private ambition, can properly mitigate outbreaks (Gopalan 2020). As we have seen with the coronavirus outbreak, the relentless pursuit of profit in some parts of the 'developed world' provides no model to emulate (*BBC* 2020). Rather, India's own state of Kerala reveals that true development entails a strong public goods regime (Kurian 2020), one that protects all of its citizens from premature death.

Pursuing prevention is the truest meaning of public health, one that would require acknowledging what one analyst, V. Geetha (2020), has correctly noted: 'We cannot tackle the coronavirus without tackling capital and its depredations.' If only the political will could be found.

References

'Coronavirus: US Death Toll Overtakes Italy as World's Highest'. 2020. *BBC*, 12 April. Available at https://www.bbc.com/news/world-us-canada-52258284 (accessed 15 November 2020).

'Helping India Combat Persistently High Rates of Malnutrition'. 2013. World Bank, 13 May. Available at https://www.worldbank.org/en/news/feature/2013/05/13/helping-india-combat-persistently-high-rates-of-malnutrition (accessed 15 November 2020).

'Indian and the Colonies'. 1897. *The British Medical Journal* 2 (1922): 1304.

'India Had World's Highest Child Mortality Rate in 2015: Lancet Study'. 2019. *Economic Times*, 15 May. Available at https://economictimes.indiatimes.com/news/politics-and-nation/india-had-worlds-highest-child-mortality-rate-in-2015-lancet-study/articleshow/69338346.cms?from=mdr (accessed 15 November 2020).

'India Tops World Hunger List with 194 Million People'. 2015. *The Hindu*, 28 May. Available at https://www.thehindu.com/news/national/india-is-home-to-194-million-hungry-people-un/article7255937.ece (accessed 15 November 2020).

'Is a Cholera-Hospital a Source of Danger to the Neighbouring Population?'. 1885. *The British Medical Journal* 1 (1261): 444–45.

'"It's a Racial Justice Issue": Black Americans are Dying in Greater Numbers from Covid-19'. 2020. *The Guardian*, 8 April. Available at https://www.theguardian.com/world/2020/apr/08/its-a-racial-justice-issue-black-americans-are-dying-in-greater-numbers-from-covid-19 (accessed 15 November 2020).

Arnold, David. 1986. 'Cholera and Colonialism in British India'. *Past and Present* 113: 118–51.

Balarajan, Y., S. Selvaraj and S. V. Subramanian. 2011. 'Health Care and Equity in India'. *India: Towards Universal Health Coverage* 377 (9764): 505–15.

Chandna, Himani. 2019. 'At 1.28% of GDP, India's Expenditure on Health is Still Low although Higher than Before'. *The Print*, 31 October. Available at https://theprint.in/health/at-1-28-gdp-india-expenditure-on-health-still-low-although-higher-than-before/313702/ (accessed 15 November 2020).

Chhabria, Sheetal. 2019. *Making the Modern Slum: The Power of Capital in Colonial Bombay*. US: University of Washington Press.

Davis, Mike. 2002. *Late Victorian Holocausts: El Niño Famines and the Making of the Third World*. Kiribati: Verso.

———. 2010. *The Monster at Our Door: The Global Threat of Avian Flu*. US: New Press.

———. 2020. 'Mike Davis on Coronavirus: "In a Plague Year"'. *Jocobin*, 14 March. Available at https://jacobinmag.com/2020/03/mike-davis-coronavirus-outbreak-capitalism-left-international-solidarity (accessed 15 November 2020).

Geetha, V. 2020. 'The Coronavirus Has Rendered the Everyday Injustice of Our Times Dramatic'. *The Wire*, 19 April. Available at https://thewire.in/rights/conquistadors-capital-coronavirus (accessed 15 November 2020).

Gopalan, Aparna. 2020. 'Covid-19: India's Decades of Deep-seated Callousness to the Poor is Going to Cost Us All Dearly'. *Scroll.in*, 9 April. Available at https://scroll.in/article/958636/covid-19-indias-decades-of-deep-seated-callousness-to-the-poor-is-going-to-cost-us-all-dearly (accessed 15 November 2020).

Koshy, Rinu. 2020. 'Conspiracy Theories, Evading Quarantine: The Bombay Plague Bore Witness to It All'. *The Wire*, 12 April. Available at https://thewire.in/culture/bombay-plague-coronavirus (accessed 15 November 2020).

Krishnan, Vidya. 2015. 'Private Practice'. *Caravan Magazine*, 1 February. Available at https://caravanmagazine.in/reportage/naresh-trehan-medanta-private-practice (accessed 15 November 2020).

Kumar, Dharma, Irfan Habib, Meghnad Desai and Tapan Raychaudhuri. 1983. *The Cambridge Economic History of India: Volume 2, C.1757–c.1970*. UK: Cambridge University Press.

Kurian, Oommen C. 2020. 'How the Indian State of Kerala Flattened the Coronavirus Curve'. *The Guardian*, 21 April. Available at https://www.theguardian.com/commentisfree/2020/apr/21/kerala-indian-state-flattened-coronavirus-curve (accessed 15 November 2020).

Lewis, Robert and Richard Harris. 2013. 'Segregation and the Social Relations of Place, Bombay, 1890–1910'. *South Asia: Journal of South Asian Studies* 36 (4): 589–607.

Mitchell, Timothy. 2010. 'Fixing the Economy'. *Cultural Studies* 12 (1): 82–101.

Mills, I. D. 1986. 'The 1918–1919 Influenza Pandemic: The Indian Experience'. *The Indian Economic and Social History Review* 23 (1): 1–40.

Polu, S. L. 2012. 'Plague and Cholera: The Epidemic versus the Endemic'. In *Infectious Disease in India, 1892–1940*, Cambridge Imperial and Post-colonial Studies Series, 50–81. London: Palgrave Macmillan.

Sen, Amartya, Raghuram Rajan and Abhijit Banerjee. 2020. '"Huge Numbers May be Pushed into Dire Poverty or Starvation … We Need to Secure Them"'. *Indian Express*, 17 April. Available at https://indianexpress.com/article/opinion/coronavirus-india-lockdown-economy-amartya-sen-raghuram-rajan-abhijit-banerjee-6364521/ (accessed 15 November 2020).

Singh, S., and S. Kumar. 2019. 'Tuberculosis in India: Road to Elimination'. *International Journal of Preventive Medicine* 10: 114.

United Nations Development Programme, n.d. 'Human Development Reports: Health Index', 1980–2013. Available at http://hdr.undp.org/en/content/health-index (accessed 15 November 2020).

Verma, Suyash. 2020. 'How the Bombay Plague of 1896 Played Out'. *Science, The Wire*, 7 April. Available at https://science.thewire.in/society/history/how-the-bombay-plague-of-1897-played-out/ (accessed 15 November 2020).

5

'The Government Will Come to Its Senses'

*Calcutta's Workers and the Plague of 1898**

Prerna Agarwal

In innumerable articles in the business press or in reportage quoting industry spokespersons, there lurks an apprehension about the response of India's workers to the Covid-19 crisis. A lot has been written about the impact of the pandemic and the ensuing lockdown on the poor and on 'migrant labour', but precious little has been revealed about how the working classes themselves see the current crisis. Commentators and politicians stood perplexed at the audacity of thousands of workers protesting in Surat and in Bandra (Mumbai), the images invading prime-time news for the first time in decades. All kinds of conspiracy theories were hatched to explain the turn of events, but not even a single worker was interviewed.

Such a mixture of apprehension, perplexity and ignorance among the ruling elite during epidemics is hardly new and, in the past, it was not without consequences. In *Colonizing the Body* (1993), David Arnold writes how during the plague epidemic of 1896–98, unprecedented and arrogant state intervention 'provoked the greatest upsurge of public resistance to Western medicine and sanitation that nineteenth-century India had witnessed'. He brings to our attention the enormous implications of social and political distance that separated the coloniser and the colonised, specifically in times of epidemics. The British had to learn a few lessons, arriving at administrative measures that were considered more acceptable by the population.

* First published in *The India Forum*, 1 May 2020.

Calcutta, capital of British India, second city of the empire, and one of the world's most profitable ports, was a site of such state interventions and popular resistance. These actions caused disruptions and disorders as Calcutta's workers resorted to riots, strikes and demonstrations during the plague. These were the first mass actions of Calcutta's working classes, demonstrating their social cohesion and their collective ability to effectively organise opposition across various occupations and industries.

By the end of the nineteenth century, Calcutta had been transformed by industrialisation and emerged as a city with a significant working-class population. As the city's poor came to dominate its physical spaces in terms of sheer numbers, and its economy by effectively running it, they also became politically dangerous. Working together in thousands in newly built factories and workshops and living in overcrowded *bustis* (slums), their means to deal with the multitude of daily problems was too often collective. Historians regard the 1890s as the first decade when strikes and communal riots assumed large proportions.

It was in such a context that the outbreak of the largest plague epidemic under British rule, from the last week of April 1898 onwards, pitched the labouring classes, the poor and the unemployed against the owners and managers of industrial and commercial concerns (both Indian and British-owned) and the colonial state. As opposed to strikes, which were related to one or several mills, and as opposed to communal riots, when solidarities amongst the poor broke down, the plague riots were a response of the urban poor as a whole towards a common threat.

The plague did not affect Calcutta with the same ferocity as it did Bombay, but even in Calcutta, colonial authorities tried to forcibly and violently implement methods of regulation. The colonised were acutely aware of such preoccupations. A rumour floated among many that the viceroy 'was willing to kill off 200,000 of the inhabitants of Calcutta so that British power could be maintained' (Arnold 1987). Early on, the government secured the loyalties of the city's bhadralok elite by making different arrangements for the people of 'better classes'. For instance, they were not to be removed to hospitals, but were isolated in their own houses (Basu 2004). The poor, of course, received a very different treatment.

The Terrorised Elites

From the last days of April 1898 until the end of May, Calcutta's elites and authorities were seized by a terror of the 'lower orders', 'evil intentioned and ignorant people', 'pilgrims, gypsies, vagabonds', and 'persons of coolie classes or people wearing dirty and torn clothes', as the city's poor were variously referred to. On 12 May, the pro-British newspaper *The Englishman* reported that:

> It is to be feared that the ignorant and uneducated of the inhabitants of Calcutta are taking up an attitude towards the plague rules ... The mob running away with the idea that it is all powerful, mistaking the concessions already made by the government as due to fear, has now apparently made up its mind that it will forcibly prevent the segregation of plague patients.

The ruling classes hardly felt in control even by the end of May. 'A citizen' wrote to *The Englishman* that:

> The position affairs have assumed seems to me to call for a drastic and prompt remedy. Half-hearted measures and continuance of the forbearance, which has reached the verge of weakness and only encourage the mob of *budmashes* and *goondas,* who are now virtually in possession, so to speak, of Calcutta, and its suburbs, are of no use whatever.

Panic among the Poor, Disorder in the Workplace

From where did such fears arise? On 3 May, after the declaration of a plague inoculation drive, panic spread among the city's poor that they would be forcibly inoculated. They believed that inoculation could even kill healthy people and prepared to defend themselves by any means.

The disorders that ensued were not merely defensive. Workers took the opportunity to temporarily overturn the existing social order.

What followed were scenes that could not be imagined in normal times, scenes of a world turned upside down.

More than a thousand workers of the Carriage and Wagon Works at Howrah went on strike on 3 May 1898. Even the remaining 2,000 workers who came to work in the morning did not go back to work after their morning meal-break. They collected at the front of the gates of the workshop and 'began discussing the inoculation question'.

The head of the department tried to convince them to return, but most of them refused because they feared that they might be forcibly inoculated. On 4 May, a general strike began. *The Englishman* wrote:

> The wild rumours of last week ... have given place to still wilder stories regarding the intentions of government to inoculate everybody forcibly ... Large number of men employed on the local mills and railways, domestic servants, gari-wallahs, cartmen, and others have gone on strike, thus inflicting the greatest injury and inconvenience on the employers themselves.

On many of Calcutta's thoroughfares, large crowds, threatening and defiant, assembled. In old Calcutta, Jaun Bazaar, Halliday Street and Entally were the principal centres. In Jaun Bazaar, *ticca garhis*, the main means of transportation for goods and men, were stopped and drivers were 'warned not to convey patients to the hospital'.

A strike by cart-men brought the transportation of goods in the city to a standstill. Loaded carts were used to block the streets. Workers struck work in various parts of the city. Complaints were heard from the gas works in Narkeldanga, the Howrah railway yard and the Calcutta port.

At Howrah railway yard, coolies were 'preventing some carters from conveying the coal belonging to the Bengal Coal Company to the workshops of Jessops and Co', *The Englishman* reported. Three-fourths of the coolies working at the jetties in the Calcutta port were estimated to be on strike. At the port, 'the cart-men have been lurking about the jetties to prevent any work being done'. They were discussing amongst each other that if the jetties were stopped from plying, 'the government will come to its senses'.

There were several instances of violent resistance. The officiating District Superintendent of Police found a large number of men armed with lathis near the Howrah Maidan, 'advancing into the town, with the intention of creating a disturbance'. *The Englishman* reported that this was because 'a doctor, *assisted by a native sergeant and two native constables* [emphasis added], had in the absence of the men commenced inoculating the women in a busti close by. The women beat off the doctor with sticks and sent to the mills for assistance.' As a result, workers of three mills stopped work and went in search of the doctor.

In another incident, workers of Burn and Company, who heard there was an inoculator in town 'rushed out of the workshop, some armed with crow-bars, sticks and sundry other weapons . . . in quest of the inoculators'. Coolies working at a coal depot in Howrah mistook a European sailor for an inoculator and chased him. Afraid of what might happen, the sailor jumped into the river. The depot's English foreman called out to the serang of a passing steam launch to save the sailor, but this crewman ignored the call and the sailor drowned, *The Englishman* reported. Three workers were charged with rioting and the murder of a European.

At Baranagore mills, north-east of Howrah, workers stopped work and asked the managers to be allowed to go to protect their families as they had heard that four inoculators had arrived from Calcutta. They were told by the manager that there was no such forced inoculation. According to one report, the workers were also told that if they found any inoculators, they were to bring them to the manager, though the manager later denied saying this. In any case, one afternoon in May, nearly 300 workers dragged in through the mill gates the body of a perceived inoculator, who had been murdered.

The strikes ensured some quick concessions for the workers. The Bengal Chamber of Commerce sent an urgent communication to the government of Bengal to assure the 'lower classes' that nobody would be forcibly inoculated. The government responded by introducing the so-called Risley ticket to be issued to the workers. On it was written: 'This is to certify that no one shall be inoculated unless he expressly desires it.'

Local officials were sent to make similar assurances to the crowds that collected in streets to discuss the plague issue (Basu 2004). The Calcutta rioting ensured that the vaccine, pioneered by Russian bacteriologist Waldemar Haffkine in 1897, was introduced slowly in the rest of the subcontinent and only used voluntarily (Arnold 1987).

The Wage Question

All was not so normal even as the coolies, carters and mill-hands started going back to work. Labour exodus continued and scarcity of labour was felt everywhere. Sections of workers, having sensed the worth of their labour and the bewilderment of their employers, used the chaotic situation to put forward demands related to pay. The wage question became a bone of contention in several instances. *The Times of India* noted that 'the cry everywhere is for more pay'.

For instance, at the Howrah coal depot, workers went back to work on the condition that they would be paid more than before. The men working at Budge Budge road camp did not go back because the contractor had refused to pay them an increased wage. A strike took place at the gram stores of Cook and Company, after workers' demand for extra wages was refused.

Mehtars, who removed and transported night soil, and sweepers, essential for the maintenance of the city's sanitation, went on a general strike across the city on 20 May. It started with an official arresting a mehtar for telling other sanitation workers that 'sweepers and mehtars of the other wards had struck work because the authorities were forcibly taking people to the hospitals, and that they should follow suit'. The following day, the strike spread to several city wards, with the strikers demanding higher wages and that 'the government gave them an undertaking to the effect that they would not remove them to hospital if attacked with plague'.

Even as the mehtars and sweepers were striking, the city's *durwans* (doorkeepers) and *jemadars* (waste contractors) circulated notices amongst themselves for a meeting on 22 May at Calcutta's Maidan, near the Ochterlony monument (now known as the Shaheed Minar). Their objective was the same as the mehtars: to force their employers not to send them to hospitals or segregation camps. One of the notices read: 'all those who don't attend will be guilty of offences equal to their sacrificing 101 cows'. Some 2,000 people ended up assembling and 'curiosity led hundreds of others to stand in groups all along Chowringhee and the Esplanade to watch the proceedings'.

Claiming the Centre of Calcutta

The Maidan, the venue of the meeting, was to become the centre of mass demonstrations for decades to come. Through the plague epidemic, Calcutta's working classes went on a series of strikes and in various places were self-conscious of their interventions. They occasionally resorted to violent action, declaring they would not tolerate oppression. The strikes and gatherings forced the government to concede that no 'members from the poorer classes' were to be taken to hospitals without consent.

Even as the government feared losing Calcutta to the plague crisis and attempted to save the city without any regard for its population, the city's labourers were able to use their collective strength to produce 'disorders' of great proportions, making sure that their voices were heard to some extent. The strikes of the plague period signalled that Calcutta's working classes had the capacity to challenge the ruling classes. Into the twentieth century, hundreds of thousands of workers would continually bring the labour question to the fore, through a series of strikes in and around Calcutta in 1920–22, 1927–29 and 1946–47.

References

Arnold, D. 1987. 'Touching the Body: Perspectives on the Indian Plague, 1896–1900'. In *Subaltern Studies V*, ed. R. Guha, 55–90. New Delhi: Oxford University Press.

———. 1993. *Colonizing the Body: State, Medicine and Epidemic Disease in India*. Berkeley and Los Angeles: University of California Press.

Basu, S. 2004. *Does Class Matter?: Colonial Capital and Workers' Resistance in Bengal, 1890–1937*. New Delhi: Oxford University Press.

6

Past and Present

*Can India Beat Corona the Way it Beat Smallpox?**

Harish Naraindas

In April 1975, an American epidemiologist, attached to the smallpox eradication team in India, stumbled upon an impending disaster (Naraindas 2003a). As part of a specially assembled international health corps, his job was to unearth cases of smallpox in what was dubbed as the last major hotspot of smallpox in the world: Bihar. But the site of his sudden confrontation with the disease was more the cause for alarm than the sizeable number of cases unearthed. It was Pawapuri near Nalanda and the occasion was the anniversary celebration of Mahavir.

Pawapuri drew to its Jain temple pilgrims from all over India. It transpired that smallpox had made its appearance as early as the first of January and had gone unreported due to a doctors' strike. The consequences were unnerving as the massive turnover of pilgrims implied that the disease would be carried far and wide. More were expected and scores would leave, many of whom would incubate the virus and show no immediate signs of the disease.

Pilgrimage, Panic and the Virtuoso

In its retrospective personal rendering in 1996 by Dr Mahendra Dutta, the central government's appraisal officer for smallpox in Bihar, this incident had all the ingredients of high drama.[1] On his arrival after

* First published in *The India Forum*, 1 May 2020.

the alarm had been raised by the American epidemiologist, Dutta realised that if not swiftly handled, Pawapuri was likely to be a major setback to India's smallpox eradication programme, which had just turned the corner and was beginning to register a declining number of cases after a huge epidemic the previous May.

But its larger fallout in terms of tracking down all the pilgrims who had passed through the portals of Pawapuri seemed easier in comparison to what confronted Dutta at the pilgrim site. While a register of pilgrims allowed the smallpox eradication cell to telegraphically notify 150 districts about the returning pilgrims and the impending outbreaks, the eradication protocol at Pawapuri ran into rough weather.

The protocol called for an immediate cordoning of Pawapuri and its conversion into a quarantine site. The impounded pilgrims were to be rapidly vaccinated, and new arrivals could gain entry only if they allowed themselves to be vaccinated. Though each of these measures came to pass, they were none too easy.

There was a momentary stand-off as the pilgrims, in a familiar scenario, refused to be vaccinated on ostensibly religious grounds. The local superintendent of police, who was at loggerheads with the district magistrate, refused to cooperate, making it difficult to throw a cordon around the village. At Dutta's behest, the state's chief secretary intervened in the dispute between his subordinates; and the pilgrims were persuaded to submit to vaccination through their religious head.

Having won, through Dutta's institutional mandate and personal charisma, and the cooperation of the local administration and the religious head, it was easy to orchestrate the rest. More than 1,000 volunteers from among the pilgrims were mobilised to act as vaccinators, run a community kitchen, keep vigil and get the rest to submit, without fail, to vaccination.

Pawapuri seems extraordinary, and certainly seemed so for Donald Henderson, the then chief of the global smallpox eradication unit of WHO. But the measures outlined were played out over and over again throughout the length and breadth of the country, especially in the four endemic states of Bihar, Uttar Pradesh, West Bengal and Madhya Pradesh. By the end of 1974, every household, village or mohalla where smallpox was detected was cordoned off, its inmates impounded, ostensibly fed and compensated for loss of wages, and contacts vaccinated.

Pawapuri was a miniature writ large with a rider. Being a pilgrim centre, it was a potential site of dissemination, made doubly difficult by the fact that the pilgrims could take umbrage in faith to register a cohesive and cogent protest. But the methods and motives at Pawapuri were part of a larger piece, which in under six months produced a singular result in modern public health: the extirpation of smallpox.

In May 1975, India recorded its last case of smallpox. Two years later, the country was certified to be free not only of the disease but of the very virus. Since human beings were the virus' exclusive hosts, the eradication of the disease meant that the virus had been extirpated from its 'natural' reservoir.

What were the measures that extirpated perhaps the most dreaded disease in the history of mankind, which killed roughly every third person who got the disease—as opposed to the novel coronavirus that in India seems to kill roughly just one out of every 30 infected persons? And is it possible to draw lessons from the past for the present?

From Reach to Incidence

Vaccination, inaugurated in India in 1802, was often falsely portrayed by the British as a monumental effort pitted against native prejudice (Naraindas 1998). Yet, as late as 1946, it touched only a small portion of British India. This was borne out by the fact that in 1951 India reported more than 250,000 cases of smallpox with 64,000 deaths. It was only in 1961–62 that the National Smallpox Eradication Programme was launched, in an attempt to cover the entire country through mass vaccination. As part of it, 80 per cent of India's population was vaccinated. While this reputedly had its effect, especially in the southern states, there was a recrudescence in 1967 with 80,000 cases, which was almost the same number of cases as were reported in 1963 when the programme started. Hence, what changed between 1967 and 1974 that led to the complete extirpation of the pox by 1975?

Till 1968, measures against smallpox were organised on *defensive* principles and concepts that could be traced to the nineteenth century. In stark contrast, Pawapuri represented a complete inversion of what had been the vaccination practice since its inception. It was an *offensive* strategy of 'search and destroy' whose purpose was to ferret out Agent Pox and railroad it—like the Americans were trying to in Vietnam to the Viet Cong—to extinction.

At the heart of the new strategy was the abandonment of the impossible dream of 100 per cent mass vaccination. It was replaced by what retrospectively seems an equally impossible dream: an attempt to unearth each and every case of smallpox.

For the first time the focus was to be on the *incidence* of disease rather than on mere reach that mass vaccination represented. Every case, as in Pawapuri, would be unearthed, isolated, quarantined and the contacts vaccinated. But this conceptual shift and its shrewd administrative reworking did not come full-blown and ready-made.

A New Calculus and a Milestone-zeal for Agent Pox

The eradication of smallpox was a global effort. And often the WHO and the US's Centres for Disease Control and Prevention (CDC) take the lion's share of the credit. But what is less known is that the brunt of the effort, the chutzpah, and the expenditure, was borne by the Third World, and perhaps a major share of it by India.

The head of the WHO called it a two-billion-dollar gift from the Third World to the First World; and not a one-off gift, but a gift given in perpetuity. According to Brilliant (1985: 134), the US, for example, recovered its investment within 26 days of the world being free of smallpox—a rate of return that is equivalent to 1,403 per cent per annum!

This calculus came from the fact that diseases in the global south were a threat to the global north even if the north was completely free of the disease. These countries, to stay 'disease free', had to keep vigil through 'infectious disease radar stations', to spot, isolate, quarantine, and vaccinate or treat what they perceived as 'importations'. The idea was to nip every importation in the bud before it led to that currently dreaded word, 'community transmission'—symbolised by the 'corona graph' that merrily putters along and then suddenly does a vertical take-off.

But keeping vigil to stay in a state of grace is an expensive proposition, which, if dismantled, can prove to be economically devastating—as we are now witnessing—apart from the human death toll. An outbreak in 1961 from a single importation cost the UK $3.6 million, while the Americans spent $150 million each year as the price for keeping vigil, according to an estimate in a WHO publication (see James Magee's piece 'A Windfall for Development', in Henderson 1980: 5). Hence, it was far better to invest in the tropical world and make it 'disease free' (unlike dealing with hunger, homelessness or unemployment, which are not contagious), thus allowing the temperate world to not only dismantle the expense and the bother of keeping vigil, but also because sustaining (to use current parlance) a 'corona wall' may be far dicier than sustaining a Mexican or Mediterranean wall.

But such tropical investments make sense only if there is a particular calculus of time. Global eradication was thus conceived as a 10-year programme, buoyed, according to Henderson, by another recent achievement: putting a man on the moon. Thus, a calculus of costs, predicated on a calculus of time, was wedded to achieving a mythic milestone: extirpating the pox and thus doing something—like the man on the moon—that had never been done before.

If the physicist Robert Oppenheimer, hero of Los Alamos, was responsible for a quarter million deaths in Hiroshima and Nagasaki, Henderson the epidemiologist—awarded the US Presidential Medal of Freedom in 2002—perhaps saw himself as saving half a million lives *every year*. But if we use 'Henderson' as a titular term of a discursive practice, we can see that most people, especially those who participated in what came to be called the Intensified Campaign (1973–75), were fired by a kind of milestone-zeal. They saw the campaign as a charismatic and redemptive adventure that would deliver a few hundred thousand people from death every year, and a few million more from the hideous after effects of smallpox.

Dutta, with his virtuoso performance at Pawapuri, was a prime example of this zeal, which in its last stages was called 'smallpox zero—point of no return!' It was a war cry that convulsed through India's entire health bureaucracy and made it almost exclusively focus on smallpox. The Indian state's monumental resources, and those of every person participating in it (like the 1,000 volunteers at Pawapuri), were put to do whatever it took to get over the finishing line and declare India—and thus the world—to be in a state of grace.

But this grand operative ballet—enacted against the backdrop of Jayaprakash Narayan's civil disobedience movement, and haunted by Oppenheimer's ghostly legacy through the detonation of a nuclear bomb at Pokharan in May 1974—was one that required thousands of people to work together with fervour and commitment, in quite the same way that the Fat Man and the Little Boy were produced at a frenetic pace by thousands working together at Los Alamos: the latter to bring redemption through mass death; and the former to put an end to mass death by ridding the earth of a scourge.

An Atlas, a Corps and an Image

Around 1973, the WHO borrowed William Foege from the CDC and shipped him to India to join the effort of globally eradicating smallpox. Foege, who also went on to win the Presidential Medal of Freedom in 2012, was credited with having stamped out smallpox in Nigeria. He had invented a new way of tackling smallpox under conditions of vaccine scarcity. Based on that experience, he drew up a new atlas of smallpox in India. It was an aspirational atlas that reconceived India as America.

Much to his surprise, Foege had found that vast parts of India, especially the southern states, were largely free of smallpox. Hence, he suggested that rather than seeing India as a Third World country where smallpox was endemic, it was better to conceive it as a largely smallpox-free country with pockets of smallpox (Foege 1975).

The new atlas not only showed large parts of India to be smallpox-free, but also allowed one to operate with the same kind of response structure that the First World operated with vis-à-vis the Third World, which rested cardinally on seeing every case as an importation that would result in quarantine, contact tracing and vaccination. If mass vaccination was an attempt to distribute water equally to an imagined fire everywhere, the new atlas showed the actual places on fire—the hotspots—and thus allowed one to concentrate scarce resources where they were most needed.

But what were these resources? While the obvious ones were a stable vaccine, a new instrument (the bifurcated needle), and a new technique that was quick and painless, there were several others that were needed to make the campaign a success. Perhaps the most important in the new scheme of things was the raising of a select band of highly committed volunteers, who were ready to ceaselessly search for Agent Pox and thwart him from his insurrectionary dreams.

This would be the task of Dr R. N. Basu, the head of India's smallpox eradication programme. Around the same time as it got Foege to India, the WHO persuaded Basu to spend time with a group of US Peace Corps volunteers in Ethiopia to see how smallpox eradication measures were being handled there. Basu's time in Ethiopia, where each person, at great personal discomfort, ceaselessly criss-crossed the countryside in jeeps looking for Agent Pox, had left an indelible mark on him. It was the very antithesis of the ossified bureaucracy that he was used to.

In an interview in 1996,[2] Basu recalled that he offered to raise one Indian volunteer for every one the WHO raised. The WHO, he said, began by raising 20 that he matched. This international corps, which grew over time and became a rotating one, spent roughly three months at a stretch in the field. They were given a quick orientation, with the most productive and the longest part being the one with the sociologists, who gave them—especially the foreign volunteers—a crash course on local mores and customs that would be cardinal if the experiment was going to work (Dutta and Foege 2004).

The volunteers—or 'commando units' as Basu described them—were then despatched in a jeep with a driver, a paramedic with needles and vaccine, and a comprehensive search protocol, along with a picture of a pox patient overrun with pustules. This image of Agent Pox, which they constantly carried with them like it was their new-found love, and showed to all and sundry in their designated beat, was an invitation to confess.

Given the long history of a capricious state, postcolonial subjects, especially the rural poor, were wary, to say the least. Hence, as an incentive, every person who confessed to having seen Agent Pox was given Rs 100 each. Soon after, perhaps to ensure that the confessor was not seen as an informer who had ratted, the victim too was given the same sum of money, which steadily grew, as the cases fell, to Rs 1,000. This grand public confessional, goading everyone through entreaty and threat, to rise from a state of fall to one of grace, was a cardinal but not the last step in the scheme of things.

The Impress, the Community and the Rumour Register

Dutta and his charismatic troubleshooting, Basu and his zealous voluntary corps, and Foege's new atlas readily suggest themselves as new conceptual tools that redrew set procedures and ways of acting and thinking. But one normally does not think of financial instruments, especially seemingly small amounts of petty cash like the imprest, as being decisive. As we will presently see, Basu's commando units would have been crippled without it.

'We were ... apart from the Jeep, the paramedic, the medical supplies, and the driver, given a generous imprest and allowed to spend it as we saw fit,' I. C. Tiwari recalled in an interview in 1996.[3] Posted as a senior epidemiologist with the voluntary corps in Champaran, Bihar, Tiwari had to ferret out Agent Pox against the backdrop of the Indian state combating the Naxalite insurgency of the time.

The Naxalite insurrection, among other things, disallowed night-time travel, and hence speed was of the essence for the volunteers. Tiwari could use the imprest to replace the vaccine, change the tyres of his jeep, or hire local enumerators and vaccinators on the spot to get the job done. His choice of examples was all suggestive of pace: replenish used-up vaccine or swap used-up tyres; get village youth to act as enumerators, stand guard, or run a community kitchen; or quickly hire them to double-up as vaccinators.

All of these became increasingly important as sometimes there were deaths after a post-infection vaccination. When cases had been found, one had to work with great pace to get the job done before there was a death. It could break community confidence and derail the exercise. Hence, the seemingly humble imprest, and the flexibility it provided, was the key.

But so was the rediscovery, given the size and scale of the operation, of the village as hallowed space and the community as coparceners in the eradication of the Pox. The community had to confess, albeit with incentives. Having done so, it had to agree to not merely passively cooperate but be actively enlisted, for a nominal fee, in getting the job done. This was fortunately enabled by the introduction of a new freeze-dried vaccine that was stable unlike the earlier liquid vaccine, and the arrival of the bifurcated needle in lieu of the painful and cumbersome rotary lancet.

These innovations, said Tiwari, allowed local youth to be trained as vaccinators in 'twenty minutes' and to create a 'containment ring' by tracing and vaccinating all contacts. And the ring grew in size as the cases fell, in quite the same way that the reward for confessing grew from Rs 100 to 1,000 each as the cases became few and far between.

But the flexible financial instrument of the imprest, so cardinal in 'getting the job done', and the reinscribing of the village and the community as instrumental to the search and containment protocol, were only possible because of a continuous refinement in the search protocol. Its acme was the rumour register that served several functions at once.

Smallpox was part of a family of exanthematous diseases marked by fever and rash, with its closest sibling being chicken pox. To ensure that no cases were missed, all cases of fever and rash were entered in a rumour register in an initial search. Tiwari's job was to start the day by looking at the rumour register and then setting out to confirm whether the cases were smallpox. This act of confirming the rumour became a second-order search and allowed the programme to finesse the search and containment protocol.

Finally, when all the district-level data from the rumour registers was collated, if it was found that there was a 'nil' district sandwiched between two districts with high incidence of fever and rash, the programme knew that there was something wrong. The corps would swing into action to investigate the anomaly. It invariably unearthed fudging, either due to 'target pressure' or corruption. This was set right by often easing personnel who operated in a business-as-usual mode to other departments, and by meticulously going through the rigmarole of search, segregate, quarantine and containment by ring vaccination in the 'nil district'.

These conceptual refinements, and an *esprit de corps*, spurred in the final stages by the attraction of achieving a historic milestone, corralled Agent Pox, inch by inch, into extinction.

The Hiatus between Person and Disease: Rendering Recalcitrant Bodies Inert

In 1665, the appearance of the plague in London resulted in the opposite of Passover. The red mark on the door of plague households was a sign, not for god to pass over and spare their first-borns, but to seal and condemn its inmates to death. While we can assume with reasonable certainty that the plague in 1665 announced itself with fever and chills, and with the characteristic swelling of the lymph nodes, we are now saddled—starting nominally in 1800 with the advent of histology—with a paradox peculiar to modern medicine: the possibility of a disease without a patient; and of patients with no disease (Naraindas 2006, 2011).

The *asymptomatic* Corona *infectee*—10 to 30 per cent of total infectees, according to different estimates—is the perfect example of the presence of disease in the absence of the patient. On becoming infected, they, like other infectees, presumably incubate the virus. But instead of exhibiting symptoms and becoming patients, they become asymptomatic *carriers* of the *virus* and silently spread the disease.

What flows from this cardinal epistemic premise (not shared by other systems of medicine) is that these persons are merely a detour to the virus. Neither their experience nor their testimony (of feeling fine, for example) necessarily counts as evidence. And if they are not willing to come forward and follow the rules laid down to ferret out Agent Corona, who they may be secretly harbouring in their person, they are committing treason against the commonweal (Naraindas 1998).

In the currently bigoted landscape, this unfortunately makes already suspect bodies hyper-suspect, and, as is currently the case, weaponises them as veritable corona-bombs on an insurrectionary run; while the bodies of the poor are made into expendable collateral.

Simulated war games and movie scripts of contagious or infectious diseases are often predicated on both of the above. The viewer's sense of impending doom is marshalled, either through a pet monkey carrying the Ebola-like virus from Congo to California in the movie *Outbreak*, or as a 'terrorist' incubating the smallpox virus and carrying it on his person to either Heathrow or O'Hare, and deliberately spreading it by walking around the airport, before curling up in a corner to die as a 'martyr to a cause'. While this provides such plots their initial insurrectionary impetus, the plot culminates in *Outbreak* with an unthinkable collateral: the possibility of nuking an entire lily-white American town to contain the virus. This is of course prevented at the last minute, unlike the ready and easy expending of an African village as collateral at the beginning of the movie. But in a retributory move for this *original sin*, a virus-infected monkey escapes the nuking, and comes home to roost.

The Epidemic Diseases Act of 1897, first put into play with great alacrity in Bhilwara, Rajasthan, was invoked on behalf of Agent Corona and his insurrectionary run, in an attempt to hunt him down and corral him. And the searching, testing, segregating, sealing and quarantining were all done, and are now being done throughout India—and the world—to railroad him into extinction.

This singular focus on Agent Corona as the *causa causans* valorises the virus and leads to an imagery of war, and concomitantly leads to a hiatus between the disease and the person, especially the *carrier*. Hence, it is none too surprising that Ludwick Fleck (1979), soon after the microbe had ascended to being the principal dramatis persona, called it the devil re-incarnate: an ontological point of view that affords us, as Canguilhem (1978) points out, a soothing certitude of a Being against which one can do battle.

Our rendering unsurprisingly follows the above trajectory, and the virus' singular agency is hypostatised and anthropomorphised by the epithet of Agent Pox or Agent Corona, as it effortlessly suggests itself by the modalities put into play to address its seemingly insurrectionary potential. This is buttressed by the fact that the Intensified Campaign was coeval in time to the Vietnam war, where the Viet Cong were also (if not principally, as that war was costlier in terms of men and money) caught up in an insurrectionary template, and the American way of dealing with them was through 'Search and Destroy'.

Such transpositions and anthropomorphisms, from a theatre of war to a theatre of disease eradication and vice versa, are quite common. This, in fact, was the final rhetorical move of the Intensified Campaign in 1974 and became *de rigueur* towards its end. Thousands of posters were printed depicting smallpox as a pox-ridden cross between a horned devil and an ear-ringed *rakshasa* (demon), who was down but not out. This creolised image, understandably, was impaled neither with a *trishul* (trident) nor by a goddess (like the *asura* was by Durga and her trident), but with the bifurcated needle that looked like a trishul, and by a man in underwear who looked like a wrestler from a rural *akhara* (wrestling academy).

This rhetorical move located the image in a rural landscape and in the realm of human possibility and science, playing all along on a readily available divine template of the smallpox goddess Sitala Mata and her understudy Jwarasur, the fever demon, but with a cardinal difference. While smallpox under the sign of Sitala led to a mode of sequestering the patient by consecrating him, as he was the repository of the deity who would leave if a regimen and a quarantine was strictly followed (Naraindas 2003b), in the new scheme of things smallpox was seen as a demon located in recalcitrant bodies that needed to be rendered inert—by vaccinating them—for the sake of *public welfare*.

But this could not be done without 'local participation', given the magnitude of the problem. Hence the village had to be reinscribed as 'hallowed space' and the 'community' had to be enlisted as coparceners. And the poster with its creolised image was a rhetorical move that attempted to signal the rural as a 'newfound arcadia', whose 'local youth', quickly trained in 'twenty minutes' to be vaccinators, would be the neophytes who would wage war and impale the Devil-Rakshasa with the bifurcated needle/trishul.

If there was collective resistance—which did happen in a tribal village, which unlike Pawapuri could not be persuaded—the state would seal it with a *cordon sanitaire* and the *disease* would be allowed to smoulder and die. And the two-thirds of the *persons* who survived the disease—given smallpox's case-fatality ratio of 30 per cent—

would be presumed to be both immune and *inert*—and hence no longer a public threat.

Coda: From an Imagery of the Kill to a Community of Coparceners?

Since this is being written in the middle of the novel coronavirus pandemic, we end by highlighting some possible differences—since the parallels are evident—between the past and the present. Although Covid-19 started as a sub-tropical epidemic in Wuhan, unlike other post-war epidemics, it did not stay true to form and move south toward the tropics. Rather, it moved north to what is now being dubbed as the (in)temperate world of 'promiscuous passports', and became a full-blown pandemic.

If we go by Event 201,[4] the eerily prescient simulation run at Johns Hopkins University in October 2019, Covid-19 may well run for 18 months with 65 million deaths—though there seem to be kinder 'predictions' lately from the US Department of Homeland Security. It will ostensibly ebb when 60 to 70 per cent of the global population has been exposed to the virus, unless old drugs, a repurposed cocktail of drugs, or repurposed vaccinations like BCG, or plasma from recovered patients, or other novel therapies step in, surprise us, and save the day.

In the absence of these, there are likely to be several moves in India that are eerily reminiscent of smallpox, with the large-scale incarceration and hosing down of the poor and the migrant with chemical disinfectants as its exemplary form; and charging clerics with culpable homicide for spreading the virus its sinister and contemporary variant.

Such moves, apart from being inhumane, are likely to be counter-productive and may come back to bite not merely the well-to-do and the bigots, but the whole country. The Indian Ministry of Health and Family Welfare has woken up to the first possibility and has issued an advisory saying that hosing down persons (read the poor) with chemical disinfectants is not advisable, as it is (i) harmful, (ii) not effective and (iii) leads to a false sense of security and may detract persons from practising either social distancing or hand hygiene.

Unfortunately, other than some muted remarks by a joint secretary, no such clear and unambiguous directive has been issued by the health ministry saying that demonising religious or ethnic minorities could (i) actively drive Agent Corona underground and thus help spread the infection, (ii) sustain the infection for much longer and (iii) delay the exit from the lockdown.

But perhaps most important, if India is to succeed and not have more deaths from the effects of the unprecedented global lockdown that has quarantined the earth, it must *socialise* and rediscover the village and communities as coparceners in this war, albeit in ways different from smallpox, which had cleverly 'enlisted' them on behalf of the vaccine.

We have already witnessed, albeit in limited ways, a concerted socialised response across sectors, such as the temporary nationalising of private hospitals, hotels and other public institutions for an impending quarantine, the setting up of homeless shelters and the running of community kitchens, the distribution of rations and protecting wages, providing health insurance and free testing, and getting our universities, industrial outfits and home-based production units into making *jugaad* masks, testing kits, personal protective equipment (PPE) and ventilators.

We have also witnessed, for example, Tamil Nadu's health secretary, Beela Rajesh, or district magistrates Adeela Abdullah in Wayanad, Kerala, and Rajendra Bhat in Bhilwara, Rajasthan, step up in amazing ways during this moment. Like Dutta in 1974, they have brought their charisma and acumen to bear with remarkable effect on a crisis situation and have been credited for either flattening the curve or stopping the virus in its tracks.

There are hundreds of others at the lower end of the hierarchy who are the counterparts of Adeela, Beela and Bhat. They have not only stepped up in unsung ways, *but as the actual feet on the ground*, are putting their lives at risk. Many of these unsung and poorly protected frontline health workers, *especially the sanitation workers*, some of whom may contract the virus and die trying to save the rest of us, are being either shunned or attacked by a spooked population, exacerbated by a trust deficit in an increasingly bigoted landscape where minority and marginalised groups are being continuously demonised.

But apart from these noble moves by well-intentioned persons and organs of the state, seemingly never enough and often thwarted by not just corruption but also by egregious rules, India may have to soon find ways in which people at large, and rural peoples in particular, may be counted as knowledgeable citizens and coparceners, rather than as recalcitrant body populations against whom and through whom, but always in whose name, one wages war against the virus.

If it does, the state may discover that people have their own ways of practising a self-imposed quarantine, as was the case with smallpox and perhaps continues to be the case with chicken pox and other exanthematous diseases, which may go by other names in native disease classifications. There are already reports of villages, especially so-called 'tribal' ones, where modes of quarantine are being practised by the villages on returning migrants from the cities, though in some cases this could easily turn into a kind of vigilantism.

Such aberrations apart, segregating and quarantining should not surprise us, as self-sequestering and abstinence of varying lengths, often regulated by the almanac, which functions as an agricultural, liturgical and prophylactic calendar, may continue to be the bedrock of rural life. In the absence of a vaccine, it may be cardinally necessary to draw upon such a repertoire. Especially so, if the battle against the coronavirus turns out to be a long-drawn-out one, or worse, fought every season.

Finally, along with sequestering, rural communities may also have ways of addressing, through their local health traditions, the so-called 'symptoms' of the 'infection' like fever and cough, including the most problematic: shortness of breath and the inability to breathe. This requires oxygen and ventilators, which India may not have enough of if the plot gets out of hand. But this may be possible only if we are open to the idea that local health traditions may be able to conceive of the present distemper in their own ways, and *translate* the Covid-19 symptoms into 'disease entities' and 'treatment protocols' of their own.

The fact that this may be already afoot, in an attempt to enfold the novel into the familiar, is the making of *papier mâché* coronavirus masks of Jharkhand. Borrowed from the idiom of the Chau dance, this mask comes with a three-ply fabric encased, thus making it a Chau-coronavirus mask. This allows the mask makers to continue their tradition, and contribute an indigenous and colourful item towards the much-needed personal protective equipment. But most importantly, it allows them to continue making a living in an idiom that is wholly their own. Perhaps in the next season they will incorporate the mask into their performance repertoire, where the coronavirus metamorphoses into *Coronasur*, like Jwarasur the fever demon, to be either impaled or cast out. By doing so they may, as has been case with smallpox and other epidemic diseases in the past, convert calamity into community, and transpose the historical into the mythical to edify transcendental truths.

Notes

1. This account is based on my conversation with him in August 1996 in New Delhi. I believe he passed away this February in Ghaziabad. I would like to thank him for his time and warmth and offer this, in part, as a tribute to him, and people like him; and also to the vast mass of people who are out there right now, providing what are called 'essential services' while the rest of us stay at home. I would also like to thank Richa Kumar, Sinjini Mukherjee and my Soc Med class for their perceptive and thoughtful comments, and the editors at *The India Forum* for their discerning comments, deft and diligent editing, and for graciously seeing this through.
2. Personal interviews, August 1996, New Delhi.
3. Personal interview, 1996, New Delhi.
4. See 'Event 201', Johns Hopkins Centre for Health Security, available at https://www.centerforhealthsecurity.org/event201/ (accessed 17 April 2020).

References

Brilliant, L. B. 1985. *The Management of Smallpox in India*. Ann Arbor: University of Michigan Press.

Canguilhem, G. 1978. *On the Normal and the Pathological*. Boston: D. Riedel Publishing Company.

Dutta, M., and W. Foege. 2004. 'A Conversation between Dr. Mahendra Dutta and Dr. William Foege'. Available at https://globalhealthchronicles.

org/files/original/2004fffab008be1051279b90bc2a4356.pdf (accessed 17 April 2020).

Fleck, L. 1979. *Genesis and Development of a Scientific Fact*, trans. and ed. Thaddeus J. Trenn, Robert K. Merton and Frederick Bradley. Chicago: University of Chicago Press.

Foege, W. H. 1975. 'Strategy of Smallpox Eradication'. *Swasth Hind* 19 (4): 119–22.

Henderson, D. 1980. 'A Victory for All Mankind'. *World Health*, May. Available at https://www.who.int/csr/disease/smallpox/WHO_RAS_SEP_ID0556_WorldHealth_May1980_ENG.pdf?ua=1 (accessed 17 April 2020).

Naraindas, H. 1998. 'Care, Welfare and Treason: The Advent of Vaccination in the 19th Century'. *Contributions to Indian Sociology* 32 (1): 67–96.

———. 2003a. 'Crisis, Charisma and Triage: Extirpating the Pox'. *Indian Economic and Social History Review* 40 (4): 425–57.

———. 2003b. 'Preparing for the Pox: A Theory of Smallpox in Bengal and Britain'. *Asian Journal of Social Sciences* 31 (2): 304–39.

———. 2006. 'Of Spineless Babies and Folic Acid: Evidence and Efficacy in Biomedicine and Ayurvedic Medicine'. In part special issue edited by Helen Lambert, Elisa Gordon and Elizabeth Bogdan-Lovis: 'Gift Horse or Trojan Horse?: Social Science Perspectives on Evidence-based Health Care', *Social Science and Medicine* 62 (11): 2658–69.

———. 2011. 'Of Relics, Body Parts and Laser Beams: The German Heilpraktiker and His Ayurvedic Spa'. *Anthropology and Medicine* 18 (1): 67–86.

Section III

Covid-19: The Initial Impact

7

India's Tryst with Covid-19*

Vikram Patel

As India endures a fourth consecutive week of a nation-wide lockdown (ranked as the most stringent in the world by the University of Oxford) to contain the spread of Covid-19, it seems an opportune moment to reflect on its rationale, its impact and where we might need to head from here.

The singular goal of the lockdown was to save lives, both by protecting every individual in the population from being infected in the first place, and by slowing the surge of cases which might overwhelm scarce intensive care resources. This is a moral goal that no one can argue with. Two questions spring to mind in relation to this goal: first, whether the lockdown will lead to reduced numbers of lives lost due to Covid-19; and second, whether a policy focused on saving lives due to one disease might inadvertently lead to more deaths due to other causes.

Let us consider the impact of the lockdown strategy on mortality due to Covid-19. Contrary to what one might have expected, the number of deaths due to Covid-19 has actually been *increasing* with each week of the lockdown. This suggests that there was much wider spread of the infection even *before* the lockdown and very limited impact of the containment policies in those crucial weeks. Still, there is no doubt that the longer the lockdown is in place, the curve of infections will ultimately flatten and then fall. After all, if everyone is forced to stay at home, there is no way for the virus to jump from one person to another (apart, of course, between those in the same home!).

---

* First published in *The India Forum*, 17 April 2020.

Such a lockdown would have an impact on all contagious diseases, that is, those that spread through direct contact with an infected person. But it is a fundamental mistake to think that the virus would then have been eliminated. Only a vaccine, or the acquisition of 'herd immunity' when a specific proportion of the community has been exposed to the infection due to its gradual spread in the population, can ultimately lead to us defeating the virus. In the absence of the former, we should expect to see more people infected, a small fraction of whom will die, whenever the lockdown is lifted, simply because the virus will, once again, have opportunities to spread in a population that remains just as vulnerable to the infection as it was before the lockdown. And, then, at some critical point in the evolution of the epidemic, transmission will stop and the epidemic will peter out. Just like it has for all similar infectious diseases in the past.

Whether more Covid-19 deaths would have occurred without a lockdown will be, at best, a speculative exercise prone to all the uncertainties inherent in modelling based on numbers with uncertain significance (which I turn to later), and we may never know the truth.

What about the impact of the lockdown on other causes of death? Since the first case was reported in late January 2020, there have been (as of 15 April) about 400 confirmed deaths. During this same period of roughly 75 days, if we extrapolate data from recent years on mortality, over 1.5 million Indians will have died due to other causes; thus, deaths due to Covid-19 account for 0.0002 per cent of total deaths in this period. Most would agree that this is a vanishingly miniscule proportion. More people would have died from virtually any of the hundreds of other deadly diseases that stalk our lives. About 1,000 persons die due to respiratory tract infections alone *every day*. These infections spread in similar ways to Covid-19 but, by forcing people into their homes, it is possible that their spread between people sharing crowded and insanitary housing would have in fact increased during the lockdown.

Simultaneously, there have been dramatic reductions in the numbers of patients seeking medical care in many parts of the country. This is because of several reasons: the prohibition of public transportation has meant that those who cannot afford private cars, the vast majority of our population, would have found it extraordinarily difficult to access healthcare; private nursing homes that are critical providers to the health needs of the poor and rural populations have been unable to function effectively because their staff cannot get to work; and scarce public health resources have been reallocated to focus on Covid-19 preparedness. Deaths due to deterioration in the care for chronic diseases such as diabetes, cancer and heart disease may have increased as a result. The number of suicides will also be expected to increase during these stressful periods, as also placing women at a higher risk of serious injury from violent partners from whom they cannot escape. And then there is the likely surge of deaths due to poverty, by some estimates affecting over 400 million workers, more than the entire population of the US, whose toll will unfold in the coming months. Malnutrition in children is estimated to kill several thousand children every day and, given the very strong association between poverty and hunger, these numbers could escalate further.

On the other hand, mortality due to at least two causes will have plummeted during the lockdown: road traffic accidents and air pollution.

The net reduction in loss of lives, the ultimate goal of the policy, may hang in the balance between these different forces, but whichever direction it takes, there is little doubt that many people, hundreds of millions perhaps, have had their lives and livelihoods devastated by the lockdown. Every policy, particularly one that ceases freedom of movement and all economic activity in a continental nation of over a billion people, requires thoughtful consideration of the balance of costs and benefits. In my reckoning, given the human tragedy that unfolded in the days following the lockdown, with epic numbers of migrants trying to get back home, evoking memories of Partition and, paradoxically, setting the stage to exponentially expand the footprint of the epidemic to rural areas, it seems that the lockdown was implemented in too much haste.

Relatedly, it is important to consider whether the lockdown should have been a progressive and dynamic policy, as is now being planned for its staggered lifting, focusing the most stringent controls in areas designated as 'hotspots' of clusters of cases and promoting less coercive strategies to contain the epidemic in other areas. These are the strategies which actually *do* work, such as testing and contact tracing. But such a strategy would have required proactively collecting real-time data on the numbers of those infected in a standardised way so that these numbers are comparable across time and space, and this has been one of the weakest links in our response to the pandemic.

Despite the importance of testing, data from the ICMR suggests that by 9 April, just about 150,000 tests had been conducted in the country, a per capita rate of testing that is amongst the lowest in the world. Even these small estimates are impossible to interpret because the number and type of people tested has varied hugely over time and place. One does not need to be a rocket-scientist to figure out that the more one tests, the more one will find; thus, the higher numbers of cases being reported in some states and as the lockdown has progressed, may, at least in part, be simply a reflection of the greater number of tests conducted.

Then, there is the question of *who* one tests. If one tests random people in the community, the numbers of infected will be much smaller because most of these individuals do not have any symptoms. On the other hand, the numbers of infected will be much higher if one tests those in a hospital who have fever and respiratory distress. Without these important caveats about the variations in the testing strategy, the daily report of the numbers heralded across our front pages, their charting across time and states, and comparisons with other countries have as much value to estimating the scale and location of the problem and what impact policies are having as, say, counting grains of rice held by fists of different sizes.

What we should have expected by now is a standardised protocol being implemented in every state, for example, testing everyone who attends nominated Covid-19 hospitals with the recognised syndrome of symptoms and signs of the infection. Indeed, simply tracking the numbers of patients coming to any healthcare facility with fever and respiratory distress could provide a more accurate picture of the unfolding of the epidemic.

Some argue that the true impact of Covid-19 would have been much worse without a lockdown. Of course they are right. But if saving lives is the sole goal of a lockdown, then this begs the question as to why the country should not also consider similar lockdowns to reduce road traffic accidents and air pollution mortality. The impacts would be even more dramatic and, in all probability, result in much larger numbers of lives saved. Yet, even as India has secured the leading place in the global ranking of mortality due to these two causes for many years, we seem to have shown no urgency at all to deal with these known, avoidable and deadly factors. This is because such stringent policies have unwanted adverse impacts and we are forced to consider all the possible scenarios and options, ultimately choosing the policy with the least likelihood of harm.

Furthermore, pre-emptive strikes in medicine are rarely justified, for example, the surgical removal of both breasts when a woman's genetic code suggests a very high risk of developing a rare form of breast cancer, because one does not want the cure to be worse than the disease for the many people who would never have developed it in the first place. And so, when one balances the vast uncertainties about Covid-19 when the lockdown was imposed, at a time when there were just 10 deaths in the entire country, with the absolute certainty that such a lockdown would massively disrupt the lives and wellbeing of most of our population, it is hard to conclude that such a pre-emptive strike was justified.

But, surely, this is not the time to quibble with what is now history. The lockdown has happened and we are in the midst of it. The nation has showed remarkable solidarity with the policy and this is to be welcomed. Instead, now is a time for us to consider the next steps and, in particular, what lessons can emerge from this epochal event. The immediate priorities must be to restore the livelihoods of our poorest, and this means restoration of public transportation and the informal economy. This will not magically return upended lives to normal and, during the difficult months ahead, the energies put into a National Register of Citizens (NRC) survey might be used to identify those who are unemployed and guarantee them a basic income pegged to the Mahatma Gandhi National Rural Employment Guarantee Act (MGNREGA) daily rates for at least a year. I am no economist, but it seems to me that such a strategy would certainly go a long way to address hunger and destitution.

Simultaneously, massive investment in active case-finding, contact tracing and humane quarantining procedures, and strengthening the capacity of the healthcare system for intensive care for future surges of infections (which will also help prevent countless other causes of deaths) is needed. Of course, I am aware that these strategies will require a lot of money that is hard to find when the economy has tanked, but I am sure money can be found, perhaps by imposing a one-year moratorium on arms purchases which exceed billions of dollars.

In the longer term, one fundamental lesson is not to plan epidemic containment policies solely on the basis of mathematical models built on assumptions and observations from other contexts. I believe the initial models that predicted apocalyptic numbers (and which have subsequently turned out to be so wildly off the mark that even just a random guess could have been more accurate) seeded some panic in the government which, knowing the shambolic state of our public healthcare system, could ill-afford to countenance mountains of dead bodies. I sympathise with the impossibly difficult dilemma and tight timelines that policymakers had to face. But there is an alternative: to make strenuous efforts from the first day to obtain accurate local estimates of the numbers of cases, which, as I noted earlier, does not need to rely only on laboratory tests as we can much more readily count the sick in the meantime.

Policies must be appropriate, dynamic and proportionate, which means that their potential for harms must also be taken into account in planning. A one-size-fits-all approach for a country with such continental diversity should be avoided. It is utterly absurd, for example, that my home state of Goa that has witnessed just seven cases in total (and zero deaths), and none in the past 10 days, should have to be locked down. We have such good experience from controlling epidemics through local action in this way in the past, from Nipah in Kerala to ZIKA in Rajasthan, and it is our past successes that we should draw upon in the future. But we do not even look so far back in time: as I write this, Kerala has shown, yet again, how to contain this particular epidemic in a manner that combines the values of both humanity and science.

The crushing of hundreds of millions of livelihoods may lead to a surge of what Angus Deaton and Anna Case (2020) describe as 'deaths of despair' when referring to the increased mortality in working-age

Americans following the last major recession in 2008. These deaths are related to poor mental health arising from hopelessness and uncertainty about one's future social and economic prospects, and are driven by suicide and alcohol abuse. India's mental healthcare system is its Achilles's heel, with fewer than 10,000 mental health professionals in the country. Yet, the ingenuity of our scientists and civil society has shown, time and again, that community-based interventions, typically involving the delivery of brief psychosocial interventions by lay counsellors and peer providers (the work of Sangath, with which I have been associated since its founding 25 years ago, is internationally recognised for this particular innovation), are effective, acceptable and affordable strategy. This is a critical moment for the state and philanthropy to invest in such home-grown solutions to stem the tide of misery looming ahead.

And, finally, a major lesson for both the government and the media is to get its messaging right. They need to communicate accurately and proportionately. They should, for example, instead of spreading panic by ghoulishly reporting meaningless numbers of those dying, promote stories that demonstrate that the overwhelming majority of those infected survive it (and indeed, most do not even know when they are infected!). Another example of needlessly stoking fear is the nonsense of generalising numbers of the dead from other countries to India without noting that the average age of mortality of Covid-19 in Europe hovers around the age of 80 years (many of whom lived in care-homes which have become clusters of death), while barely 1 per cent of India's population is in this age group (and almost none live in care-homes)! Communicating the age-stratified risk of mortality and indicating that the vast majority of our youthful workforce would not have been significantly affected by the virus, might have stopped the biblical migration of millions to their villages and prevented the stigmatisation of those who are infected or at-risk. Such an understanding would also have emphasised physical distancing *in the home* to minimise the risk of transmission to vulnerable elders.

India's tryst with Covid-19 is far from over. It will continue to fester away for months, even years, and only time will tell what long-term impacts the lockdown has had and whether the government was able to catch the balls still hanging in the air. But, even beyond this particular tryst, this will certainly not be the last epidemic of a novel infectious agent to hit our shores. It is so very important that we ensure that the lessons we have learned from this experience will enable us, the next time around, to be better prepared to, at the very least, do no harm.

Reference

Deaton, Angus and Anne Case. 2020. *Deaths of Despair and the Future of Capitalism*. Princeton, NJ: Princeton University Press.

8

The Twin Crises of Covid-19 and How to Resolve Them*

Ananda Lal Roy and Maitreesh Ghatak

With the spectre of Covid-19 haunting the world, every country is faced with an impossible choice—public health or the economy? Given that this is a global public health crisis, an economic recovery will not be possible unless the health crisis is resolved first and public fear is alleviated.

Imagine the consequences if the economy is 'opened' prematurely before we know firmly that the risk of viral spread is eliminated or at least minimised. This could result in a new wave of infection, create fear and panic, and end up in a loss of public trust. It would drive markets down and lead to a fresh round of job losses. Therefore, the importance of dealing with the public health side of the crisis is paramount. For that, normal economic activity has to be suspended, except for essential services.

On the other hand, suspending normal economic activity results in shortages, layoffs and closure of businesses. This puts millions of people at subsistence risk—many more than the number directly or potentially affected by the disease. Therefore, the public health and the economic sides of the problem are closely interrelated. Instead of a sequential solution—public health first or economy first—the way forward must be guided by solutions based on a clear understanding of the connections between these two aspects of the crisis.

The problems of public health and of the economy are interdependent, even in countries that are relatively rich and without

* First published in *The India Forum*, 24 April 2020.

extreme inequality. Where incomes are lower and inequality is greater, this interdependence is significantly accentuated.

Other things held constant, lower-income groups are more vulnerable to Covid-19 because of co-morbidities that are worsened by poor pre-existing health conditions as well as due to a lack of healthcare access. This is especially true in India where the healthcare system is generally under-resourced, and where a large section of the population lives on the margins of subsistence and suffers from a low level of health. High population density, especially in urban areas, and a large number of poor people who have no means to practise proper hygiene, all make physical distancing and the enforcement of a lockdown difficult, if not impossible. This further raises the risk of contagion. If the contagion spreads widely in a population of the size of India, it would put an incredible amount of pressure on the healthcare system.

Hence, for the same set of natural factors such as climate, biological characteristics and demographic composition, higher economic inequalities will amplify the likelihood of contagion and stretch the public health system to its limit. At the same time, given that around 90 per cent of the workforce in India is in the informal sector and so does not have a regular salary or sufficient savings, the economic shock from the lockdown is going to be quite severe.

There is thus a real danger that deaths and serious illnesses due to starvation may outnumber those due to Covid-19 itself. The poor state of the healthcare system is going to exacerbate this problem. This is the two-way feedback loop that works from the public health aspect to the economic aspect of the crisis.

Dealing with the Crisis

Three broad categories of medical options for Covid-19 are being explored: They are (i) developing vaccines; (ii) developing novel antiviral drugs; and (iii) repurposing existing drugs. Although a vaccine is the most effective option in the long run, it would take 12–18 months to be developed, as it has to be tested not only for efficacy, but also for safety. Apart from these options, Covid-19 patients are being treated with antibodies isolated from recovered patients.

While all these options are being explored globally at a rapid rate, it will take some time to have an effective and safe treatment. The novel coronavirus spreads via humans, so unless travel and human contacts are prevented, its spread will not be stopped. For the time being then the most effective mitigation strategy is physical distancing to the extent possible.

The extremely mobile nature of this virus also makes it futile to shut down one region at a time. But in India mitigation through a country-wide lockdown has to be balanced with the risk of starvation that stares at a population where large numbers live close to the margins of subsistence. This was visibly demonstrated by the plight of migrant workers trying to find their way back to their villages after the lockdown was announced. In the absence of a universal social safety net, continuing the lockdown indefinitely and uniformly is not an option either.

We need to have a policy that balances a selective relaxation of a lockdown (say, based on the incidence of reported cases by districts) with an overall stop-and-go approach as has been proposed in many developed countries.

The number of confirmed Covid-19 cases or deaths was relatively low in India in the early months since the pandemic broke. However, now this is no longer true—in terms of absolute numbers, it is now one of the worst-affected countries. The caseload has increased significantly due to a confluence of several factors, including relaxing lockdowns, the natural tendency of general public to not adhere to strict public health guidelines for long periods and an extremely high population density in India. However, the severity of the disease, including mortality rate, remains surprisingly low. Whether this is due to gross under-reporting or other factors (like previous exposure to milder forms of seasonal coronaviruses) remain unknown. Given the size of India's population, as one had anticipated in the early stages of the outbreak, if a sizeable number of people who are infected exhibit severe symptoms and require hospitalisation, the healthcare systems would be hard-pressed to deal with such a surge. The situation will be even more dire if the infection spreads in rural communities where there are few proper facilities to treat critically ill patients.

The experience from other countries suggest that there are effective mitigation strategies, such as tracking and tracing, in addition to physical distancing and frequent handwashing that could bring the numbers down. Implementing these measures has nevertheless proved to be difficult. High population density and crowded housing make physical distancing difficult in many places. Also, poverty, inadequate sanitation and the lack of public health education at the local community level would constrain the feasibility of frequent handwashing. Although far from ideal, perhaps providing masks and gloves in large enough quantities remains more practical as a mitigation strategy in these communities.

The Short Term

The solutions to the problems in both public health and economic aspects of the crisis are also interdependent, in the short run and in the long run.

In the short run, public health intervention must focus on preventing contagion by imposing selective and flexible lockdowns, depending on the contagion threat, and with results from aggressive testing (both to assess infections and recovery). This approach might require multiple rounds of lockdowns until transmission slows down. But if the lockdowns are working, they can be of progressively shorter durations. However, given the nature of the epidemic, these lockdowns cannot be entirely local and will require close coordination between the central and the state governments in order to synchronise their respective lockdown policies.

While providing a timeline for reopening the country would not be prudent at this stage, it would be possible to provide a plan for a controlled relaxation of physical distancing. This could be achieved by wide-reaching but targeted serological testing for the presence of antibodies against the coronavirus—serological testing indicating recovery from Covid-19 and likely protection against immediate reinfection—and perhaps providing health certificates to those who are seropositive against the virus, allowing them back into the workforce. Testing could be accompanied by incentives of food and money. Facilitating the movement of a critical mass of seropositive people would also help in acquiring herd immunity sooner rather than later.

Let us consider a few examples. Sweden did not mandate a country-wide lockdown or a stay-at-home order, although the population has adhered to a voluntary physical distancing guideline. Sweden has so far reported around 97,000 cases with a reported mortality rate of around 6 per cent, a fatality rate that is among the highest in the developed world. Germany, which instituted a lockdown, has a death rate of 3 per cent. Given its past experience with SARS, Singapore moved aggressively to mandate a lockdown, thereby lowering both the total number of cases and the mortality rate. The mortality rate in India is still very low (1.5 per cent) despite the reported number of cases being over 6.9 million. Once again, this could be gross under-reporting or due to other factors like previous exposure to milder seasonal coronaviruses (thereby developing some immunity against Covid-19).

The problem with the highly infectious Covid-19 is that it does not stay in one place—it moves before one realises it. So, a more synchronised strategy of selective lockdowns and testing is the way forward, coupled with measures to provide subsistence support. To begin with, essential workers who have been working through the lockdown need to be tested and if found infected, quarantined. In a graded way, less-essential workers need to be tested too, and if found virus-free or with acquired immunity, they should be able to get back to work.

An essential component of this strategy has to be an economic package involving the provision of basic food and fuel rations needed for survival and a certain amount of cash for other essential items. Any form of lockdown policy has to be accompanied by a strengthening of the safety net. Without this it will be hard and perhaps impractical to enforce a lockdown, and there will be a higher risk of a large number of deaths due to starvation.

The size of the support package (Ghatak 2020) as well as the policy announcements and their implementation, all so far leave a lot to be desired (visibly demonstrated by the plight of migrant workers, for example). On the other hand, without a lockdown, the contagion could spread at a rate that would make any economic support package infeasible as well as impractical.

The Medium and Long Term

In the medium run, the obvious way forward seems to be to build on the complementarity between public health and economic interventions, to both revitalise the economy and expand the capacity of the public health system in terms of personnel, equipment and healthcare facilities. For example, once the immediate fiscal crisis is dealt with, there is an overwhelmingly strong case for focusing public expenditure on recruiting and training healthcare workers capable of doing basic tests and providing rapid and initial responses, especially in areas not well served by health services. It would generate both a critical first line of defence for our healthcare system, as well as provide training and employment opportunities as the economy re-emerges from a period of massive losses.

It is easy to see that an immediate reaction to the crisis would be to close borders and turn the clock back on globalisation. In the long run, that would be misguided and counterproductive. After all, pandemics have occurred in the past when the world was less globalised. The virus does not recognise borders, the solution should not either. The collective scientific, medical, technical and financial resources of the world are needed to combat the spread of Covid-19. No country can go it alone.

Airline disasters that were common in the early stages of the airline industry, or more recently, the terrorist attacks of 9/11, did not mean we had to forego air travel. Rather, the solution was to ramp up technical safety and personal security standards internationally and to have a mechanism and policy of monitoring and coordinating these across countries. In the present scenario too, the way forward should be similar. We need to proactively raise global health awareness and safety standards related to maintaining an ecological balance within countries, as well as raise public health protocols to contain and limit the spread of infectious diseases once there is an outbreak. This would require much closer cooperation and strategic coordination among countries on public health policies, rather than a retreat into isolationism.

The origin of the Covid-19 outbreak also clearly suggests that environmental conservation and an ecological balance are now essential. The 'jumping' of viruses from natural hosts (bats in this case) to humans via other intermediate host animals is recent and primarily due to human encroachment upon natural habitats. These activities include deforestation, modern agro-industrial practices and ever-expanding urbanisation. Drastic climate change has 'opened up' formerly uninhabitable areas, resulting in significantly altered natural habitats of various species and profoundly engendering ecological imbalances. These events have brought humans into closer contact with various species and their resident viruses and other pathogens. The virus did not come looking for us, but we went to the virus.

One of the biggest economic lessons of the crisis is that without environmental and ecological safeguards, the process of growth can crash spectacularly. We are witnessing this right now. There is a direct threat of setting back the decades of progress owed to a certain model of growth that (for all the criticism it has faced) pulled large numbers of people out of poverty in countries such as China and India. Climate change disproportionately affects the poor. Hence, a renewed emphasis on dealing with climate change and on instituting ecological safeguards while dipping into land and natural resources is not a luxury of green-leaning elites, but a necessity for avoiding in future the kind of twin economic and public health disasters that we are now experiencing.

Outlook

No matter how dire the situation appears right now, there is no doubt that the current Covid-19 crisis will eventually be mitigated. Vaccines and/or other drugs will be developed for treatment and people will ultimately develop herd immunity. After all, modern medicine is very recent. It is our natural immunity that has protected us against viruses and other pathogens and kept us alive for thousands of years. Regardless of what new pathogens emerge, it is ultimately this natural immunity that will ensure in the long run that humankind persists, even if we suffer many deaths and face immense misery in the interim.

How should we prepare for the future—because it is merely a matter of time before the next pathogen emerges?

The first and best option is to prevent an infectious disease becoming a pandemic. If despite our best efforts a pandemic occurs, we should have strategic and comprehensive containment and mitigation plans firmly in place. Proactive measures will be required to increase national stockpiles of PPE (such as masks, gloves and disposable gowns), hand sanitisers and ventilators.

Finally, we should work towards an eradication strategy with mass testing, vaccination and wide-scale community engagement. Rather than just a top-down approach, public policy based on grassroots community engagement must be adopted to better educate people on health hazards and the mitigation strategies associated with such pathogens. Furthermore, community organisers can convince and incentivise people to help with testing and immunisation. These measures can be seen effectively carried out in regions and countries that dealt with past pandemics like HIV and tuberculosis.

Economic drivers could include development of gadgets and devices using new technologies (for example, wearable thermometers, wearable oxygen-sensing and other monitoring devices), although such devices would raise important privacy issues, as well as give too much surveillance power to governments or to large corporations. The development of new technologies could also include cheap and easy-to-use test kits both for virus detection and for antibody tests to monitor immunity.

These measures might require large-scale coordinated and strategic public–private partnerships between research institutions, government health agencies and pharmaceutical companies. Public and publicly supported academic enterprises can conduct and facilitate research to develop a drug or a device.

While there are grounds to be cautious about private corporations, they are much better equipped to quickly manufacture and widely distribute a drug, vaccine or a medical device. These could be done with government-decreed stipulations on affordability. Indeed, the public–private partnership model has been effective in dealing with large public health crises, as during the ZIKA virus infection and in dealing with malaria. These partnerships are also helping with Alzheimer's disease, type-2 diabetes, rheumatoid arthritis and Parkinson's disease.

We must be far better prepared for the next pathogenic menace. If there is one abiding lesson to be taken from this crisis, it is the need for preparation.

Reference

Ghatak, Maitreesh. 2020. '3 Points of Concern on Government's Much-needed Economic Package'. *NDTV*, 28 March. Available at https://www.ndtv.com/opinion/3-points-of-concern-on-governments-much-needed-economic-package-2201707 (accessed 22 November 2020).

Section IV

The Law, the Judiciary and Covid-19

9

Exodus Constitutionalism

*Mass Migration in Covid-19 Lockdown Times**

Upendra Baxi

Exodus, marking the liberation of the people of Israel from slavery in Egypt under the leadership of Moses, is the foundation of the Hebrew Bible. But as a meaning of dispossession or forcible mass movement of people, it constitutes a universal historical experience.

I

It is estimated that in 2019 international migrants comprised 272 million (United Nations 2020). Well over 41 million were internally displaced persons, and the United Nations High Commissioner for Refugees (UNHCR) now uses the concept of nexus dynamics to refer to 'situations where conflict and/or violence and disaster and/or adverse effects of climate change exist in a country of origin'. Recently, the United Nations Human Rights Committee (2020) stated that 'countries may not deport individuals who face climate change-induced conditions that violate the right to life'. It is estimated by the World Bank that 143 million people from South Asia, Latin America and Sub-Saharan Africa will constitute climate-driven migrants by 2050 (Lewis 2020).

A quick recitation of well-known global statistics is no substitute for a sensitive real-life understanding of the challenge that migrants face in cheating their way into existence and survival. As Hannah

* First published in *The India Forum*, 19 June 2020.

Arendt reminded us all on the eve of the Universal Declaration of Human Rights, the abstract figure of the human person obscures from view, almost to a vanishing point, the lived reality of the stateless and asylum-seeking refugees constituting the real horror of abject rightlessness. She stressed the basic human right to natality, a right to belong to a political community, and expected it to follow the entailments of the 'right to have rights' (see Birmingham 2006; Michelman 1996; Parekh 2004).

We are treated to abundant and elaborate televisual news and views, constitutionally enriched judicial *suo motu* phrases, elaborate rhapsodies of party political performances, social media comments, activist lawyer and citizen petitions to the courts, a forest of administrative policy and programmes, and the din of dissent, plus more. All this may not carry the authentic migrant voice. To borrow the words of the famous rock musician Jethro Tull, all this is 'but a whisper' which can 'make us feel', while our 'deafness a shout' that cannot 'make us think'.

And the poet says: 'In the tidal destruction the moral melee/ The elastic retreat rings the close of play', and 'sandcastle virtues are all swept away'. The migrant workers walk endless miles and miles while all 'wise men don't know how it feels/To be thick as a brick'. Nor ever will they know fully what it means to die on a suitcase in a railway station and have a toddler uncover the dead body of a migrant mother; or be mowed away on the tracks by a speeding train while succumbing to a fatigue-induced slumber; or be gang raped while on the move or in a state shelter.

Jethro Tull and his companions lived in an era in which no social media images went viral, but they developed a lyric and song where some unwise folks at least sensed what it was 'to be as thick as a brick'. The phenomenon of the Covid-19 migrant on the move was all about the senseless social suffering that thingified human beings and converted their suffering into commodities in markets of governance, justice, development and human rights.

II

Of necessity, this conversation mainly engages a peculiarly poignant set of contexts, conditions and circumstances of what I call 'exodus constitutionalism'. But in order to get there a few preliminary points need to be made.

First and most crucial, no one in the world could claim recipe-knowledges that may address a sinister global pandemic. The state and society have a common agenda to fight a global pandemic. No state action can hope to succeed without the intelligent cooperation of citizens and no constitutionally sincere citizen may justifiably think that state managers and institutions are dispensable.

Indeed, the state must exercise great vigil over the situation and seek to provide conditions adequate to the security of a right to life and living with dignity and security. What is also needed besides rights-based consideration is 'resilient' politics based on empathy.[1]

Epistemic humility is then a first virtue of the tasks and labours of governance, development, rights and justice. What matters is not the willingness to strike accompanied by the fear of being wounded, but the willingness and ability on all sides to learn from manifest and latent mistakes in law, policy and governance accompanied by rapid course correction.

Second, not just the social activists, but the bureaucracy, security and political elites too need always to accept the accumulated constitutional wisdom of the judiciary. A subservient judiciary and a sycophantic legal profession (and media) are no friends of a democratic order. If the Supreme Court is to remain a 'last resort of the bewildered and the oppressed' (in the immortal words of Justice P. K. Goswami),[2] adjudicatory co-governance of the nation (the wisdom of the people speaking through courts, or demosprudence) is as essential as is legisprudence (the wisdom of the legislators) and jurisprudence (the wisdom of the jurists). Pooling these wisdoms is the need of the hour in combating Covid-19.

Third, this pandemic renders political one-upmanship or hyper-partisanship entirely superfluous and downright dangerous. Epistemic humility requires us all to learn from and listen to each other, and not take recourse to antagonistic politics that divides people into the friend and the enemy. If nothing else, Covid-19 should teach us to care for each other and co-learn from fellow citizens, rather than use the arsenal of law to silence or punish free and responsible acts of speech and expression, howsoever inconvenient or irritating these may prove to those who hold power. To accuse each other of defamation, hurting religious or cultural sensitivities, sedition or even treason is an undemocratic vice not to be celebrated.

III

All policy formulations must rely on the postulate that constitutional and core human rights are not an adversary but an ally in the fight against Covid-19 and related evils. An infected body is not just a source of contagion but also a human citizen, a being with basic rights. The Lancet-O'Neill Institute Commission on Global Health and Law in its recent (2019) report stresses that the capacity of the law to act as 'a social determinant' of health has been 'underutilized', and also stresses 'evidence-based legal interventions', which should 'build the research case for legal action'. It appeals to the 'global health community' to 'oppose laws that undermine the right to health and to equity', especially those laws that 'stigmatize or discriminate against marginalised populations', as these are 'especially harmful and exacerbate health disparities'.

We also need to attend to the views that tend to place migrants into homogenous and heterogenous categories for different purposes. For example, the United Nations International Organisation for Migration (IOM) regards a migrant as broadly 'any person who is moving or has moved across an international border or within a state away from his/her habitual place of residence, regardless of (1) the person's legal status; (2) whether the movement is voluntary or involuntary; (3) what the causes for the movement are; or (4) what the length of the stay is'.

This agency-specific wide definition is useful to map out cross-border and within-nation voluntary and forced migration. On the other hand, there is another view that accentuates differentiation between voluntary and involuntary, free or forced, migration. In this sense, we preserve distinct categories such as immigrants, asylum seekers, other necessitous migrants, internally displaced persons (IDPs), stateless peoples, persecuted religious minorities and ecological exiles. Further, 'migrants' form a heterogeneous mass who have not merely the same basic material needs (food, clothing, shelter, health, literacy and numeracy) and non-material needs (dignity, privacy, freedoms, participation, information and access), but also such vertical needs. There is, also, no such thing as 'migrants', but only persons and groups with distinctively (and often disturbingly) different needs and abilities: divided by age (from infants to senior citizens), sex and gender, health (the coexistence of earlier morbidity), disability, and ways of belonging to religious, cultural, spiritual and civilisational communities.

We concern ourselves here with forced migration of IDPs. Indeed, every time we use the general appellation 'migrants' or 'internally displaced persons',[3] we must fully know the existential horror reflected in their individual and social biographies: the economic, social and political conditions and contexts which make people move from the domicile of birth to the domicile (of their necessitous and precarious) 'choice'.

IV

How do the anti-Covid strategies and contexts in India cope with both individual human and social suffering? Some imposition of this suffering has been considered as a necessary evil, and bearing it gracefully is considered a badge of national unity and patriotism. Some suffering, however, must be classified as 'surplus' or unnecessary suffering.

Such suffering occurs when every individual person is regarded as a potential carrier of disease and exposed to state and social management. Epidemiology regards each person as a unit of contagion and the law becomes the instrument for management of contagion, followed by testing, treatment, isolation, distancing and therapy. Law emerges as an adjunct of intense public health management, in turn morphed into a public culture of self-care (frequently washing hands, wearing masks in public places and 'social' distancing). Is sheer survival of individuals and society as a whole to be considered as paramount to the management of a global pandemic in which all constitutional values remain secondary? Or, should it also be the case that anti-Covid performances must not violate basic human rights? For example, the human right to health may not be held incompatible with the human right to live with dignity, or the new penal laws and action should also bear in view social stigma as a mechanism of instant control.

Difficult questions are raised concerning the imposition of the lockdown or its partial lifting. Epidemiologists and health experts continue to differ on different models of scientific uncertainty. But no education in the obvious is necessary to say that even the simple rules of hygiene are not observable in conditions of extreme impoverishment or in migrants on the move. Governments have done well to launch a campaign for civic education and in supplying masks, soaps and even water. But these can do very little in reducing physical distancing in slums or slum-like conditions which manifest the malaise of unconstitutional mass impoverishment. To point out to some structural limits of the anti-Covid programmes is surely not to indulge in any anti-national, seditious or treasonable conduct. Rather, it highlights the importance of more intense implementation of the Directive Principles of State Policy and the performance of fundamental duties as provided by Part IV-A of the Constitution of India.

Second, the pressing need to put an anti-Covid framework in place makes unusually difficult a fresh legal start for managing the nation. Drastic measures like lockdowns and zoning require taking the toxic dust off from the four-section colonial Epidemic Diseases Act, 1897,[4] and naming the happening as a 'disaster' within the meaning of the Disaster Management Act (DMA), 2005. This did help governments acquire an arsenal of discretionary police powers, enforce social discipline, introduce many new measures of epidemiological surveillance, and resort to volatile forms of biopower and biopolitics. However, it is good to come across normative constitutional and statutory limits. For example, Section 61 of the DMA prohibits 'discrimination on the grounds of sex, caste, community, descent or religion' in the administration of compensation and relief to the victims of disaster, but this should not remain a prescription more honoured in breach rather than compliance.[5]

In a deep constitutional irony, a command and control–planned national economy law (the Essential Commodities Act, 1955) now helps neoliberal India combat Covid-19. It enabled the Union government on 13 March 2020 to declare masks and hand sanitisers as essential commodities until 30 June. This law's vast potential to control production, supply, distribution, and to secure their equitable distribution and availability at fair prices, is once again writ large on the economy and the nation. So remains its potential for use in life after Covid-19.

Third, whatever one may say about its design and detail, the principle of federalism as an essential aspect of the basic structure of the Constitution remains necessary to sustain social diversity and human dignity. Asymmetric federalism is not always irredentist or secessionist; it also promotes 'the conditions of an enlarged democratic setting' by leveraging group 'equality, inclusive participation and justice', which 'deepen the legitimacy and strengthen the functionality of multinational states' (Hausing 2014: 89). Unsurprising is the fact that 'extensive empirical case studies ... conclusively show that all durable multinational states also happen to be federal democratic states' (ibid.).

V

An endemic feature of Indian politics, and probably all party-political systems everywhere, is the processes of politicisation of catastrophe. The term 'catastrophising' has been long used by social psychologists to characterise a social disposition, but Adi Ophir (an Israeli political philosopher whose work should be better known in India) explicitly links it with the distribution of evils, including (if I may use my words) radical suffering of the constitutional have-nots. Ophir describes this political process of 'the sudden or gradual rise in evils', its 'quantity, quality, frequency, span of distribution, and durability'—in short, a rise in 'the volume of evils' and the 'accompanying decline in the availability and effectiveness of means of protection, healing, and restoration'. Indeed, such internal processes where natural and man-made disasters often work conjointly to 'create devastating effects on a large population' and represent the 'very avalanche of evils that injure entire populations' (Ophir 2010). Cognate insights are offered by the Nigerian thinker Clade Ake (1994) in speaking about the 'democratization of disempowerment', and the Cameroonian philosopher Achilles Mbembe (2019) who has accentuated the 'necrophiliac' nature of public power.

This combination of multiple disasters and mass catastrophe is on abundant display in the migrant crises, first in the policy inadvertence which lasted till 29 April, and second in the difficulties since then in making transport and related facilities available to migrants on the move. We all know of the costs to be borne by the originary states of migrant workers, the so-called 'bus politics' or 'train politics', and the repatriation of some migrant workers to the host states. If the spread of a global pandemic was an act of misfortune, its catastrophisation has to be located in the injustices of social structure and policy. On the other side, the spectacular emergence of new communities of belonging (social groups trying to meet the many needs of migrants on the move), which counter the politics of creating communities of danger, hopefully will become a post-Covid future, ending forever the production of social indifference.

VI

The Covid-19 styles of law and administration all over the globe enhance the powers of the administrative biopolitical state. But since its inception, India's apex court has acquiesced in the constitutional fact of vast powers to make law and policy. The presumption of the constitutionality of state laws and policies still stands. The judicial doctrine of harmonious construction in the sphere of conflicting rights in Parts III and IV of the Constitution still prevails. Administrative *mala fides* remain difficult to prove; and the courts in interpreting the Constitution still hold that the mere possibility of abuse of power is not a ground for not conferring it. Further, several draconian security and anti-terror and related economic offences have been held constitutionally valid. And let us recall that as late as in the *Kesavananda Bharati* case (1973),[6] six Supreme Court justices ruled in favour of Parliament's absolute power to change the basic structural constitutional identity, and many justices even today believe in judicial self-restraint.

Yet the indictment of judicial overreach survives and grows, as an example of successful political (and even academic) propaganda since the dawn of the Constitution! But (without further exploring here my writings), it must be reiterated that the conflict between the legislative/executive combine and adjudicative constitutional interpretation stands ingrained in the Constitution itself as a vital aspect of republican democracy. We may learn from it but cannot eliminate it.

And the differences between competitive power politics and the constitutional politics of courts needs to be always re-explored. The latter may be occasionally jurispathic (rulings that are coercive) but is never self-interested. Justices do not decide disputes or contentions on considerations of personal benefit, even when the quality of justice they produce may be contested.

The heightened use of *suo motu* proceedings by the Supreme Court and the high courts has been quite remarkable in the time of Covid-19. Aggressive monitoring by as many as 19 high courts of administrative schemes and local institutional management procedures is an aid, rather than an obstacle, to more effective anti-Covid action (as, for example, in situations of domestic violence, inadequate nutrition and release of undertrial prisoners on bail).

How to make the invisible socially visible is another name for social action litigation (SAL), still conflated with the so-called public interest litigation (PIL). Even if considered identical twins, each has a different constitutional visage. SAL is dialogical, not adversarial. The protracted 'hope and trust' jurisdiction is inherent to SAL and not an aberration, even though in PIL we may prefer certain instantly desired outcomes.

Still the SAL power and process may be criticised when the dismissal of well-reasoned petitions amounts to judicial abdication. Whether such abdication has occurred or not in relation to the migrant labour exodus is a hotly contested issue, both inside and outside the court. A Supreme Court bench has referred to the central government the detailed 2020 Stranded Workers Action Network (SWAN) report on stranded migrant workers, and articulated 'hope and trust' in SAL jurisdiction to trigger appropriate policy and on-the-ground action.[7] Sometime later, a different bench took urgent *suo motu* action and issued some interim directions.[8] Welcome though this step is, on a better-late-than-never principle, it is too soon to make even informed guesses on how these directions will work in the daily life of those on the move. We may also ask whether the adversarial litigation is more to be preferred compared to *suo motu* action.[9]

The vast executive and administrative structures claim, and rightly so, to be sensitive to people's misery in a global pandemic. But does that necessarily mean that courts and justices may not speak *at all?* Is not there a difference between a rights-based solicitude and the more routine policymaking tasks? Judicialising the issue of mass public health, monitoring of the supply of essential medicines and testing, conditions in public hospitals and costs in private ones, for example, mark judicial itineraries of normative cooperative action to sensitise and redirect the local executive regarding specific issues otherwise solely left to health and other experts.[10]

There is lots to be learnt on all sides from those who decided to walk across the length and breadth of India that is Bharat; this mass civil disobedience met with some law and order type preventive or punitive response. But undeterred, they marched on very long distances on foot, gambling with exhaustion, hunger, disease, fatigue and even death. Neither policy, nor political, actors thought that such 'mass illegalities' (to use a striking phrase of Michel Foucault) were ever possible and therefore did not anticipate legal ways to solicit compliance. We should also accept that the migrant labourers acted as individual moral actors, rather than as an inert mass of moral patients.

VII

While not offering any full-fledged theory of this form here, I suggest that our constitutionalism may truly be called *exodus constitutionalism,* acting as the other of ordinary democratic constitutionalism. In a sense, border control is the insignia of the sovereignty of a modern state and marks the beginning of geopolitics. The good side of this is what Arendt was to call natality: a political community to which one may belong. The flip side is the terrible reality of statelessness: a being without any national identity and having the status of a global pariah as a refugee or asylum seeker, quintessentially a rightless human being.

Exodus constitutionalism is not only born and thus always at work with ordinary constitutionalism, but it also often stands at the crossroads of political and judicial power. One may here usefully borrow from the life sciences the imagery of the host and parasite, to learn how the latter begins the dance of its own destruction while populating the host. I know that the analogy is stressful in Covid-19 days, but as the great French philosopher Jacques Derrida once described it, this relation constitutes a viral trajectory: 'an inert code that replicates itself by using a host', by making 'an unsuspecting host ingest it; to force the host's internal machinery to make new copies of the virus; and to spread as many of these copies as possible, in order to maximize the possibility of infecting new hosts'. The virus 'requires a more complex host to invade and destroy but cannot live by itself'. The 'virus being many things ... in part a parasite that destroys, that introduces disorder into communication ...; it derails a mechanism of the communicational type, its coding and decoding ... [it] is neither alive nor dead ...' (Derrida, quoted in Burnett and Wills 1994: 12; Salingaros 2003).

Extended to the constitutional text, Covid-19 and the epic tragedy of mass migration, we find the same disease of a 'combinational type' that introduces 'disorder' and death 'in communication'.

The Constitution of India may well be said to provide a leading contemporary text of exodus constitutionalism. Composed in the poignant times of the partition of India, the Constitution itself was written with blood. It bears many birthmarks of its foundational violence—20 million people; Hindus, Sikhs and Muslims constituted the largest mass migration in human history. Since then many exoduses have happened, marked with considerable violence. The Planning Commission of India in 2012 stated that since Independence (1947), about 60 million people had been displaced by development projects. And the 2017 *India Migration Report* acknowledges that apart 'from conflicts and disasters, over the years, development projects, including urban redevelopment and beautification, have displaced large numbers of people from different parts of the country' (Rajan 2018).

The constitutional development has been thus haunted by many an involuntary mass migration, from the mass exodus of the Kashmiri Pandits to now Covid-19 threatened mass migrants often walking to their distant homes from many populous Indian states they had once made their own. It is estimated that in the first phase of the lockdown, this number was about 5 million (see the complex analysis by Nomaan Majid in Chapter 14 of this volume), although the statistical scenarios fluctuate widely and are as diasporic as the migrants on the move (Chishti 2020).

Exodus constitutionalism crystallises the dilemma of dates. Our citizenship provisions stipulated in Articles 3–5 of the Constitution expose this. So do the recent memories of the conjoint working of the Citizenship Act of 1955 and its amendments, the 1946 Foreigners Act, the 1964 Foreigners (Tribunal) Order, and the adjudicatory leadership of the Supreme Court resulting in some forcible detentions and migrations in Assam.[11]

What may one say are the main characteristics of an exodus constitutionalism? First, at the heart of every constitution there pulsates a distinction between 'us' and 'them', the constitutional self and the constitutional others. In this sense, even when the other may not always be regarded as an enemy, constitutional identity depends a great deal on the distinction (rendered famous by Carl Schmitt) between the 'friend' and the 'enemy'. The US is often cited as an example of restricted citizenship because no foreign-born naturalised citizen can run for the office of president, but restrictions based on citizenship for contesting or voting at elections and occupying public offices are common to most societies.

Second, the status of citizenship is available through Articles 5–9 of Part II of the Constitution, and Parliament may make further law (which it has through the Citizenship Act or Foreigners Act). But citizenship is a sovereign decision of the state and not a fundamental right. Parliament by simple majority may decide who may count as citizen, and the supreme judiciary seems in no constitutional hurry to decide thorny constitutional issues thus arising and now raised by a few states and social action petitioners.

Third, exodus constitutionalism enhances the vulnerabilities of the populations affected. Even the term 'Covid-19 migrant workers' does not fully disclose various vulnerabilities specific to the very young as well as very old, women at work (notably sex-work and domestic labour), and married women. According to the 2011 Census, about

205.8 million women in India migrated for marriage, an extraordinary fact illustrating how marriage is related to migration. The demography of migration also varies strikingly, as we all know.

Fourth, a devaluation of citizenship is typical of exodus constitutionalism. IDPs (whether victims of natural disasters or of conflict and violence, or certain practices of development *as* governance) are often treated as *objects* rather than *subjects* of governance. This distinction has been affirmed by the United Nations Declaration on the Right to Development (Baxi 2007). IDPs signify kaleidoscopically changing situations in which constitutional othering always takes place, often making the culmination of the process of 'thingification'.

Many other variations exist. But it is high time that we recognise ways in which we continue to repudiate the foundational postulate of the Declaration of Philadelphia in 1919 that birthed the International Labour Organisation (ILO). It enunciated a century ago that 'labour is not a commodity' and that 'all human beings, irrespective of race, creed or sex, have a right to pursue both their material well-being and their spiritual development in conditions of freedom and dignity, of economic security and equal opportunity'. These are also the solemn pledges of the Constitution of India. Shall we allow forms of exodus constitutionalism to further override it?[12]

Notes

1. See the Gujarat High Court decision of 22 May 2020 by Justice B. Pardiwala and Justice Ilesh J. Vohra, who summoned 'resilient' and 'dynamic' leadership and the role of 'emotional intelligence' in these 'testing times' for the ruled and rulers alike. See *Suo Motu versus State of Gujarat*, 22 May 2020, available at https://indiankanoon.org/doc/119863050/ (accessed 22 November 2020).
2. *State of Rajasthan & Ors etc. etc versus Union of India etc. etc*, 6 May 1977, 1977 AIR 1361, 1978 SCR (1) 1, available at https://indiankanoon.org/doc/174974/ (accessed 22 November 2020).
3. It is surprising that the constitutional protection accorded to IDPs by Justice Gita Mittal in *P. K. Koul versus Estate Officer & Anr*, 30 November 2010, available at https://indiankanoon.org/doc/84234324/ (accessed 22 November 2020), is insufficiently put to use now. That landmark 2010 decision of Delhi High Court not merely reiterated the right

to housing as a core human right, but also reiterated (paragraph 34 onwards) the famous principles enunciating the human rights of IDPs. She also bemoaned the 'hyper-technical' approach adopted by the Union government in relation to the housing of the violently displaced Kashmiri Pandits.

4. The Epidemic Diseases Act No. 3 of 1897, available at http://legislative.gov.in/sites/default/files/A1897-03.pdf (accessed 22 November 2020).
5. As late as 27 May 2020, Chief Justice S. A. Bobde, and Justices A. S. Bopanna and Hrishikesh Roy took serious notice of a Jamiat Ulama-i-Hind averment that 'communal colour being given to the outbreak of the Covid-19 pandemic by certain sections of print, electronic and social media' poses 'a threat to the life and liberty of Muslims infringing their fundamental rights under Article 21 of the Constitution (Talwar 2020). The demonization is also an infringement of the right to live with dignity which is also covered under Article 21 of the Constitution.' The News Broadcasters Association (NBA) as well as Additional Solicitor General K. M. Natraj were directed to file a reply explaining inaction by the government under Sections 19 and 20 of the Cable Television Networks (Regulation) Act, 1995.
6. *Kesavananda Bharati … versus State of Kerala and Anr*, 24 April 1973, available at https://indiankanoon.org/doc/257876/ (accessed 22 November 2020).
7. As per Justices N. R. Ramana, Sanjay Kishan Kaul and B. R. Gavai on 24 April 2020. The situation of the stranded migrant workers was highlighted in public discourse by three petitions by: (i) Mahua Moitra and Swami Agnivesh, on behalf of migrant workers seeking various other reliefs; (ii) Aruna Roy and Nikhil Dey, seeking payment of wages to registered MNREGA households by the government, in consonance with the Ministry of Labour's direction of 20 March 2020 to chief secretaries of all states directing that during the coronavirus pandemic, all workers be paid 'full wages without any deductions'; and (iii) Harsh Mander and Anjali Bharadwaj. See Uday Singh (2020) and Mander (2020).
8. See an altogether different *suo motu* order by Justices Ashok Bhushan, Sanjay Kishen Kaul and M. R. Shah on 26 May 2020 concerning 'the problems and miseries of migrant workers', available at https://main.sci.gov.in/supremecourt/2020/11706/11706_2020_34_42_22217_Order_26-May-2020.pdf (accessed 22 November 2020).
9. We would never know for certain whether the late-night letter (Rajagopal 2020) by some superannuated justices of the Supreme Court and the

high court, and by some eminent senior counsel addressed to the court made a vital difference to the judicial attitudes the next morning.

10. Yet the judiciary may not always speak with one voice; the US Supreme Court on 29 May 2020, for example, denied relief to the church that had asked for the Pentecost Sunday celebrations. Chief Justice John G. Roberts held that 'when restrictions on particular social activities should be lifted during the pandemic ... is a dynamic and fact-intensive matter subject to reasonable disagreement' (Howe 2020). But dissenting Justices Clarence Thomas, Neil Gorsuch and Brett Kavanaugh maintained that the restrictions were not justified when others are permitted; 'malls, pet groomers, hair salons and marijuana dispensaries—are comparable to gatherings at houses of worship, and California has not shown a good reason for treating houses of worship differently', and notably that religious organisations are 'comparable secular businesses'.
11. See the magisterial study by Niraja Gopal Jayal (2013). There, she speaks, among other valuable things, of how cherished and at the same time contested the concept of citizenship has become, and of 'legal' and 'aspirational' citizenship, and the conflicts between the individual and collective dimensions of citizenship and identity.
12. Kalpana Kannabiran (2020) suggestively evokes the concept of 'constitutional commons', appealing to 'a robust memory of the Constitution, of the directive principles', and counsels that we 'act on that basis alone', subjecting all forms of state action to '*empathy* and a *deep ethical commitment* to constitutional morality'. Constitutional commons are not achieved or preserved by action that escalates 'the assertion of prerogative and the distribution of largess'. We return to Mbembe's (2019: 40) quest, then, of 'a politics that no longer necessarily rests upon difference or alterity but instead on a certain idea of the kindred and the in-common'.

    The idea of constitutional commons is one way to roll back 'exodus constitutionalism', but perhaps we need to ask: (i) how the 'in-common' deals with the politics of identity and difference, and (ii) how the practices of subaltern nonviolent normative insurgency may begin to reshape politics and bring democracy near to people's constitutionalism. This set of themes form many a challenge for the post-Covid world.

References

Ake, Clade. 1994. *Democratization of Disempowerment in Africa*. Lagos: Malthouse Press.

Baxi, Upendra. 2007. *Human Rights in a Posthuman World: Critical Essays*, Chapter 4. New Delhi: Oxford University Press.

Birmingham, Peg. 2006. *Hannah Arendt and Human Rights: The Predicament of Common Responsibility*. Bloomington: Indiana University Press.

Burnett, Peter and David Wills. 1994. *Deconstruction and the Visual Arts: Art, Media, Architecture*. New York: Cambridge University Press.

Chisti, Seema. 2020. 'Explained: How Many Migrant Workers Displaced?: A Range of Estimates'. *Indian Express*, 8 June.

Government of India. 2005. 'The Disaster Management Act, 2005'. Available at https://www.ndmindia.nic.in/images/The%20Disaster%20Management%20Act,%202005.pdf (accessed 22 November 2020).

Hausing, Kham Khan Suan. 2014. 'Asymmetric Federalism and the Question of Democratic Justice in Northeast India'. *India Review* 13 (2): 87–111.

Howe, Amy. 2020. 'Court Declines to Lift Restrictions on Crowds at Church Services'. *SCOTUS Blog*, 30 May. Available at https://www.scotusblog.com/2020/05/court-declines-to-lift-restrictions-on-crowds-at-church-services/ (accessed 22 November 2020).

Jayal, Niraja Gopal. 2013. *Citizenship and its Discontents: An Indian History*. Cambridge, Massachusetts: Harvard University Press.

Kannabiran, Kalpana. 2020. 'Justice and Rights in a Viral Contexts in India'. *The India Forum*, 2 May.

Lancet Commissions. 2019. 'The Legal Determinants of Health: Harnessing the Power of Law for Global Health and Sustainable Development'. Available at https://www.thelancet.com/pdfs/journals/lancet/PIIS0140-6736(19)30233-8.pdf (accessed 22 November 2020).

Lewis, Sophie. 2020. 'Millions of Future Climate Refugees May Need Protection, U.N. Committee Warns'. *CBS News*, 21 January. Available at https://www.cbsnews.com/news/climate-change-refugees-united-nations-rules/ (accessed 22 November 2020).

Majid, Nomaan. 2020. 'How Many Casual Workers in the Cities have Sought To Go Home?'. *The India Forum*, 5 June.

Mander, Harsh. 2020. 'Migrant Workers, the Lockdown, and the Judiciary'. *India Forum*, 11 May.

Mbembe, Achilles. 2019. *Necropolitics*. Durham: Duke University Press.

Michelman, Frank. 1996. 'Parsing "A Right to Have Rights"'. *Constellations* 3 (2): 200–09.

Ophir, Adi. 2010. 'The Politics of Catastrophization'. In *Contemporary States of Emergency: The Politics of Military and Humanitarian Interventions*, ed. Didier Fassin and Mariella Pandolfi, 40–61. New York: Zone Books.

Parekh, Serena. 2004. 'A Meaningful Place in the World: Hannah Arendt on the Nature of Human Rights'. *Journal of Human Rights* 3 (1): 41–53.

Planning Commission. 2013. *Twelfth Five Year Plan (2012–2017): Faster, More Inclusive and Sustainable Growth, India.* New Delhi: Sage Publications.

Rajagopal, Krishnadas. 2020. 'Hours Before Taking Up Migrant Workers Issue, Supreme Court Got Stinging Letter from Senior Lawyers'. *The Hindu*, 27 May. Available at https://www.thehindu.com/news/national/hours-before-taking-up-migrant-workers-issue-supreme-court-got-stinging-letter-from-senior-lawyers/article31685187.ece (accessed 22 November 2020).

Rajan, S. Irudaya (ed.). 2018. *The India Migration Report 2017: Forced Migration*. New Delhi: Routledge India.

Salingaros, Nikos. 2003. 'The Derrida Virus'. *Telos* 126: 66–82.

Stranded Workers Action Network. 2020. '21 Days and Counting: COVID-19 Lockdown, Migrant Workers, and the Inadequacy of Welfare Measures in India'. Available at https://www.thehindu.com/news/resources/article31442220.ece/binary/Lockdown-and-Distress_Report-by-Stranded-Workers-Action-Network.pdf (accessed 22 November 2020).

Talwar, Sanya. 2020. '"Don't Let People Instigate Law and Order Issues", SC Observes While Seeking Centre's Response on Plea against Communalization of Nizamuddin Markaz Isue'. *LiveLaw*, 27 May. Available at https://www.livelaw.in/top-stories/nizamuddin-markaz-dont-let-people-instigate-law-order-issues-sc-s-157389 (accessed 22 November 2020).

Uday Singh, Chander. 2020. 'The Supreme Court is in Thrall of Government'. *The Wire*, 28 May.

United Nations. 2020. 'International Migrant Stock 2019'. Available at https://www.un.org/development/desa/en/news/population/international-migrant-stock-2019.html (accessed 23 November 2020).

United Nations Human Rights Committee. 2020. 'Historic UN Human Rights Case Opens Door to Climate Change Asylum Claims'. Available at https://www.ohchr.org/EN/NewsEvents/Pages/DisplayNews.aspx?NewsID=25482&LangID=E (accessed 22 November 2020).

10

Gendering the Pandemic in the Prison*

Pratiksha Baxi and Navsharan Singh

That the prison system needs reform and that its conditions are inhuman is a matter of state record and acknowledgement. The legal principle 'bail not jail' frames every legal commentary on bail (*LiveLaw* 2020a). The law therefore intends for undertrial prisoners (UTPs) to be a numerical custodial minority in the prison. However, the 2018 National Crime Records Bureau (NCRB) data shows that of the 4,66,084 prison inmates in our prisons, 1,39,488 (30 per cent) are convicted and 3,23,537 (70 per cent) are undertrials. Yet, no moratorium on fresh arrests that would stop new admissions of undertrials into prisons has been announced during the pandemic.

In *Contagion of Covid 19 Virus in Prisons,*[1] the Supreme Court of India directed the constitution of High Power Committees (HPCs) headed by each high court to oversee the de-congestion of prisons during the pandemic. The court noted that 'prisons can be fertile breeding grounds for incubation of COVID-19'. Despite a national de-congestion drive, even on 22 June 2020, as per the e-prison dashboard, the total prison population stood at an extraordinarily high 4,64,127. This would include UTPs, convicted prisoners, and detenues or civil prisoners. The legal system has the responsibility to devise ways to avoid mass contagion in custodial institutions, failing which the system would be hit by a catastrophisation of a disaster, for as Upendra Baxi argues (see Chapter 9 of this volume), 'if the spread of a global pandemic was an act of misfortune, its catastrophisation has to be located in the injustices of social structure and policy'.

* First published in *The India Forum*, 10 July 2020.

The threat of mass contagion in prisons poses specific challenges to women, children, and gender and sexual minorities in prisons and other custodial minorities (Carissimo 2020). Older women prisoners, detenues and undertrials in overcrowded pandemic-struck prisons have been denied bail, while pregnant women, lactating mothers, and mothers and their children, women with disabilities, and women with co-morbidities continue to be incarcerated in overcrowded prisons. Why should courts be mindful of women inmates *as* women?[2] We argue that all women inmates should be released, whether or not they are pregnant, and outline why we think that a disaster could become a catastrophe if the legal classification of women prisoners and undertrials deserving of release or bail is not altered.

Are Women 'Custodial' Minorities?

Curious about what percentage of the overall prison population comprises women, we collated the figures available on the e-prisons dashboard[3] on 20 June 2020 and found that this platform showed that there are 22,927 women inmates in all prisons in India (Table 10.1). This forms 4.1 per cent of the total inmates, an increase from 3.3 per cent in 2000 as per the NCRB statistics[4] available until the end of December.

Table 10.1: Age of Women in Pandemic-struck Prisons, June 2020

Total No. of Women Inmates	*Below 20 Years*	*20–30 Years*	*30–40 Years*	*40–50 Years*	*50–60 Years*	*60–70 Years*	*Over 70 Years*
22,927	1,093	4,922	5,917	4,963	3,116	1,379	1,627

Source: These figures, which change everyday, have been collated from the e-prisons dashboard as of 20 June, collected on 21 June 2020 at 13:00 hours.

We argue that all women inmates may be defined 'custodial' minorities. As per the 2020 statistics we collated, there are 68 persons incarcerated under the category 'others'. No grave threat is posed to society by UTPs belonging to sexual and gender minorities that non-custodial alternatives cannot be found for them, while they wait for investigations and trials to be over. And alternatives to the prison system need to be innovated for all convicted women, and gender and sexual minorities. There does not seem to be an attempt to recognise that their right to health and life is made far more precarious in a transphobic prison-medical complex. They must be counted and accounted for.

Women inmates in male-defined prisons governed by male rules of incarceration experience specific forms of discrimination, deprivation and violence. Their dignity is stripped as women—menstruating bodies are made to leak and vaginal infections allowed to fester. Their souls broken *as* women, with strip searches and cavity probes.[5] All women in prisons without distinction of charge, crime or sentence, whether pregnant, lactating, menstruating or menopausal, differently abled or ailing, may be thought of as 'custodial' minorities. Muslim women face terrible targeting and blame, as do Dalit women who face intolerable discrimination and bear the brunt of misuse of law against them. Similarly, Muslim and Dalit male undertrials are also subjected to sexualised forms of torture in police and judicial custody. And policies that exclude foreigners from interim bail position them as custodial minorities, who face institutionalised racism. However, the law has difficulty in 'seeing' these prison inmates, especially undertrials, as custodial minorities.

The penal policy during the pandemic found critique as a number of students, activists, human rights dissenters, bloggers, journalists and ordinary people found themselves being detained and arrested during the lockdown, without easy recourse to the legal system (*The Polis Project* 2020). Most of these women and men are now confined in prisons and denied bail by different courts. In such instances, the pandemic is not considered as a ground for bail even for those UTPs who are ill, and likely to die if infected by Covid-19. These arrests were especially critiqued since the lockdown had ensured that no one could flee or escape police investigation, and the need for incarcerating a suspect in overcrowded pandemic-infested prisons seemed punitive. The application of the draconian terror law against young Muslim women and their detention in prisons has been condemned as persecution of Muslim women for leading the protests against the citizenship law (Sharma 2020). These shifts in the penal policy are accompanied by the consolidation of legal autocrats (Scheppele 2018), the emergence of newer forms of legal 'reasoning', which Gautam

Bhatia (2020) characterises as 'imprisonment by metaphor', and are marked by the rise of particular forms of autocratic legalities, while creating an institutional crisis for the prison system. These custodial minorities are seen as undeserving of release during the pandemic.

Classification by the HPC: The Case of Delhi

Following the Supreme Court, the HPC chaired by Justice Hima Kohli met to devise a method for de-congesting prisons in Delhi. This resulted in a number of decisions starting from 26 March 2020.[6] Delhi has 16 jails located at Tihar, Mandoli and Rohini, with 17,440 inmates (consisting of 2,997 convicts, 14,355 UTPs and 88 civil prisoners, as on 27 March 2020) against a holding capacity of 10,026 prisoners. 'Deserving' undertrials such as first-time offenders, those arrested for an offence punishable up to seven years or in custody for over three months could be released on interim bail. For instance, interim bail was permitted for women undertrials in custody for 15 days or more. However, this rule did not apply to all women. Those women who were foreigners, or undergoing trial under the drug law, child sexual offence law, rape law or corruption were denied interim bail. Further, those women who were accused with 'cases investigated by CBI/ED/NIA/Special Cell Police and Terror related Cases, cases under Anti-National Activities and Unlawful Activities (Prevention) Act etc.' stood excluded from interim bail.

Neither did the HPC look at women prisoners as a class, nor did it order the release of all pregnant women or mothers with babies as being a high-risk category. There was no moratorium on fresh arrests of pregnant women or mothers with babies during the pandemic. The classification of women prison inmates was according to nationality, nature of offence, investigation agencies and *etc*. This 'etc.' classification rests on a penal policy that sorts women inmates into *deserving* and *undeserving*. The classificatory practice is not based on protecting high-risk populations, irrespective of offence or sentence.

'It is a Very, Very Sorry State of Affairs'

By June 2020, in Maharashtra at least 10 prisons reported that 292 inmates and 72 prison staff had tested positive. At least four inmates have died due to Covid-19 in Maharashtra (*The Citizen* 2020): two in Taloja central prison, one in Yerawada and another in Dhule prison. The women's prison in Byculla also reported one positive case (Hafeez 2020a). Yet undertrials locked up in these jails continue to be denied bail.

The Maharashtra Department of Prisons and Correctional Services put in place the process of de-carceration and de-congestion aiming to release 17,000 inmates. If this target is achieved, then prisons in Maharashtra will be filled to only 60 per cent to 70 per cent of their capacity (Kulkarni 2020), assuming new arrests are not made and prison transfers do not take place. This process was accelerated when the contagion hit the Arthur Road jail where (in mid-June) a shocking 181 inmates and 39 staff were afflicted by Covid-19. Yet bail to all vulnerable populations is not being given (*The Hindu* 2020) in spite of the risk of the contagion.

In the PUCL case filed in the Bombay High Court against overcrowding in jails in Maharashtra (Chaudhari 2020), it was put on record in mid-June that even after four Covid-19 deaths, prisons did not have space to quarantine, and no testing was being done. And temporary prisons are in a deplorable state (Modak 2020; *Scroll.in* 2020). As the Bombay High Court remarked, it is 'a very sorry state of affairs' (Modak 2020).

In May, merely 1,700 women had been released from prisons in eight states, a meagre 8.3 per cent of all women inmates.

Reading Section 61 of the Disaster Management Act, 2005

Reading the Disaster Management Act, 2005, into prisons as hotspots of mass contagion with overcrowded and vulnerable populations, one might argue that the DMA's provisions for mitigation as well as relief and rescue come into operation. The 2008 National Disaster guidelines define an epidemic as a biological disaster. Therefore, the question of de-congesting prisons is not only a question for the judiciary, but it is equally a question for the disaster authority to contain mass contagion, prevent fatality and treat affliction in an affected area. Further, prison inmates' right to health and right to life are protected by a plethora of laws. If the application of disaster law is legally valid, then the classification of the prison population, and the grounds of mitigation, rescue or relief (remission, bail or parole), must be read with Section 61 of the DMA. Section 61 prohibits discrimination by holding that 'while providing compensation and relief to the victims of disaster, there shall be no discrimination on the grounds of sex, caste, community, descent or religion'.

The 2007 National Disaster Management Guidelines, which state the principles for the state disaster management plan, insist that such plans must recognise: '... the differential needs of all sections of the society, including marginalised groups such as the elderly, pregnant and lactating mothers, children, physically and mentally challenged persons etc. It should specifically address the concerns of women.'

The National Disaster Management Plan of 2019 outlines critical guidelines for inclusiveness, including the directions that prohibit discrimination against women, gender and sexual minorities, Dalits, tribals and religious minorities. Therefore, the state disaster management plan must recognise the differential needs of women and other custodial minorities in prisons. The disaster law must be read with prison rules so that *all* women prisoners are considered most vulnerable populations, who deserve rescue and relief, mitigation and compensation.

One compelling interpretation of the non-discrimination principle crystallised in the disaster law is to read it as a law that prohibits discriminating between the rights of an undertrial accused of murder as compared to the rights of an undertrial accused of terror or sedition, for mitigation, relief and rescue during a disaster.

Coercing Incarcerated Pregnancies and Custodial Childbirths

The utter lack of concern for pregnant inmates has not shocked judicial conscience. No *suo moto* proceedings followed the reports from the Thane jail in Maharashtra (Hafeez 2020b), outlining the plight of a pregnant prisoner who was infected by Covid-19.

The most recent debate on incarcerated pregnancy and the misuse of terror law has been about Safoora Zargar who was first arrested on 10 April 2020. The state has filed 26 criminal charges against her, including various sections of the Unlawful Activities (Prevention) Act (UAPA), 1967, a law that has been critiqued for serious violations of fundamental rights. The state opposed her bail applications in lower courts thrice. None of the bail courts contemplated the law on the question of forced childbirth in prison, especially at the time of the risk of mass contagion in a prison (*LiveLaw* 2020b). Rather, the Patiala court merely 'requested' the jail administration to provide Zargar 'adequate medical (sic.) aid and assistance' given her 'precarious medical condition' (*State versus Safoora Zargar* at p. 9, order dated 4 June 2020). The court did not address the question: should pregnant prisoners or undertrials be coerced into giving birth in prisons?

On 23 June 2020, Zargar was granted bail after the Solicitor General of India decided not to oppose the bail on humanitarian grounds. The Solicitor General of India argued that this act of humanity was not to be treated as a legal precedent (Tripathi 2020). Bail was granted with conditions. Was this a concession? There have been different views on the prosecutorial acknowledgement of humanitarian grounds (Raza 2020). Some reason that if the case had been argued, the question of the applicability of the terror law and the very question of the legality of incarcerated pregnancies would have had to be addressed. Whether the bail order is read as an example of autocratic legalism (Scheppelle 2018) that allows humanitarian acts to interrupt the grammar of politics, or it is read as a welcome sociological precedent that allows the law to fulfil its quest for humanity, the fact remains that the courts have yet to rule that all incarcerated pregnancies and custodial childbirths are inhuman, cruel and degrading to women in every custodial institution.

We suggest that the law's quest for humanity should be especially attentive to the cruelty inflicted by the exception. Exceptional law such as the terror law by virtue of its application already imbues the accused with hyper-criminality, and justifies cruel, inhuman and degrading treatment of terror suspects. We know this from Ujjwal Kumar Singh's (2007) magisterial book on terror law; or the lacerating account of routinisation of torture in police remand and judicial custody by Nitya Ramakrishnan (2013). Jinee Lokaneeta offers a chilling account of policing, forensics and torture in her recent book, *The Truth Machines* (2020). Vrinda Grover (2018) has held a powerful brief against encounter killings of women and custodial torture, while insisting that the aggravated impact of state impunity on women and sexual minorities must remain central to any constitutional understanding of custodial violence. Taking our cue from these germinal works, we argue that incarcerated pregnancies and custodial childbirths must be thought of as cruel, inhuman and degrading treatment of women in all contexts without exception.

In 2018, the Ministry of Women and Child Development held that 'pregnant women should be given bail to facilitate childbirth outside the prison', and that 'information about a woman's pregnant status should also be made known to the court that has ordered the detention, to enable the court to grant bail (where appropriate) or modify the detention order as deemed necessary'. The state therefore is also of the view that incarcerated pregnancies and custodial childbirths are not desirable. Yet the ministry's recommendations of 2018 have not yet been adopted.

Nor has the National Commission of Women's (NCW) advisory of 22 April 2020 been heeded. It states that

> even the cases of those women under trials who are charged for non-bailable offences leading to a penalty of death or life imprisonment, if found guilty, needs to be processed for bail under proviso to the Section 437 (1) (ii) of CrPC., which provides for special dispensation to women and children below the age of 16 years in the matter of grant of bail.

Hence, even women UTPs who are charged with life or death can be given bail. The NCW has not only failed to ensure that all women inmates, including pregnant and lactating mothers are rescued from prisons as an urgent measure, but it has also not stopped new arrests and remand during the pandemic.

Not only has Section 61 of the disaster law, which defines non-discrimination, not been applied, but no reasons have been given for why non-custodial alternatives cannot not be found for women undertrials as provided in international law (*LiveLaw* 2020c). Surely, Article 51 of the Constitution obliges courts to follow international law. The United Nations General Assembly's adoption of the United Nations Rules for the Treatment of Women Prisoners and Non-custodial Measures for Women Offenders (also known as the

Bangkok Rules; *vide* Rule 24) states that 'non-custodial means should be preferred for pregnant women during the pre-trial phase wherever that is possible or appropriate'. Incarcerated pregnancies and coercing custodial childbirth violate Rule 24. Furthermore, the principle of non-discrimination obliges states to find alternatives to imprisoning women (United Nations Office on Drugs and Crime 2011).

Moreover, does a pregnant woman who has decided to carry the pregnancy to full term not have the right to bail on the grounds of her right to protect the needs of her unborn child? Why is an incarcerated pregnancy and a custodial childbirth per se not a denial of reproductive justice? Bail should be given to women on the grounds of reproductive justice (Centre for Reproductive Rights 2019) and law must not inflict reproductive harm to women in custody. Recognising this implicitly, in its judgement of 2016, the Gujarat High Court, after finding a pregnant woman guilty of murdering her sister-in-law in a dowry related case, allowed the woman to surrender after she had delivered her baby.[7]

Custodial childbirth and incarcerated pregnancy then is a specific form of cruel, inhuman and degrading punishment that is inflicted on women in prisons. Any incarcerated pregnancy and custodial childbirth is a fundamental violation of reproductive justice. To rescue some pregnant women and not others during a disaster amounts to condemning some pregnant inmates to a death sentence. In our law, no death sentence can be given to a pregnant woman; nor can the technique of execution be cruel, degrading or inhuman. Section 416 of the Criminal Procedure Code (CrPC) holds that an execution may be postponed or commuted if the woman on death row is found to be pregnant. Yet scores of pregnant women are still to be released from our prisons and remain deprived of law's humanity. The law's quest for humanity lies in the face of what it finds intolerable, and yet humanity stands defeated by law's cruel attachment to reasonable classification based on offence and sentence.

Custodial Reproductive Violence

Why are reproductive rights of some women prisoners more important than of others? There is a lengthy and sad litany of the literal miscarriage of justice in our legal history that has inflicted more sexual and reproductive harm on some women. We know that women who are 'othered', such as Phoolan Devi, were forced to undergo a hysterectomy (Ramanujan 2008; Sen 1991). Her consent to remove her uterus was deemed irrelevant, for the prison officials decided that she should not give birth to more Phoolan Devis. This targeted reproductive violence that aimed to extinguish a woman's reproductive capacity is an act of gross custodial violence against all women prisoners. Who is liable for irreversible reproductive harms like non-consensual sterilisation, coerced miscarriage or maternal or infant mortality, especially against women who are imprisoned to be 'taught a lesson'? This precedent of injustice is reason enough for courts to rethink jurisprudence of bail and custody of all women undertrials and prisoners.

The question of reproductive justice is not an issue when reproductive politics *others* women—Muslim, Dalit, Kashmiri—to deny an entire community a reproductive future. These discourses index differential treatment of differently situated pregnant bodies. The sexual and reproductive violence on Soni Sori in prison (Rabha 2020) highlights how torture itself is sexualised and directs reproductive violence on the bodies of Adivasi women. The public vilification campaigns against all these women aim to portray them as exceptionally criminal and dangerous, who deserve to be taught a lesson through cruel, inhuman and degrading punishment. A media that repeats the police-prosecution framing of accused women normalises and justifies state excess.

Another routine and heartbreaking illustration of custodial reproductive violence is the shackling of pregnant prisoners. From women's perspective this is a form of custodial reproductive violence that is a grave violation of women's right to life, as of the right of their unborn or newborn child. In keeping with international law, as recently as 2018 the Ministry of Women and Child Development has recommended that 'instruments of restraint, punishment by close confinement or disciplinary segregation should never be used on pregnant or lactating women'.

Our courts tend to forget that prisons are male spaces where women are fitted in and many women prisons have reported stories of indignity, decay and torture. Women face the indignity of strip searches, cavity searches and routine abuse that is directed at their being as women. The techniques that discipline and punish menstruating bodies, lactating bodies, pregnant bodies, menopausal bodies, ailing bodies and young bodies of women inscribe a terrifying gender code. This is not to argue that women prisoners do not have agency or politics, nor to suggest that they be reduced to their biological beings. Rather, this is to underline that prisons are foundationally male spaces, designed to reduce all women to biological degradation (Ministry of Women and Child Development 2018).

Conclusions

Justice Krishna Iyer famously said that 'prisons are built with the stones of law'.[8] However, for women, prisons are built with stones of 'patriarchal' law. It is time to campaign against incarcerated pregnancies and custodial childbirths as making for cruel, inhuman and degrading treatment of women. We must fully trace the impact of the sexual and reproductive politics of the state on practices of carcerality normalised under the sign of the nation. To do otherwise, is to direct violence at women. It is time to campaign for an urgent moratorium on all fresh arrests of women, and of gender and sexual minorities, wherein no coercive action should be taken against women and gender and sexual minorities, and no custodial sentences should be handed out to such persons. All women and gender and sexual minorities should be released during the pandemic.

It is time to rethink the prison system as it exists from the point of view of gender and sexual minorities, a question that should concern all kinds of publics and movements, jurists and academics, people and their courts.

Notes

1. In *Re: Contagion of Covid 19 Virus in Prisons*, 16 March 2020, SCC OnLine SC 320.
2. *R. D. Upadhyay versus State of AP & Ors*, 13 April 2006, available at https://indiankanoon.org/doc/1258611/ (accessed 25 June 2020).
3. National Prisons Information Portal, available at https://eprisons.nic.in/Public/DashBoard.aspx (accessed 21 June 2020, at 13:00 hours).

4. World Prison Brief data, available at https://www.prisonstudies.org/country/india (accessed 21 June 2020).
5. See Uma Chakravarti's compelling film, *Prison Diaries* (2019), on Snehalata Reddy's account as the only woman political prisoner who spent eight months in solitary confinement, https://psbt.org/films/prison-diaries/ (accessed 25 June 2020).
6. See the minutes of the meeting, dated 18 May 2020, available at https://images.assettype.com/barandbench/2020-05/452d97d7-dd6f-4ec3-80d7-ee3a1a3284fc/2020_5_18_Delhi_Minutes_of_Delhi__HPC_Meeting_.pdf (accessed 25 June 2020).
7. *State of Gujarat versus Jadav @ Jatin Bhagvanbhai Prajapati*, 1 February 2016, available at https://www.legitquest.com/case/state-of-gujarat-v-jadav-jatin-bhagvanbhai-prajapati/190D60 (accessed 25 June 2020).
8. *Sunil Batra versus Delhi Administration*, 20 December 1979, 1980 AIR 1579, 1980 SCR (2) 557, available at https://indiankanoon.org/doc/778810/ (accessed 25 June 2020).

References

'"Above All, There Should be Dignity and Respect in the Affairs Related to the Birth or Death of Human Beings": A Profile of Varavara Rao'. 2020. *The Polis Project*, 28 May. Available at https://thepolisproject.com/profiles-of-dissent/#.X7e2q2gzZPb (accessed 25 June 2020).

'Bail is Rule and Jail is Exception: SC Reminds HC that Denied Bail to Accused Even After Police Filed Closure Report'. 2020a. *LiveLaw*, 19 March. Available at https://www.livelaw.in/top-stories/bail-is-rule-and-jail-is-exception-154102 (accessed 25 June 2020).

'Bhima Koregaon Case: Delhi HC Criticises NIA for Transferring Gautam Navlakha to Mumbai in Haste'. 2020. *Scroll.in*, 28 May. Available at https://scroll.in/latest/963199/bhima-koregaon-case-delhi-hc-criticises-nia-for-transferring-gautam-navlakha-to-mumbai-in-haste (accessed 25 June 2020).

'Bombay High Court Seeks Details of Bail Applications from Trial Courts in Maharashtra'. 2020. *The Hindu*, 12 June. Available at https://www.thehindu.com/news/national/other-states/bombay-high-court-seeks-details-of-bail-applications-from-trial-courts-in-maharashtra/article31813951.ece (accessed 25 June 2020).

'Pregnant Student Safoora Zargar Denied Bail by Delhi Court in UAPA Case Alleging Delhi Riots Conspiracy'. 2020b. *LiveLaw*, 4 June. Available at https://www.livelaw.in/top-stories/pregnant-student-sarfoora-zargar-denied-bail-by-delhi-court-157839 (accessed 25 June 2020).

'Release Sudha Bharadwaj, Shoma Sen from Covid-19 Hit Byculla Jail: Citizens Appeal to Committee'. 2020. *The Citizen*, 24 May. Available at https://www.thecitizen.in/index.php/en/NewsDetail/index/15/18788/Release-Sudha-Bharadwaj-Shoma-Sen-From-Covid-19-Hit-Byculla-Jail--Citizens-Appeal-to-Committee (accessed 25 June 2020).

'Safoora Zargar's Detention Against International Law Standards: American Bar Association Appeals for her Immediate Release'. 2020c. *LiveLaw*, 13 June. Available at https://www.livelaw.in/news-updates/safoora-zargars-detention-against-international-law-standards-american-bar-association-158262 (accessed 25 June 2020).

Bhatia, Gautam. 2020. 'Imprisonment by Metaphor: The Safoora Zargar Bail Order'. *Indian Constitutional Law and Philosophy*, 4 June. Available at https://indconlawphil.wordpress.com/2020/06/04/imprisonment-by-metaphor-the-safoora-zargar-bail-order/ (accessed 25 June 2020).

Carissimo, Justin. 2020. '8 Pregnant Women to be Released from New York Prison over Virus Fears'. *CBS News*, 6 May. Available at https://www.cbsnews.com/news/coronavirus-new-york-prisons-pregnant-women-freed-covid-19/ (accessed 25 June 2020).

Centre for Reproductive Rights. 2019. 'Reproductive Rights of Incarcerated Persons'. In *Securing Reproductive Justice in India: A Casebook*, 283–312. Delhi: Centre for Constitutional Law, Policy and Governance, National Law University. Available at https://reproductiverights.org/sites/default/files/2020-02/SecuringReproductiveJusticeIndia-Chpt08.pdf (accessed 25 June 2020).

Chaudhari, Kanchan. 2020. 'Very Sorry State of Affairs: HC on Covid-19 Tests in Maharashtra Prisons'. *Hindustan Times*, 17 June. Available at https://www.hindustantimes.com/mumbai-news/very-sorry-state-of-affairs-hc-on-covid-19-tests-in-maharashtra-prisons/story-7ovxQVf5TFkNv2P58m2GUJ.html (accessed 25 June 2020).

Grover, Vrinda. 2018. '"It's Time Police Learnt that Custodial Torture is Unacceptable"'. *The New Indian Express*, 19 August. Available at https://www.newindianexpress.com/thesundaystandard/2018/aug/19/its-time-police-learnt-that-custodial-torture-is-unacceptable-1859556.html (accessed 25 June 2020).

Hafeez, Mateen. 2020a. 'Maharashtra: Four Constables Test Covid-19 Positive in Thane'. *Times of India*, 21 June. Available at https://timesofindia.indiatimes.com/city/mumbai/maharashtra-four-constables-test-covid-19-positive-in-thane-jail/articleshow/76497959.cms (accessed 25 June 2020).

———. 2020b. 'Maharashtra: Pregnant Woman Inmate Tests Covid-19 Positive in Thane Jail'. *Times of India*, 30 May. Available at https://timesofindia.indiatimes.com/city/thane/maharashtra-pregnant-woman-inmate-tests-covid-19-positive-in-thane-jail/articleshow/76113274.cms?utm_source=contentofinterest&utm_medium=text&utm_campaign=cppst (accessed 25 June 2020).

Kulkarni, Sushant. 2020. 'Covid Hits 10 Prisons in Maharashtra, Nearly 300 Inmates Infected'. *Indian Express*, 16 June. Available at https://indianexpress.com/article/india/maharashtra-covid-prisons-6462126/ (accessed 25 June 2020).

Lokaneeta, Jinee. 2020. *The Truth Machines: Policing, Violence, and Scientific Interrogations in India*. Hyderabad: Orient BlackSwan.

Ministry of Women and Child Development. 2018. 'Women in Prisons: India'. Government of India. Available at https://wcd.nic.in/sites/default/files/Prison%20Report%20Compiled.pdf (accessed 25 June 2020).

Modak, Sadaf. 2020. 'Maharashtra: Temporary Jail Condition Deplorable, Navlakha Tells Partner, Lawyer'. *Indian Express*, 22 June. Available at https://indianexpress.com/article/cities/mumbai/maharashtra-temporary-jail-condition-deplorable-navlakha-tells-partner-lawyer-6469938/ (accessed 25 June 2020).

National Commission for Women. 2020. Press Note, 22 April, New Delhi. Available at http://ncw.nic.in/sites/default/files/NCW%20Recommendation%20to%20DG_IG%20of%20Prisons_0.pdf (accessed 25 June 2020).

National Disaster Management Authority. 2007. 'National Disaster Management Guidelines: Preparation of State Disaster Management Plans'. Government of India. Available at https://nidm.gov.in/PDF/guidelines/sdmp.pdf (accessed 25 June 2020).

Rabha, Anubhuti. 2020. 'Police Brutality against Women: From Soni Sori to Safoora Zargar'. *Feminism in India*, 10 June. Available at https://feminisminindia.com/2020/06/10/police-brutality-against-women-soni-sori-safoora-zargar/ (accessed 25 June 2020).

Ramakrishnan, Nitya. 2013. *In Custody: Law, Impunity and Prisoner Abuse in South Asia*. New Delhi: Sage Publications.

Ramanujan, Anuradha. 2008. 'The Subaltern, the Text and the Critic: Reading Phoolan Devi'. *Journal of Postcolonial Writing* 44 (4): 367–78.

Raza, Danish. 2020. 'M.Phil Student Safoora Zargar Gets Bail after 70 Days'. *Article14*, 23 June. Available at https://www.article-14.com/post/denied-3-times-safoora-zargar-now-gets-bail-after-70-days (accessed 25 June 2020).

Scheppele, K. L. 2018. 'Autocratic Legalism'. *University of Chicago Law Review* 85 (2): 545–83. Available at https://lawreview.uchicago.edu/publication/autocratic-legalism (accessed 25 June 2020).

Sen, Mala. 1991. *India's Bandit Queen: The True Story of Phoolan Devi*. New Delhi: HarperCollins.

Sharma, Betwa. 2020. 'The Week that Safoora Zargar Made Bail, Gulfisha Fatima's Petition for Freedom was Dismissed'. *Huffpost*, 24 June. Available at https://www.huffingtonpost.in/entry/gulfisha-fatima-safoora-zargar-delhi-high-court_in_5ef2cfffc5b601e5995653e0 (accessed 25 June 2020).

Singh, Ujjwal Kumar. 2007. *The State, Democracy and Anti-terror Laws in India*. New Delhi: Oxford University Press.

Tripathi, Karan. 2020. 'Delhi HC Grants Bail to Safoora Zargar as Delhi Police Agrees to Her Release on Humanitarian Grounds'. *LiveLaw*, 23 June. Available at https://www.livelaw.in/top-stories/safoora-zargar-centre-agrees-for-release-humanitarian-grounds-delhi-hc-158771 (accessed 25 June 2020).

United Nations Office on Drugs and Crime. 2011. 'The Bangkok Rules'. Available at https://www.unodc.org/documents/justice-and-prison-reform/Bangkok_Rules_ENG_22032015.pdf (accessed 25 June 2020).

11

Migrant Workers, the Lockdown and the Judiciary*

Harsh Mander

From the midnight of 24 March 2020, India went into what has been rated as the most stringent lockdown of physical movement and economic activity in the world in response to the Covid-19 pandemic (Daniyal 2020; *Economic Times* 2020).

Three weeks later, a survey of 11,159 migrant workers by SWAN (2020a), reported on 20 April 2020 by *The Hindu*, opened a troubling window to the intense distress of migrant workers stranded by the lockdown.

The first SWAN survey revealed an urgent hunger crisis. Fifty per cent of the workers had rations left for less than one day; 72 per cent of the people the team spoke to said that their rations would finish in two days. Because they had little or no cash in hand and were continuously beset by uncertainty about the next meal, many had been eating frugally. Ninety-six per cent had not received rations from the government and 70 per cent had not received any cooked food from any source.

Along with food, cash had almost run out for most of the workers: 78 per cent of people had less than Rs 300 left with them. About 70 per cent were left with less than Rs 200 (less than half a single day's wage) for the rest of the lockdown period. Around 98 per cent had not received any cash relief from the government.

---

* First published in *The India Forum*, 8 May 2020.

I am grateful for the generous research support from Cheryl D'Souza and Misbah Rashid. A shorter version of this chapter was published in *Scroll.in*, 5 May 2020.

Eighty-nine per cent had not been paid by their employers at all during the lockdown; about 9 per cent had been partially paid. Some who had been given rations by the employers were told that the money for the rations would be deducted. Some workers have also been threatened and told not to complain.

Into the second phase of the lockdown (15 April–3 May), a second report from SWAN (2020b) covered the period until 26 April and was titled '32 Days and Counting'. The report showed that precarity remained high. During the second phase, half of the workers had rations left for less than a day; 46 per cent reported being with no food or money. More than four out of five persons had still not received rations in the second phase. Sixty-four per cent had less than Rs 100 of cash with them, while 74 per cent had less than half their daily wages with them to see them through for the rest of the lockdown. Only 6 per cent had been fully paid and 16 per cent partially paid.

Seventy-eight per cent had not been paid by their employers at all during the second phase of the lockdown; 89 per cent had not been paid at all in the first phase. Ninety nine per cent of the self-employed have had no income during the lockdown period.

Among the migrants surveyed, 41 per cent said they would stay in the city because they were anxious about unpaid rent and loans, and had no cash to travel or survive even at home. One-third planned to continue in the same line of work or with the same employer; another one-third were unsure about what to do. Roughly 16 per cent planned to leave and then return after some time, about 13 per cent planned to find work back in their hometowns, and about 5 per cent want to earn some money and leave.

Distressed by the indignity meted out to the migrant workers, a particularly anguished migrant labourer from Jharkhand working in Mumbai said: '*Modi ki nazron mein hum keedein hi hain na, waisi maut marenge*' (We are after all insects in the eyes of Modi so we will have to die that kind of death) (SWAN 2020a: 9).

Petition for Relief

A week into the lockdown, lawyers Prashant Bhushan and Cheryl D'Souza filed a public interest petition in the Supreme Court, seeking the upholding of the right to life with dignity under Article 21 of the Constitution for the migrants who were badly hit by the sudden and severe lockdown. The petitioners were Anjali Bhardwaj and this writer (Saxena 2020).[1]

The petition pointed to the humanitarian crisis created by the lockdown. Its central demand was that the central and state governments must 'jointly and severally' ensure payment of minimum wages to all migrant workers within a week, for the entire period of the lockdown. This should be agnostic to whether they were employed in an establishment, engaged by contractors or self-employed. The petition also demanded that this must be done by self-attestation and self-identification, because the state has no comprehensive record of employed workers, let alone casual and self-employed workers.

The petition detailed first what it felt were grave inadequacies and gaps in the financial package of Rs 1.70 lakh crore under the Pradhan Mantri Garib Kalyan Yojana. The Union government maintained to the Supreme Court that this package would ensure that citizens were not deprived of the basic amenities of food, drinking water, medication, etc.

We replied that Rs 1.70 lakh crore constitutes just over 1 per cent of the GDP of India. Further, many elements of the scheme merely front-load instalments of existing schemes, or provide for disbursement of cess funds already earmarked for the welfare of particular sectors, or programmes. For instance, the scheme includes a daily wage increase of Rs 20 under MGNREGA, which is a regular adjustment against inflation made every year and, therefore, in no way, can be reasonably considered an additional resource to deal with the lockdown distress. Similarly, the announcement that emergency support will be granted through the Building and Other Construction Workers' Cess funds is not an additional resource. The funds (accumulated to Rs 52,000 crore) are specifically earmarked for the welfare of construction workers, and in fact the non-utilisation of these funds has even been raised in the Supreme Court.

The Union government announced that public distribution system (PDS) card holders would be given 5 kg of foodgrains and 1 kg of pulses free of cost every month for three months. We replied that a large section of migrant workers is excluded from the PDS because the system is a domicile-based entitlement that requires proof of permanent address. There is no scheme or law for inter-state portability of ration cards. We maintained that the only way to ensure a modicum of food security to migrants would be to universalise access to foodgrains, pulses, cooking oil and soap, and provide them to everyone who seeks them, irrespective of whether they have a ration card or not.

We also pointed out that the *ex gratia* of Rs 500 to 20.4 crore women who have Jan Dhan accounts is extremely inadequate, both in terms of the quantum and its inclusion only of those with functional accounts. Once again universal cash transfers equivalent to minimum wages would alone assist households to hold hunger at bay.

The Union government claimed that construction workers (most of whom, according to the government, are migrant workers) would receive financial assistance through the 'Welfare Fund for Building and Other Construction Workers' and would cover 3.5 crore registered workers. However, the petitioners pointed out that the vast majority of construction workers are not actually registered under the Building and Other Constructions Workers (Regulation of Employment and Conditions of Service) Act, 1996, and therefore only a very small percentage of construction workers would benefit. A rapid survey conducted by Jan Sahas in March–April of 3,196 migrant construction workers from north and central India found that 94 per cent of its respondents did not have cards registered under the 1996 act (Jan Sahas 2020).

The Union government claimed overall that its financial package took care of the daily needs of every poor person, which include migrant workers and their families, so there was no imperative for migrant workers to rush to their villages. Their daily needs were being taken care of wherever they were working, and the needs of their families were being taken care of in the villages. It added that the central government had directed states to provide food, shelter and medical facilities to migrant workers who have been quarantined en route to their places of origin.

The petitioners contested this last claim as well, stating that the figures of the number of active relief camps and shelters for migrant workers submitted by the government themselves laid bare the complete inadequacy of the official provisions made for migrants. The government informed the Supreme Court in its first reply to the petition that there are a total of 26,476 active relief camps and shelters in which 10,37,027 persons are housed. From the government's own data, it was apparent that Kerala alone accounted for 59 per cent of the relief camps and shelters, even though the state's population constitutes only 2.6 per cent of India's population. Of the number of persons housed in relief camps, Kerala and Maharashtra together accounted for 72 per cent of the total. Large states like Uttar Pradesh, Bihar and Jharkhand, which saw huge numbers of people moving back because of the hardships caused by the lockdown, together accounted for only 12 per cent of the active relief camps and shelters and persons housed.

Of around the 15 lakh persons who had been given food, two states—Haryana and Delhi—accounted for 51 per cent of the total, showing the wide regional variation and the overall compete inadequacy of such facilities.

Limited Support for Migrant Workers

The Union government, under the Disaster Management Act, 2005, directed all public and private employers to continue to pay workers their wages through the period of the lockdown. It also prescribed that landlords should not seek rent from workers during the lockdown. It observed adversely that 'the movement of a large number of migrants have taken place in some part of the country so as to reach their home towns. This is in violation of the lockdown measures on maintaining social distance' (Ministry of Home Affairs 2020).

As petitioners, we argued that the two main protections for migrant workers during the lockdown as contained in the 29 March order in effect shifted the entire burden of protecting the earnings of migrant workers and preventing their eviction from rented homes to the employers and landlords. The order instituted no mechanism to secure the implementation of this order, nor for redress when it was flouted.

Moreover, many migrant workers are employed in micro, small and medium enterprises (MSMEs). The petition argued that the small employers of modest means would not be in a position to pay workers their salaries because their businesses and establishments had been abruptly closed by the lockdown. The government also does not have any accurate or comprehensive record of workers employed in the informal sector, and therefore, would also not have the necessary information to enforce the order. The same would apply also to their landlords for rent waivers. As most migrant workers live in slum settlements, in *jhuggies* or at worksites such as construction sites and small restaurants, there would be no formal rent agreement to prove that they were staying there; and once more, the government would also have no record of this, making enforcement again untenable.

There was also no reason why employers and landlords—many of whom would incidentally be of limited means—had to bear the economic costs of a lockdown which they did not order or a pandemic which they did not create or spread.

Further, this order of 29 March, as the petition points out, makes no provision for the financial security of the large proportion of migrant workers who are self-employed and are therefore not paid any salaries, such as street vendors, rickshaw pullers, *dhobis*, petty service providers, ragpickers and sex workers. It also ignores completely one of the most vulnerable segments of the labour market, namely casual daily wage workers. Studies show that only 17 per cent of workers in the informal sector have identifiable employers (Rajan 2008: 92). The earnings of the remaining 83 per cent would not be protected even if every employer obeyed the 29 March order.

It is noteworthy that in all its responses to the petition, the Union government at no stage gave any information about the numbers of migrant workers who had been paid wages by their employers, or the numbers who had not been evicted by their landlords, and any action that had been taken against those who violated its 29 March instructions.

Government of India, while issuing this directive, neither provided any funds for wage support to the employers, especially small employers, nor any income support for self-employed workers. Contrasting responses and measures by governments worldwide show the way forward (Gopalan 2020). The Denmark government had announced it would cover 75 per cent of the wage bills, Canada had introduced a wage subsidy scheme, England had provided for 80 per cent of average earnings subsidised, and Australia had framed a 'job keeper' wage subsidy plan.

Judiciary's Response

In the course of the hearing on 7 April, the Chief Justice asked that since the workers were being provided meals, why would they need money?

The bench stated that in times of such crisis, it did not want to interfere with government decisions. On complaints raised by the lawyer Prashant Bhushan about inedible food in crowded shelters or the lack of access to food at the feeding centres opened by the government, the court dismissed this stating that it would ask the government to put in place a helpline for complaints.

In this and subsequent hearings, the court did not pay heed to the additional affidavits by the petitioners about starving families; police brutality towards workers who attempted to leave their homes to access food in the feeding centres; employers' associations writing to the court about their inability to pay wages; and about landlords evicting their worker-tenants because of their inability to pay rent.

The abysmal condition of shelters for migrants in Delhi was confirmed from an unlikely official source: the Delhi police. The *Indian Express* quoted the key observations of 10 Delhi police station house officers (SHOs) who were tasked to prepare a report on these shelters:

> Fans not working and no power back-up; sanitisation of toilets rarely done; most of the migrants want to leave as their families cannot survive. Rude behaviour of civil defence staff; food quality not good; no hand wash and sanitizers; foul smell in toilets; water supply in toilets only between 7 am and 11 am; one soap for bathing and no detergent for washing clothes; mosquito bites. (Barman 2020)

Despite many pleas for urgent redressal, the Supreme Court adjourned the two next hearings on 7 and 13 April (all held by video-conferencing) without passing any order.

In the final hearing, a newly constituted bench (therefore not fully versed with the petitioners' submissions in the previous hearings) very briefly heard the case. In this hearing, the petitioners additionally placed on the record of the Supreme Court the SWAN study. The court, however, was still not persuaded by the grim picture of distress, destitution and hunger which, the lawyer stated, was mounting dangerously with every day of the hearings.

The bench said it could not rely on studies by private bodies when the government portrayed a completely different picture. They accepted instead the assurance from the Solicitor General that a 'helpline number has been provided' and that 'whenever any complaint is received, the authorities are attempting to address the same immediately'.

With this, they chose to finally close the case, without giving any relief to the migrants during the lockdown. The final order simply read: 'we call upon the respondent – Union of India – to look into such material and take such steps as it finds fit to resolve the issues raised in the petition'.

Whither a Life with Dignity?

In past decades, the Supreme Court of India on many occasions has ruled that the fundamental right to life guaranteed by Article 19 is the fundamental right of every citizen to a life more than 'mere animal survival', to a life with dignity.[2]

For millions of migrant workers stranded in cities without work and food in the lockdown, confined to overcrowded and underserved shelters, standing in long lines for every meal, walking hundreds of miles with the single aspiration in this uncertain time of suffering and crisis to be with their families, uncertain about how they will ensure food and medicine for their children and parents, the prospect of a life with dignity has become even more remote.

Notes

1. For the petition, see '*Harsh Mander and Anjali Bhardwaj versus Union of India*, available at https://www.livelaw.in/pdf_upload/pdf_upload-372004.pdf (accessed 3 December 2020).

2. *Francis Coralie Mullin versus The Administrator, Union Territory of Delhi and Ors*, 13 January 1981, 1981 AIR 746, 1981 SCR (2) 516, available at https://indiankanoon.org/doc/78536/ (accessed 3 December 2020).

References

'Data: 96% Migrant Workers did not get Rations from the Government, 90% did not Receive Wages during Lockdown: Survey'. 2020. *The Hindu*, 20 April. Available at https://www.thehindu.com/data/data-96-migrant-workers-did-not-get-rations-from-the-government-90-did-not-receive-wages-during-lockdown-survey/article31384413.ece (accessed 3 December 2020).

'World's Biggest Lockdown May Have Cost Rs 7–8 Lakh Crore to Indian Economy'. 2020. *Economic Times*, 14 April. Available at https://economictimes.indiatimes.com/news/economy/finance/worlds-biggest-lockdown-may-have-cost-rs-7-8-lakh-crore-to-indian-economy/articleshow/75123004.cms?from=mdr (accessed 3 December 2020).

Barman, Sourav Roy. 'Delhi Police Report on Migrant Camps: Fans Not Working, Bad Food'. *Indian Express*, 28 April. Available at https://indianexpress.com/article/india/delhi-police-report-on-migrant-camps-fans-not-working-bad-food-6382213/ (accessed 3 December 2020).

Daniyal, Shoaib. 2020. 'Not China, Not Italy: India's Coronavirus Lockdown is the Harshest in the World'. *Scroll.in*, 29 March. Available at https://scroll.in/article/957564/not-china-not-italy-indias-coronavirus-lockdown-is-the-harshest-in-the-world (accessed 3 December 2020).

Gopalan, Anand. 2020. 'What are the Legal Obligations to Pay Wages During a Lockdown?'. *BusinessLine*, 5 April. Available at https://www.thehindubusinessline.com/opinion/what-are-the-legal-obligations-to-pay-wages-during-a-lockdown/article31262286.ece (accessed 3 December 2020).

Jan Sahas. 2020. 'Voices of the Invisible Citizens: A Rapid Assessment on the Impact of COVID-19 Lockdown on Internal Migrant Workers'. Recommendations for the State, Industry and Philanthropies. Available at https://freedomfund.org/wp-content/uploads/Voices-of-Invisible-Citizens.pdf (accessed 3 December 2020).

Ministry of Home Affairs. 2020. MHA Order Restricting Movement of Migrants and Strict Enforcement of Lockdown Measures. Government of India, 29 March, New Delhi. Available at https://www.mha.gov.in/sites/default/files/MHA%20Order%20restricting%20

movement%20of%20migrants%20and%20strict%20enforement%20of%20lockdown%20measures%20-%2029.03.2020.pdf (accessed 3 December 2020).

Rajan, S. Irudaya (ed.). 2008. *Social Security for the Elderly: Experiences from South Asia*. New Delhi: Routledge.

Saxena, Akshita. 2020. 'Covid-19: Supreme Court to Hear Plea for Payment of Wages by Government to Migrant Workers'. *LiveLaw*, 1 April. Available at https://www.livelaw.in/top-stories/covid-19-sc-to-hear-plea-for-payment-of-wages-by-government-to-migrant-workers-read-petition-154634 (accessed 3 December 2020).

Stranded Workers Action Network (SWAN). 2020a. '21 Days and Counting: COVID-19 Lockdown, Migrant Workers, and the Inadequacy of Welfare Measures in India'. Available at https://www.thehindu.com/news/resources/article31442220.ece/binary/Lockdown-and-Distress_Report-by-Stranded-Workers-Action-Network.pdf (accessed 3 December 2020).

———. 2020b. '32 Days and Counting: COVID-19 Lockdown, Migrant Workers, and the Inadequacy of Welfare Measures in India'. Available at https://covid19socialsecurity.files.wordpress.com/2020/05/32-days-and-counting_swan.pdf (accessed 3 December 2020).

Section V

The Lockdown and After

12

India's Lockdown*

Debraj Ray, S. Subramanian and Lore Vandewalle

On 24 March 2020, Government of India ordered a nation-wide lockdown for 21 days as a preventive measure against the spread of the novel coronavirus. The lockdown—in full force as we write—restricts 1.3 *billion* people from leaving their homes. Transport services are suspended, educational institutions are closed and factories are shut down.

This is in line with the measures imposed in most European countries and in the US, but the sheer scale of the measure—as in the case of most policies in India—is intimidating. Add to this the grim truth of Indian occupational structure and poverty, and you would likely predict what we now see: unending streams of migrants trying to find their way home, the fear of loss of *all* income, deep privations, and even (in the space of days) hunger, starvation and death.

The Indian experience highlights, in a visceral way, both the Scylla of widespread viral infection and the Charybdis of socio-economic lockdown. It is not a choice between lives on the one hand and loss of economic production on the other. Because India is so poor and because her occupational structure so un-amenable to being shifted online, it is a question of *lives versus lives*: the nightmarish culmination of all those philosophical trolley problems that we so wish were innocently confined to the classroom.

---

* Published in *The India Forum*, 10 April 2020.

This chapter was first published with the same title as the CEPR Policy Insight No. 102, April 2020. It is reprinted here with permission of the Centre for Economic Policy Research.

We want to be explicit about this ethical approach: lives versus lives.

One view—implicit, for instance, in arguments made in certain quarters in the US—is that there must be some allowable tradeoff between *economic* well-being and human lives. We do not subscribe to that view, and entertain no such tradeoff. Therefore, our first choice in the fight against Covid-19 would be for governments to implement a comprehensive general lockdown, *provided* that this is accompanied by comprehensive state support for compensating welfare measures aimed at protecting the health, nutrition and psychological well-being of *all* households. Many have called for such measures. But calling for them is one thing, and implementing them another. What if the state is unable or unwilling to provide that support to all families under lockdown? Then households are exposed to the profound morbidity and mortality risks that stem from the loss of incomes and jobs, not to mention their constricted freedom of mobility, heightened psychological stress, enhanced prospects of domestic violence, and indeed, perhaps greater vulnerability to the virus itself. What then?

Vulnerability to Lockdown

The vulnerability of the population—especially the poor—to a generalised lockdown is accentuated in India by three specific structural features of the population.

The first has to do with occupational configurations. The latest report based on the Periodic Labour Force Survey (PLFS) is instructive in this regard (National Statistical Office 2019). Over 2017–18, about 52 per cent of rural households received their main income from self-employment. The share of rural households with a major source of income from casual labour was 25 per cent. Regular wage/salary earners accounted for 12.7 per cent of rural households. For observers in developed countries, the corresponding figures for urban India's households are less surreal—32.4, 11.8 and 41.4 per cent, respectively—though it is worth bearing in mind that close to two-thirds of India's population is rural. Many of these self-employed rural households are marginal cultivators or small artisans.

In the urban areas, many are engaged in running local shops, small businesses or in minor intermediation activities. It would therefore be very conservative to treat only the casual labour category of households as especially vulnerable. Even if we did, then a simple combination of the numbers above would reveal that casual households *alone* account for over 20 per cent of all Indian households. We are thus speaking of at least a fifth of the household population that is particularly fragile in its ability to cope with an indefinitely imposed economic lockdown, and most likely many more than that. This heightened vulnerability is, of course, common in all poor countries, but it is particularly worrisome in a society of 1.3 billion people.

A corollary of this sort of occupational structure is that it is highly 'informal'; that is, it belongs to that penumbra of the economy in which transactions are largely outside the fiscal reach of the government, both in terms of taxes (a concern, perhaps, in normal times) and transfers (the overwhelming concern now). Well over half of India's GDP is produced in this informal sector. In contrast, countries in western Europe have 10–20 per cent of their national output produced in the informal sector (Kelmanson et al. 2019). The Indian informal sector is not a sector that can transit to online existence with ease—it cannot start holding business dealings on Zoom or provide internet-based services to replace their ongoing activity. It is possible that some fraction of them have long-term relationships with other better-placed Indian households, and can rely on them for assistance or a continuation of their economic relationships. We do not have an estimate of how widespread these ties are.

Another correlate of vulnerability is low savings. From a study by one of us in rural Chhattisgharh,[1] we observe that the median household spends Rs 345 per week on food items *alone* (this does not include other essentials such as soap or kerosene). That median household has liquid savings of just Rs 881, though. If we divide these savings by the weekly expenditure on food, we see that half the households do not have enough liquid savings to get through a lockdown of 21 days. If we add the value of grain stocks, livestock and jewellery, the median climbs to Rs 1,818, but it is still the case that 38 per cent of households do not have the wherewithal to get through a 21-day lockdown. Moreover, such forms of savings are very hard to liquidate under a correlated shock, because the prices of the assets plunge at the same time that they need to be sold.

Reaching the Vulnerable

How might we leverage the existing arms of the state to reach these households? Even for the best-motivated Indian government, this is a tricky proposition. Cash transfers come first and foremost to mind, but transfers to whom? We would need to credibly separate the vulnerable from the protected, the low-income earners from the high. We do not have the income data to implement this separation. (For instance, no more than 3 per cent of Indian citizens pay income taxes.)

In response, one might throw one's hands up and ask for *universal* transfers. This is related to the Universal Basic Income debates that have recently occurred the world over, India included. The Rangarajan Committee's 2014 thresholds ask for Rs 972 (rural) and Rs 1,407 (urban) per person per month, a number that appears to be pitiably outdated. Nevertheless, with these low estimates, a universal transfer would call for a budget a bit north of Rs 1.43 trillion. The annual GDP for India is around Rs 200 trillion, so that comes to over 0.7 per cent of the annual GDP *per month*, a not infeasible but still hefty price tag with bad leverage properties—everybody would need to be paid to avert a crisis for those truly in need. To place the number in context, the Indian government has budgeted 1 per cent of annual GDP under all expenditure headings for the coronavirus crisis—more on this below.

Finally, note that the lockdown will come with significantly lower output—the US has been staring down the barrel of a 25 per cent drop in GDP quarter over quarter. While a universal transfer would still have a progressive component, the associated real transfer would be significantly diminished by the prospects of widespread hoarding, speculation and inflation.

Better, then, to exploit channels that are already self-selected by the poorer public. Options such as India's massive rural employment guarantee scheme (the MGNREGA), and the PDS operating through

India's ration shops, come to mind. As Reetika Khera (2020) has argued, MGNREGA could expand its work guarantees well beyond 100 days per annum, and she has called for 20 days per month during the crisis. India has a buffer stock surplus; now is the time to run that surplus down by increasing rations through the PDS. These are eminently sensible suggestions, and they take advantage of the self-targeting that is built into these networks.

As MGNREGA is implemented in rural areas only, it has to be suitably complemented in cities in order not to prolong the human tragedy of the first week of the lockdown. Thousands of poor migrant workers have been frustrated by the shutdown of transport facilities and closed state borders in their effort to return to their village homes. Many have been forced to undertake foot journeys of several hundreds of kilometres, with limited cash in hand, and little access to food, water or shelter. Trekking labourers have been rounded up and locked up in crowded enclosures. In one shocking incident, a contingent of migrants was showered with corrosive disinfectant. Significant reports of deaths are beginning to come in, including the deaths of children. There is little doubt that these will multiply as the coming difficult days go by.

The relief measures proposed by Government of India to help its citizens over the initial three-week period of the lockdown have been both delayed and relatively scanty. In its 'relief package' the government allocated just a little under 1 per cent of GDP for corona-related assistance. In addition, some components of the Indian relief package refer to provisions already made in the Union Budget, while others are scarce in relation to their intended purpose. Consider, for instance, the proposed allowance of Rs 500 per month per family: the average monthly *per person* consumption expenditure is itself about two-and-a-half times this amount; and, indeed, even the average per person expenditure of the poorest 20 per cent of the population exceeds the allowance (Subramanian 2019). The specific purposes for which assistance has been earmarked do not necessarily tally—in terms of either quantum or priority—with painstaking lists which various commentators with specialised knowledge in the field have drawn up (see, for instance, Drèze 2020).

Confronting the Tradeoff

It is the job of epidemiologists and specialists in infectious disease to warn about the dangers of a virus. The novel coronavirus SARS-CoV-2 belongs to that category of viruses which are highly contagious, and often lethal in their effects. It can (and will) cause many deaths. Because contagion is front and centre in these considerations, social externalities are a matter of first-order importance. It is little wonder that in countries that have enforced a lockdown, the plea to 'self-isolate' or engage in 'social distancing'—household phrases now—are based more on the implied threat to *one's own health*, rather than the implied threat to *others* of one's own actions. These phrases—and the associated priorities of containing the viral spread over all else—have percolated to India. They inform the thought processes that underlie India's own lockdown. They inform the general sense of threat and fear that guides India's policymakers. They also inform the terror that appears to swamp the public when faced with a Covid-19–positive individual, or even with healthcare workers and medical personnel on the frontlines of this crisis. Such individuals have been ill-treated in the most demeaning ways.

In India, these effects are particularly palpable because much of the country lives side by side in the closest possible quarters. People are being advised to maintain a distance of six feet from one another in a setting where slum dwellers and inhabitants of shelters live in cramped and unsanitary conditions. The context, too, is ominous: the requirement of physical distance as a sanitary precaution often translates, in Indian society, to the maintenance and accentuation of hierarchies based on notions of ritual purity and caste- and gender-based disparities. The potential for abuse and maltreatment is enormous. (We hasten to add that the same potentials exist all over the world, but population densities and cultural context can amplify them.)

It is with this background in mind that it is worth taking a second look at the current crisis. We ask you to forget Covid-19 for a second and imagine an incredibly nasty season of the common influenza, one in which (say), half the population is affected in a given year rather than the customary 10–15 per cent.[2] Look at this first from the 'micro' perspective of an average individual who gets the flu in this particularly virulent year. The conversation between friends and acquaintances can readily be imagined—'oh, it's a terrible season this year, everyone's getting the flu.' It would be unfortunate, but from our average individual's point of view, this is scarcely a cause for panic, even though the flu has a known a fatality rate of around 0.1 per cent or perhaps slightly more. Except for the very old, we do not give it the time of day.

Now switch mirrors and consider the same scenario in 'macro' perspective. The number of influenza-related deaths in our imaginary scenario would *triple*. In the US, for instance, the 2017–18 flu season was on the high side: according to the Centre for Disease Control, an estimated 45 million people came down with influenza, and 61,000 died. Scale this up for our imaginary monster flu year—then 180,000 people would die. The additional 120,000 would place enormous stress on the health system—there would be a shortage of hospital beds and ventilators, or PPE, and the need for triage would skyrocket. This 'macro' nightmare is to be contrasted with the individual or 'micro' viewpoint which is no more threatening than getting the flu in a given season.

It is possible to argue, and in fact it *has* been argued (by one of us, Ray 2020, among others) that Covid-19 may not be substantially different from our imaginary setting. It is surely far more contagious than the flu, but conditional on being affected, the mortality rate may be not that much higher than that of the flu. However, widespread understanding of this fact by the general public is not in the interests of a social planner. In the hypothetical scenario of a contagious flu, it is just as important (as it is now) to maintain social distancing, to practise self-isolation, and to take all steps to reduce contagion. The strain on overall society would be just as immense. However, all individual actions would need to be taken with society in mind, and not with a sense of great personal threat. That is much harder to implement. As a result, it is far more useful—from a social perspective—to convey the impression that Covid-19 is a highly lethal disease, so that self-preservation can be invoked to implement socially desirable outcomes.

These are understandable strategies from the point of view of an economically advanced country, where the economic fallout from lockdown can (and should) be shouldered without complaint. After all, lives come first. But in the 'lives versus lives' setting in which India now finds herself, and given the panic-induced social attitudes that now fester among the public, it is imperative that there should be a more nuanced understanding of these truths; at least on the part of policymakers.

With this in mind, consider again the moral dilemma we come up against when we contemplate alternative approaches to the pandemic—namely, more or less stringent forms of lockdown, with associated packages of transfers in cash or kind. Especially in poor and unequal societies such as India's, both the lockdown and no-lockdown extremes entail triage. A comprehensive lockdown will differentially assist those whose fall-back options in a time of confinement are better, and those who can afford the pecuniary and spatial luxuries of social distancing. Effectively, the lockdown picks out the non-poor for favourable treatment vis-à-vis the poor.

In a relatively relaxed environment with freer mobility, the virus attack would be more evenly distributed *across* socio-economic groups. The criterion for differential outcomes under the relaxed alternative is more likely to be age, with the elderly, implicitly, now becoming the prime candidates for adverse selection. In the absence of a complete, first-best package of social protection, *neither a comprehensive lockdown nor a relaxed lockdown is free of ethical complications.* An uncompromising insistence on a thoroughgoing lockdown under any circumstances is far from being a morally straightforward stance. These complications are heightened when we add the micro and macro considerations described earlier.

A Possible Compromise for India

In such a time of crisis, it is absolutely necessary (i) to concentrate our effort on policies that are feasible; (ii) to avoid measures which are unaffordable for most citizens; (iii) to not criminalise individual actions triggered by the need for survival; and (iv) to communicate state intent in credible, unambiguous and specific terms. Against this background, we would like to place the following proposal on the table for critical evaluation.[3] We are not dogmatic about it. Like every other proposal, this has its limitations; see especially the discussion surrounding item 4 below.

1. The micro perspective adopted above and the accompanying discussion together suggest that the death rate from Covid-19 for people between 20 and 40 years of age is *significantly lower* than the overall death rate for all ages from influenza. Indeed, as can be argued, even the overall mortality rates (averaging over age) could be comparable across the two diseases—though Covid-19 is far more contagious. Therefore, it is possible to cautiously advance the proposition that if it is acceptable for people of all ages to move around freely in the presence of influenza, it should be acceptable to *allow* (not force) all adults under 40 in India to work freely at the present time. Again, this is not an ideal outcome, but it is a reasonable compromise to work with, and it can be readily monitored (for instance, an Aadhaar card states the year of birth).[4]
2. This measure can—and must—be supplemented by serological testing as such testing becomes widely available, and as antibody stocks in the population build up. This must be seen as being crucial and indispensible. Everyone certified under an antibody test should be permitted to work, in addition to the 20–40 population.
3. Later, as the infection rate subsides, new measures can be taken to move 'up the age distribution' for work permits.
4. Protection of the elderly must be left (though not entirely) to households, who will possess the incentives and motivation to provide for and monitor such protections. We need to rely on *intra-household* motivation, where some degree of altruism is to be reasonably hoped for, even expected, as opposed to *inter-household* altruism, on which it would be foolhardy to repose an equal burden of faith.
5. Transfer of massive funds to the public health system, with an explicit emphasis on the testing, isolating and treatment of older patients. This should be aided by state provisioning of home-site visits by health workers. It should be understood that the core crisis is a public health crisis, and not necessarily

an individual one. This appears paradoxical, but in the light of our discussion in the previous section, it should not be.

What is involved is a form of self-selection: people who can afford the luxury of staying at home will do so, while those that cannot will opt to go to work. As with many self-selection outcomes, this one too is unfortunately mediated by the inherently inequitable prospects confronting our citizens: the labouring poor will exercise the option of working, unlike those with more secure fall-back options. But at least the former will not be confronted with the *involuntary* contingencies of hunger, undernutrition and life-threatening economic shortfall.

The immense advantage of this proposal is obvious enough: it allows most Indian families to keep a lifeline open, and in so doing it suggests a measure that is equitable, balanced and usefully implementable. We highlight here two points on which a final evaluation must rest.

1. What are the guarantees that the elderly will be adequately protected under this policy?

The answer is that there are no guarantees. Intergenerational contact cannot be fully avoided under any policy. Widespread poverty and inequality, both distinctive features of India, constitute a poor environment for realising the anti-disease objectives of a lockdown. The bulk of the population lives in cramped conditions with full interpersonal exposure, with large families often confined to a single room.

That said, consider an outright lockdown. No one among the poor can afford to obey it. Barring draconian orders such as shoot-on-sight, shops and small businesses will reopen, *with both young and old working*. Compare this to a situation in which the young are legally permitted to work. Then the locus of transmission shifts to the household and the family.

How the two loci compare is a matter of debate. We do not have the data to assuredly predict which measure poses the greater transmission risk to the elderly. But here is what we can say. Our proposal gets the older individuals out of the direct workforce, and it asks for protective measures primarily within the family, supplemented by state-assistance across families.

Once again, going by recent reactions in the community to medical personnel and to individuals suspected of having been infected, we would be extremely wary of any steps that rely on the social altruism of private agents across families. There could be feasible, decentralised measures that families could adopt, perhaps with the help of a small cluster of neighbouring and friendly families. For instance, there is the option of using two families to reallocate living quarters between old and young. But the entire strategy should rely on small, voluntarily formed groups to internalise externalities. While no measure is ideal, ours relies on the self-interest of households rather than a generalised notion of the social good. Finally, we should also note that in India, the elderly constitute a relatively small fraction of the population. The population of India aged 65 or older is just 5.1 per cent of the total, a figure nearly one-fifth as small as the corresponding number for Italy, which is 23 per cent.[5]

2. In any case, young versus old aside, will this proposal not increase the overall incidence of Covid-19, relative to a comprehensive lockdown?

Alas, it will. The best of all worlds cannot be achieved. The one assured way to minimise the incidence of the disease is to have *a complete and fully implemented lockdown*. But—given the impossibility of the highlighted phrase in the previous sentence—is that really what we want to do? Must we neglect the immense burden—not merely economic, but in terms of human lives and suffering—that a comprehensive lockdown must place on the majority of the Indian population?

The considerations above must be supplemented by the micro and macro perspectives introduced earlier. The added burden placed on the health system at an aggregative level could coexist with a much smaller burden at the individual or micro level, particularly if it turns out—as some evidence suggests that it might—that fatality rates from the coronavirus are of the same order of magnitude as the flu. There is certainly a case to be made for massively funding the health system in this time of crisis, while loosening the lockdown in the manner proposed above. In the years to come, this improved health system will be a blessing.

Conclusions

Epidemiologists and infectious-disease specialists correctly emphasise the dangers of a lethal virus spread. It is their job to do so. With the prisoner's dilemma that pervades any such situation, it is also their job to warn the public that the *personal* dangers of an infection are high.[6] But that should not obscure the vision of a broader social ethic. The objective is to save lives *on the whole*, not just to reduce pandemic deaths.

In some societies with widespread and comprehensive safety nets, the two alternatives in the previous sentence coincide. A lockdown will not kill, especially with a well-articulated and well-targeted strategy of economic compensation. (There could be vociferous objections from business groups, but that is another matter.) But in societies like India, a lockdown *can* kill: via job loss, increased vulnerability to economic shocks, and via social stigma and misinformation. Then the objective of saving lives as a whole may or may not be achieved by a draconian lockdown.

We have contended here that the problem of which strategy to invoke to combat the pandemic is not only a complicated one, but one which does not necessarily, and always, resolve itself in favour of the option that seems currently to command a considerable measure of international consensus. In the context of a large developing country like India, where both poverty and inequality are ingrained structural features of the economy and society, there may be a case for a relaxed version of the stringent universal lockdown approach. Stated without nuance, this is an approach that would—over the long haul—allow the relatively less vulnerable working-age population some latitude in the matter of going to work, in order to minimise the costs of unemployment, starvation and income loss. Responsibility for the welfare of the elderly could be decentralised to the level of individual households, but must also be very robustly shared by the state through an organised, old age–targeted policy of special care—through testing, quarantining and treatment.

We conclude on a final note of philosophical interest, one in which the political aspect of the problem also acquires a certain salience. The debate of 'lockdown versus economy' (crudely put) assumes very different political hues in the 'West' and in India.

In Europe and in the US, one would be inclined to support a lockdown without hesitation, because Covid-19 is highly contagious—much more so than the flu. Even if an individual's risk of mortality is about the same across Covid-19 and the flu (conditional on being infected, that is), the strain on the health system is enormous because Covid-19 is far more contagious. While the economic effects are large—certainly so in a high-inequality, restricted-social-net country like the US—one has the informational and targeting capacities needed to make people whole: starvation is not first-order. In India, it *is* first-order. The same progressive support for a lockdown in the 'West' may need to be entirely reallocated in a different context. It is in this context that our suggestions are offered—in a genuine spirit of shared enquiry that invites opinion and discussion, and not with assertive confidence or dogmatic certainty.

Notes

1. Authors' calculations using data from Somville and Vandewalle (2015).
2. For instance, the Centre for Disease Control in the US estimated that between 37.4 million and 42.9 million people contracted the flu during the 2018–19 season.
3. This section repeats, almost verbatim, parts of an article published in *Ideas for India* by a subset of the present authors: Ray and Subramanian (2020).
4. As in the case of employees still at work in other parts of the world, it is important to keep them informed through public awareness campaigns and to encourage employers to take precautions (for example, through the provision of hand sanitiser and respecting social distance).
5. Statistics from the Census of India and the World Bank.
6. For instance, it is not uncommon to make statements that the young could also be lethally affected by Covid-19. Such arguments are often best made by highlighting the *absolute numbers* of the young that could be affected, especially in highly populated metropolitan areas.

References

Drèze, J. 2020. 'View: The Finance Minister's Covid-19 Relief Package is Helpful, but there are Gaping Holes in it'. *Economic Times*, 28 March.

Kelmanson B., K. Kirabaeva, L. Medina, B. Mircheva and J. Weiss. 2019. 'Explaining the Shadow Economy in Europe: Size, Causes and Policy Options'. IMF Working Paper 19/278.

Khera, R. 2020. 'Covid-19: What Can Be Done Immediately to Help Vulnerable Population'. *Ideas for India*, 25 March.

National Statistical Office. 2019. Annual Report, PLFS 2017–18, Government of India.

Ray, D. 2020. 'The Micro and the Macro of Covid-19, or the Case of the Invisible Denominator'. *Chhota Pegs*, 30 March.

Ray, D., and S. Subramanian. 2020. 'Covid-19: Is there a Reasonable Alternative to a Comprehensive Lockdown?'. *Ideas for India*, 28 March.

Somville, V., and L. Vandewalle. 2015. 'Savings Behaviour and the Introduction of Mobile Banking in India'. Research project (2013–16) coordinated by Somville and Vandewalle, funded by a research grant from the Research Council of Norway.

Subramanian, S. 2019. 'Letting the Data Speak: Consumer Spending, Rural Distress, Urban Slow-Down, and Overall Stagnation'. Arena Papers of The Hindu Centre for Politics and Public Policy, 11 December.

13

Hunger Grows as India's Lockdown Kills Jobs

*Results of a Survey from 12 States**

Rahul Lahoti, Amit Basole, Rosa Abraham, Surbhi Kesar and Paaritosh Nath

The Covid-19 global pandemic and its associated containment measures have taken a heavy toll on economies and societies worldwide. In India, the national lockdown, imposed on 24 March 2020 and subsequently extended four times to 31 May, has had a profound effect on employment and earnings.

Livelihoods have been devastated at unprecedented levels. Food insecurity and economic vulnerability have increased to staggering proportions. Hunger deaths and suicides linked to economic stress are being reported from various parts of the country.[1]

Any recovery from this crisis will be slow and very painful. The immediate relief measures do not appear to be in proportion to the severity of the situation on the ground.

In a survey of nearly 5,000 self-employed, casual and regular wage workers across 12 states of India, conducted in collaboration with civil society organisations between 13 April and 23 May, we have found a massive increase in unemployment and an equally dramatic fall in earnings.[2] Two-thirds of our respondents have lost work. The few informal workers who were still employed during the lockdown saw their earnings drop by more than half. Almost 8 in 10 are eating less food than before. The impact of job losses and food insecurity has been higher for certain groups of people: Muslims, Dalits, women and those with lower levels of education.

* First published in *The India Forum*, 29 May 2020.

As late as May, even the grossly inadequate government relief measures, in the form of cash transfers or increased rations, had not reached large sections of the economically vulnerable population. Half of our respondents reported not receiving any cash transfers.

Three structural characteristics of the Indian economy and decades of underinvestment in public goods have combined with the sudden and severe lockdown to generate widespread misery. First, for India's predominantly informal labour force, which earns income day-to-day, any stoppage of economic activity instantly destroys employment and earnings. Second, the lopsided nature of economic growth has created a large divide between rich and poor states. Third, the same uneven growth process has created employment opportunities in larger cities much faster than in smaller towns and villages.

This unequal development manifests as migration flows of millions of workers, creating dense populations of the urban poor. When these long-run factors are put together with India's persistent underinvestment in health and housing, our vulnerabilities to the present crisis become painfully clear.

The vulnerable population in urban areas has been severely impacted, but relief measures have not reached them. The Union government should follow the lead of states such as Odisha and Himachal Pradesh, which are trying out an urban employment generation programme, and Kerala, which already has such a programme running. State finances may not allow effective urban employment guarantees, but the central government can certainly do this.

The measures recently announced by the government go some way in addressing the crisis, but they fall well short of what is required, since the bulk of the stimulus package focuses on increasing liquidity rather than direct spending.

Survey Coverage

We partnered with 10 civil society organisations for phone surveys in 12 major states of India. They provided us with a list of telephone numbers from their databases, from which we randomly selected households for the organisations to interview.

The sample is purposive and non-representative of the states and regions it covers. However, we ensured that the sample was diverse by selecting respondents across rural administrative blocks and by talking to respondents across diverse occupations. In total, we completed 4,879 interviews across rural and urban areas in 12 states.[3] Our survey covered 161 districts and seven large cities (Ahmedabad, Ajmer, Bengaluru, Bhubaneshwar, Delhi, Jaipur and Pune). Respondents interviewed in urban areas spanned over 30 different occupations. Our findings are broadly consistent with what other similar surveys reveal.[4]

Since our respondents are in the network of civil society organisations, they are more aware and have more access to government schemes. They are not among the most economically vulnerable sections in the country. Hence our results are a conservative estimate of what the most vulnerable population might be experiencing. The results presented are not weighted, and the conclusions below are not generalisable. But with the paucity of representative data, they present a useful broad picture to guide policy.

In some of the states, our sample is predominantly rural or largely urban, as is indicated in the labels in Figure 13.1.

Overall, 58 per cent of our respondents were in rural areas, 52 per cent were women, 79 per cent were married, and the average

Figure 13.1: State-wise Distribution of Respondents, 2020

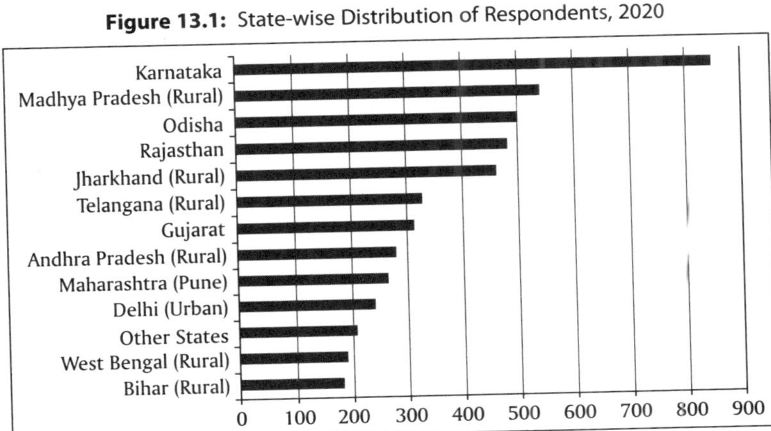

Source: Survey results.

age was 38 years.[5] About half of the sample was illiterate or had only primary education. Of those interviewed, 85 per cent were either the main income earners of the household or spouses of the main income earners. More than 8 in 10 households had a monthly income of less than Rs 10,000 in February 2020.

In rural areas, more than half of our respondents were either farmers or casual workers. About 7 in 10 households in rural areas owned some cultivable land. In urban areas, more than 4 in 10 respondents had been non-agricultural casual workers in February (Figure 13.2). A majority of the workers in urban areas were service providers or construction workers. They worked as ragpickers, domestic helps, tailors, sanitation workers, street vendors, plumbers, painters, carpenters, taxi or auto drivers, balloon sellers, cleaners, beedi makers, construction labourers or security guards.

Impact on Livelihoods

The lockdown has resulted in unprecedented levels of losses in livelihoods and earnings.[6]

Amongst those who had been working in February, 66 per cent reported they lost employment during the lockdown. They could

Figure 13.2: Work Activity Status of Respondents Prior to Lockdown, 2020

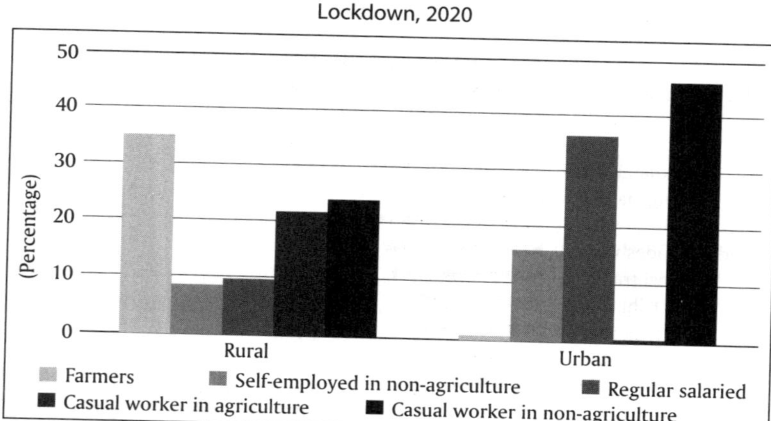

Source: Survey results.

not find even a single day's work during the lockdown or had to completely stop their self-employment activities. The loss of employment was more severe in urban areas, with almost 8 in 10 respondents reporting losing work, compared with just over half in rural areas (Figure 13.3).

About half of the regular wage workers contacted by us received a reduced salary or no salary during the lockdown period. This was higher for those in urban areas (54 per cent) than those in rural areas (39 per cent).

'I have worked for so many years in the factory, I should get paid at least a little amount for now. The government should also help. Otherwise how will we bear daily expenses?', asked a 39-year-old male regular salary worker from Uttarakhand.[7]

Figure 13.3: Loss of Employment for those who were Working in February 2020

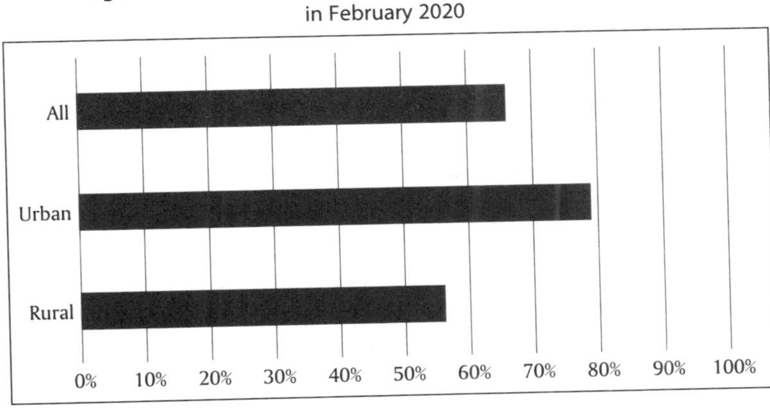

Source: Survey results.

The non-agricultural sector experienced more losses in employment than the agriculture sector, with casual workers and the self-employed being the worst-off (Figure 13.4).

Individuals who had some degree or diploma, or belonged to the Other Backward Castes (OBCs), as opposed to the Scheduled Castes (SCs) or Scheduled Tribes (STs), seemed to have experienced relatively lower loss in employment. Muslims in our sample have experienced substantially larger losses in employment than Hindus, at 81 per cent versus 65 per cent.

Figure 13.4: Employment Loss by Work Activity Status in February 2020

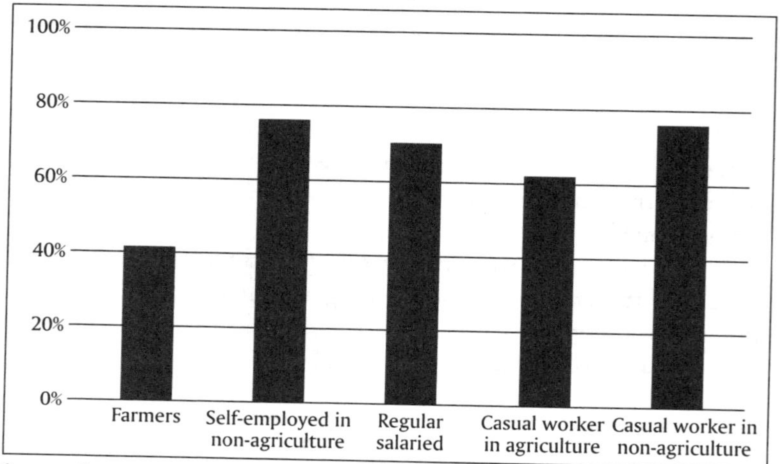

Source: Survey results.

Respondents living in vulnerable urban households—those with a monthly income of less than Rs 10,000 in February—have seen greater levels of loss of employment (79 per cent) than those in higher-income households (76 per cent). In rural areas, fewer respondents from land-owning households reported loss of work, relative to those from landless households: 67 per cent versus 51 per cent.

For those who managed to retain work during the lockdown, incomes were more than halved. For casual workers, median monthly earnings dropped to Rs 1,727 from Rs 3,750, and for the self-employed in the non-agriculture sectors, to Rs 2,165 from Rs 5,000. The median drop in earnings was higher in rural areas than in urban areas. Among farmers, as many as 85 per cent faced severe difficulties in harvesting and selling crops. They were unable to harvest due to the lack of machinery or labour. They could not sell their harvest or had to sell at reduced prices due to the lack of transportation.

Impact on Households

The lockdown has led to severe levels of food insecurity, depleted savings and increased household borrowing. In urban areas, 83 per cent reported consuming less food than before. In rural areas, the corresponding figure was 73 per cent. Food insecurity was higher among women, Muslims, SCs, people with lower educational qualifications, and those in vulnerable households.

'Living has become hard. We have two children and are unable to provide them three meals a day. During many instances, we go hungry or eat one meal to give food to them,' said a 31-year-old female casual worker from Karnataka. 'There is no help from the government.'

Almost half of our respondents reported not having enough money to buy even a week's basic essentials. The contrast here between rural and urban areas is stark: the lack was reported by 65 per cent of urban respondents and 35 per cent of rural respondents. This probably reflects the greater dependence of urban respondents on market-provided goods and services.

More than 8 in 10 respondents did not have money to pay the following month's rent. More than a third were taking loans to cover daily personal expenses during the lockdown. The median size of such loans was Rs 5,000. Urban respondents were more likely to take loans (41 per cent) than rural (33 per cent) (Figure 13.5). Less than a tenth of these loans were taken from formal sources, indicating the limits of banks to reach out at times of distress. Half of the respondents

Figure 13.5 Impact on Households, 2020

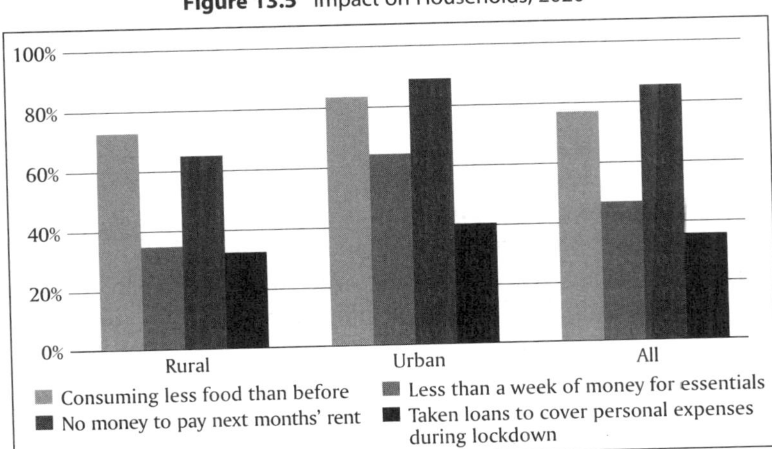

Source: Survey results.

borrowed from friends and family. About 2 in 10 borrowed from moneylenders.

Reach of Relief Measures

Large sections of the economically vulnerable population had not received any government relief (Figure 13.6). Almost 2 in 10 vulnerable households were unable to get any rations. Muslim respondents were also more likely to not be able to procure rations as Hindus: 27 per cent versus 17 per cent. The median quantity of grains obtained by those able to access rations was 5 kg per person, far less than the promised quantity.

Figure 13.6: Reach of Relief Measures, 2020

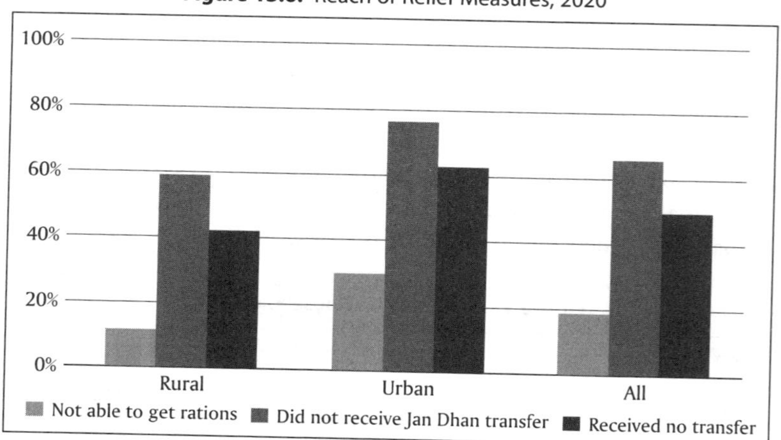

Source: Survey results.

'The villages are in bad shape. We can't buy essentials even. And we can't go to the town for work or for buying items for daily needs,' said a 37-year-old male self-employed worker from Rajasthan. 'Savings are also getting depleted. It will be difficult to keep going for months like this.'

Since our respondents are connected to civil society organisations, they are more likely to be able to access the ration system than other socio-economically similar households. The inability to get rations would likely be worse for other groups.

The saga is far worse when we examine the reach and extent of the promised cash transfers.

Half of our respondents reported not receiving any cash transfer under central or state-specific schemes.[8] The reach of cash transfers was particularly weak in urban areas, where 63 per cent did not get even a single cash transfer.

In absolute terms, on average, our respondents had lost Rs 2,000–3,000 of income per month. The announced cash transfer that is supposed to reach most households is grossly inadequate to compensate for this loss.

For instance, the central government announced cash transfers of Rs 500 per month for three months for every woman with a Jan Dhan bank account. This translates to Rs 4 per person per day, assuming the eligible woman has a family of four. Compare this to the poverty line of Rs 50 per person per day in rural areas and Rs 73 in urban areas (based on the Rangarajan Committee estimates of 2011–12, converted to current prices).

Even the reach of Jan Dhan accounts is very limited. Only 1 in 3 vulnerable households reported receiving the promised cash transfer. This was mostly because a large majority did not have Jan Dhan accounts. Overall, 6 in 10 vulnerable households did not have women Jan Dhan accounts.

The suspension of MGNREGA work has deprived the vulnerable of a safety net. 'We want to work in MGNREGA but no work is available ... The contractor has not started work this year,' said a 40-year-old female casual worker from Jharkhand. 'My payment from last year's work is also pending, it was wrongly deposited in someone else's account.'

Recommendations

The disruption from Covid-19 and the lockdown in the economy and labour markets is enormous. Any relief measure for this crisis should at minimum consist of three prongs: a universalisation of the PDS, the expansion of direct cash transfers, and an expansion of the rural employment guarantee scheme and its introduction in urban areas. We expand on these recommendations here.

The PDS has the widest reach in providing relief. But there still are a large number of households, especially the most vulnerable groups, that do not receive rations due to a lack of ration cards. Governments should issue temporary ration cards or through other means universalise PDS for the next six months. India has enough food reserves for this (Drèze 2020a). Governments should also open cooked meal centres for the hungry. The mid-day meal scheme in schools, Anganwadi centres and public feeding programmes existing in several states can be utilised for this effort.

To cover the income losses, governments should provide a monthly cash transfer of at least Rs 7,000 for the next three months to households by combining administrative lists of welfare schemes such as MGNREGA, PDS and Ujjwala. To relieve pressure on the rural banking system, panchayats could be used for cash transfers, as done in Odisha.

There is large a demand for work, both from returning migrants and from those who have lost jobs. Large-scale worksites under MGNREGA should be started immediately (Drèze 2020b). The allocation for MGNREGA work should be increased by at least Rs 1 lakh crore. The number of days of guaranteed work per household should be raised to 150 days. MGNREGA workers should be paid without delays, preferably through cash-in-hand, and their past dues should be cleared. To provide relief to the urban poor, a nation-wide large-scale employment guarantee programme should be launched, expanding on the experiments in some states with urban wage employment programmes.[9]

The pandemic and the resultant economic distress is likely to stay with us for some time. This unfortunate situation has already caused a lot of suffering for many. We as a society need to realise the scale of the problem, be empathetic to the plight of the underprivileged, plan for it, and provide much-needed direct and immediate relief.

Notes

1. See the public database of reported deaths that have happened as a result of the lockdown, maintained by Thejesh G. N., available at https://thejeshgn.com/projects/covid19-india/non-virus-deaths/ (accessed 15 May 2020).

2. Data and details of the survey and the organisations that administered the survey are available at https://cse.azimpremjiuniversity.edu.in/covid19-analysis-of-impact-and-relief-measures/ (accessed 15 May 2020).
3. We made 7,000 telephone calls and our response rate was close to 70 per cent. This response rate is far higher than response rates obtained in random-number telephone dialling. This was partly because respondents were called by organisations with whom they had a prior relationship. We have 12 states where more than 180 respondents each were interviewed. Overall we have observations from 15 states.
4. See a compilation of Covid-19 lockdown impact surveys, available at https://cse.azimpremjiuniversity.edu.in/covid19-analysis-of-impact-and-relief-measures/#other_surveys (accessed 15 May 2020).
5. The distribution of the sample by gender is not uniform across states. In a few states like Gujarat, our sample is mostly women, while for some others it is dominated by men.
6. The findings reported here differ slightly from the ones presented in the Centre for Sustainable Employment (CSE) webinar conducted on 12 May 2020 as they have been updated with results from about 1,000 households that have been surveyed since then. The broad patterns remain the same.
7. Respondents were interviewed on conditions of anonymity, hence they are not named here.
8. Detailed results by each cash transfer scheme are available on https://cse.azimpremjiuniversity.edu.in/covid19-analysis-of-impact-and-relief-measures/ (accessed 15 May 2020).
9. A detailed proposal for this has been made by CSE, available at https://cse.azimpremjiuniversity.edu.in/wp-content/uploads/2019/04/SWI2019_Urban_Job_Guarantee.pdf (accessed 15 May 2020).

References

Drèze, Jean. 2020a. 'Excess Stocks of the Food Corporation of India Must be Released to the Poor'. *Indian Express*, 9 April. Available at https://indianexpress.com/article/opinion/columns/coronavirus-lockdown-food-for-poor-migrants-mass-exodus-jean-dreze-6353790/ (accessed 15 May 2020).

———. 2020b. 'The Need for a Million Worksites Now'. *The Hindu*, 25 May. Available at https://www.thehindu.com/opinion/lead/the-need-for-a-million-worksites-now/article31665949.ece (accessed 15 May 2020).

14

How Many Casual Workers in the Cities Have Sought To Go Home?*

Nomaan Majid

The public focus on 'migrant labour' emerged almost as soon as the Covid-19 lockdown was announced on 24 March. Many poor workers, who found they were without work and very short of funds, took it upon themselves to walk to their villages; some with families, many more on their own.

Most of these persons began their journey on foot. Their miserable state was caught on camera, and there has been considerable discussion of their plight. It can be said without doubt that these persons were very poor urban workers who had lost their jobs.

However, how many of them were on the road, whether they represented the bulk of redundancies in urban areas, whether they were all migrants and, if so, of which kind—these questions began to stick to the images of workers walking out of the cities. The violence that some of these workers met with during their journey emotionally charged the issue further.

That they were going out of urban areas to the perceived safety of their non-urban destinations in itself does not mean that they are all or mostly short-term migrants. Similarly, the fact that most of these workers are very poor and had been dismissed from their jobs, tells

---

* First published in *The India Forum*, 29 May 2020.

The author would like to thank Abhishek Kumar for research assistance, and Ajit Ghose and Radhicka Kapoor who discussed some aspects of the topic with him. The views expressed in the text are the author's and not of the organisation he works for.

us little about how much they represent others who had been made jobless in urban areas.

Loss of Jobs

The scale of job losses at the all-India level and indeed in urban India from where these persons have been moving out are difficult to ascertain, as there are not many current surveys. The estimate of job losses is distinct from the estimate of persons who potentially may have incurred damage to livelihoods. This number can be inferred from the baseline data we do have of the workers, as in the Periodic Labour Force Survey (PLFS) of 2017–18. The headcount of the poor or the self-employed and casual workers is an obvious upper limit. Some evidence that is emerging now suggests that very large sections of the working population have indeed lost jobs.

One survey that we must rely on is the Centre for Monitoring Indian Economy (CMIE) survey (Vyas 2020). It estimates that 122 million workers lost their jobs in April 2020. This is more than a quarter of all employed persons. Of these, it identifies 91.3 million as labourers and small traders—the corresponding category in standard employment data being casual workers and the self-employed.

While the scale of estimated job loss is huge according to CMIE, the survey does not give an urban–rural split. Researchers at Azim Premji University (APU) have done another much smaller purposive survey, which is very useful (the 'APU survey', Centre for Sustainable Employment 2020). This survey gives a breakdown of jobs lost by location and employment type. We are, of course, interested here in the urban jobs lost.[1]

As far as urban jobs are concerned, the APU survey shows that by mid-May 2020, 81 per cent of casual workers, 84 per cent of self-employed and 76 per cent of regular salaried workers had lost their jobs.

The PLFS urban shares and employment estimates are given in Table 14.1. Therefore, if we apply APU's 81 per cent to the PLFS estimate of 18.96 million casual workers (Usual Principal Status or UPS), we get 15.35 million. This is a large number of casual workers in urban India who may have lost their jobs.

Table 14.1: Size and Distribution of the Workforce (UPS), 2017–18

PLFS 2017–18 Population-adjusted Estimates (in Number)	*Urban*	*Total*
Self-employed	4,88,88,488	22,85,33,506
Casual workers	1,89,63,028	11,18,32,733
Regular salaried workers	6,15,13,763	10,42,87,666
All workers	12,93,65,279	44,46,53,905
PLFS 2017–18 Shares (%)	*Urban*	*Total*
Self-employed	37.8	51.4
Casual workers	14.7	25.2
Regular salaried workers	47.6	23.5
All workers	100.0	100.0

Source: PLFS 2017–18.

The figure is slightly higher in the Usual Principal + Subsidiary Status (UPSS) estimates of workers.[2] The number is, of course, going to get slightly higher if we further take the 2020 adjusted population estimate as opposed to the estimate for 2017–18. The absolute number clearly depends on the population estimate we take, but the difference is not much.

The Identity of Urban Workers Who Are Leaving

There are many poor people living in urban areas. They include workers of many descriptions. Many self-employed are very poor, and almost all casual workers are poor.[3] There are also poor regularly employed persons without social security who too are affected by the lockdown. It is our view that in the first round of the lockdown, it is the casual workers who have been affected the most.

The PLFS numbers suggest that in urban areas, casual workers were around 14.6 per cent of total urban employment in 2017–18—the 18.96 million number. This would indeed be the count if all casual workers were to leave, all 18.96 million. As we saw, applying the APU survey-based percentage of urban casual labour job loss (81 per cent) to this number would bring the affected casual worker population count to 15.35 million.

Many casual workers are persons who either have accommodation arranged for them for which they pay through contractors or live on work premises (as on construction sites), rent rooms on an informal basis, or make do in temporary spaces for which they pay directly. In any event, it is safe to assume that a considerable minority of casual labour in urban areas does not live in premises that have properly written rent leases with emergency clauses, or in owned premises.

Moreover, these casual workers who have adverse accommodation arrangements are likely to be the poorest and must be amongst those who lost their jobs after the lockdown was imposed. After all, it is most of the casual workers that we suspect have lost jobs.

The National Sample Survey (NSS) Housing Survey of 2018[4] allows us to identify urban casual workers, their sectors of occupation, their duration of stay in residence on a premises, and their residential contractual arrangements.[5] The latter also allows us to distinguish owned, owned-leased and rented accommodation with written contracts. We term these non-adverse accommodation arrangements. This is in contrast to less formal arrangements that are based on employer-provided spaces (like construction sites or spaces near factory compounds or makeshift quarters) and informal rentals without written contracts. We call these adverse accommodation arrangements.

While the bulk of urban casual workers in all sectors live in what we call non-adverse conditions of accommodation, a significant minority, around a quarter, live in adverse accommodation arrangements (Table 14.2). We estimate that number to be 25.69 per cent of the 18.96 million casual workers as in PLFS 2017–18. This comes to about 4.87 million living under adverse accommodation arrangements.[6]

Table 14.2: Accommodation Arrangements of Casual Workers (Percentage Distribution), 2018

	All	*Rural*	*Urban*
Non-adverse accommodation arrangement	74.3	97.13	74.31
Adverse accommodation arrangement	25.7	2.87	25.69

Note: Non-adverse: owned and leased or dwelling with contract; adverse: employer-provided, dwelling without written contract, or no dwelling.

Source: From the Housing Survey of 2018.

The other point to note here is that those who have non-adverse accommodation arrangements and who live in owned and leased abodes are in a majority. Around 74.3 per cent of casual workers in urban areas live in owned and leased accommodation. It is inconceivable that these casual workers who are long-term occupiers or quasi-owners of their urban abodes would give up their foothold in urban areas, or immediately start to move out after they lose their jobs.

We can now look at the duration of stay in premises for casual workers. Tables 14.3 to 14.5 show three things.

First, Table 14.3 shows that as we increase the duration of stay, there is a decrease in the share of casual labourers living in premises that are under adverse arrangements. Thus, as expected, shorter period rentals and stays correlate with less secure accommodation arrangements. Adverse accommodation arrangements decline as the period of stay of casual workers lengthens.

While this is not a guarantee for identifying short-term migrants, it is still plausible to infer that short-term migrants, under the Census definition, will be amongst those who live in an accommodation for less than 1 year, especially the ones who are also living under adverse accommodation contractual arrangements.

Table 14.3: Distribution of Accommodation Arrangements of Casual Workers by Period of Stay, 2018

Casual Workers' Period of Stay by Accommodation Arrangement	*Adverse Accommodation Arrangements (%)*	*Non-adverse Accommodation Arrangements (%)*
Less than 1 year	78.47	21.53
1–2 years	75.46	24.54
2–5 years	66.03	33.97
(Up to 5 years)	(71.22)	(28.78)
5–10 years	36.94	63.06
10–20 years	21.41	78.59
20–40 years	9.25	90.75
40–60 years	5.21	94.79
60 years or more	4.68	95.32
Not known	34.51	65.49
Total	25.54	74.46

Source: Estimates from the Housing Survey of 2018.

The adverse contracts are clearly bunched in accommodation arrangements for stays of fewer than 5 years. They are not just located in the under 1-year category but can go up to the 5-year group. Table 14.4 shows the distribution of adverse accommodation arrangements for casual workers by duration.

Table 14.4: Distribution of Adverse Accommodation Arrangements of Casual Workers by Duration, 2018

Period of Stay	*Percentage of All Adverse Accommodation Contracts*
Less than 1 year	10.17
1–2 years	17.02
2–5 years	24.07
(Up to 5 years)	(51.26)
5–10 years	19.15
10–20 years	14.60
20–40 years	9.26
40–60 years	3.62
60 years or more	1.29
Not known	0.82
Total	100.00

Source: Estimates from the Housing Survey of 2018.

Table 14.5 shows us the shares of select classifications of casual workers in the 2018 Housing Survey and the inferred absolute numbers from the estimates of the casual labour population as in the 2017–18 PLFS.

The worst-off group comprises casual labourers with less than 1-year accommodation and adverse housing contracts. They are around 4,92,000, say, half a million. According to our reasoning, this is the category in which short-term migrants will most likely be.

The next category does not bind the group to adverse accommodation arrangements, but retains the restriction of a stay of less than 1 year. This number is larger, around 6,27,000.

Finally, we have that category of urban casual workers that has adverse accommodation arrangements without the restriction of period of stay. This is the 4.8 million number. If we use the estimates for population in 2020, the ball-park figure should be around 5 million.

Table 14.5: Size of Select Casual Labour Categories, 2017–18

	As a Percentage of All Casual Workers in the 2018 Housing Survey (%)	*PLFS Urban Casual Workers (Population-adjusted)*
1. All urban casual workers with less than 1-year stay and living under adverse accommodation contracts	2.60	4,92,276
2. All urban casual workers with less than 1-year stay	3.31	6,27,363
3. All urban casual workers living under adverse accommodation contracts	25.54	4.84 million

Note: The PLFS-adjusted numbers are the percentage in the second column, multiplied by the absolute number of urban casual workers (population-adjusted).

Source: Author's estimates from PLFS 2017–18 and the Housing Survey of 2018.

These casual workers, numbering 4.8 to 5 million, are the ones who are likely to have found themselves without work post the lockdown and who, living on premises with adverse accommodation arrangements, would have been compelled to leave the cities in the first wave of movement home.

This estimate clearly looks conservative in light of the speculation that has been going on. It also suggests that the group of leaving workers is less likely to comprise the very short-term workers, but rather a wider range of workers.

One extension to these estimates may be to examine all workers rather than just casual workers. This is tantamount to saying that we are not focusing on one worker type. After all, the APU survey also says that 84 per cent of the self-employed and 76 per cent of the regular employed were made redundant.

Our view in this context is that there is no exclusivity of worker group amongst those returning, but it is likely that casual workers dominate the first wave. The reason for this is that we think self-employed persons may have a slightly longer staying power than casual workers. On an average their consumption levels are higher.

Keeping the restriction of short term of the stay (less than 1 year) and those with adverse accommodation contracts, the number of all urban workers (casual, self-employed and regular salaried) in this category is 3.45 million. The number of urban workers with under 1-year stay and without adverse contracts increases to 5.28 million. (Table 14.6, row 2)

Table 14.6: All Urban Workers with Adverse Accommodation Contracts, 2017–18

All Urban Workers with Adverse Accommodation Contracts	*As a Percentage of All Workers in the 2018 Housing Survey*	*All Urban Workers in the Population (Adjusted, Million) in PLFS 2017–18*
1. All urban workers with adverse contracts	25.10	32.48
2. All urban workers with less than 1-year stay	4.08	5.28
3. All urban workers with period of stay of less than 1 year and adverse accommodation contracts	2.67	3.45

Note: The PLFS-adjusted numbers are the percentage in the second column, multiplied by the absolute number of urban workers (population-adjusted) in Table 14.1.

Source: Author's estimates from PLFS 2017–18 and the Housing Survey of 2018.

Of course, by removing the restriction of time of stay altogether, we get a high number of 32.5 million workers who have adverse accommodation arrangements (Table 14.6, row 1). It must be noted that because we have removed the time constraint, it would be difficult to argue that short-term migrants dominate the larger number even if it was close to the actual exodus number.

In our view, this is a large but plausible number of 32.5 million workers with adverse accommodation arrangements who include 3.45 million short-term migrants with adverse contracts. This is because there is rampant urban poverty in India, and there are many permanent residents in urban areas who are poor and who do not have secure accommodation arrangements, and yet stay put in urban areas. Needless to say, over time if there is a weak recovery, many persons amongst them will be without shelter too.

Some Remarks

Our considered estimate of workers initially wanting to move out of urban areas is around 5 million. This would tend to include around a half million short-term migrants—the indicator being the interface between casual work, adverse accommodation arrangements and a short period of stay. A further slowdown and the incapacity of the economy to restart may bring a second wave with more self-employed and some regular workers (without security), some of whom will no doubt wish to leave urban areas.

Given that these numbers are based on many assumptions, it is expected that they are not plausible to some researchers. This is natural in a situation of limited data. New data, especially the Census of 2021, will shed light on this issue when it comes out. There are, however, two distinct sources from which confusions can arise that can be addressed even at present.

The first point we need to make is that one should recall that 81 per cent of casual workers in urban areas have lost their jobs according to the APU survey. This comes to roughly 15.3 million. If we assume that the proportion of these 15.3 million who are in adverse accommodation arrangements is the same as in the 2018 Housing Survey, that is, 25.1 per cent, then the absolute number of workers in adverse accommodation arrangements who have lost their jobs comes to around 3.84 million. So, the number when extrapolated even from the APU survey is on the low side and close to our estimate. This is despite the fact that the overall job-loss percentages from the APU survey, if translated into absolute numbers, would be very high.

So a low estimate of casual workers with adverse accommodation arrangements (the proxy for those who are walking out of urban areas) is not inconsistent with estimates of very high job losses.

Inter-state and intra-state demarcations, in conjunction with alternative classifications and definitions of migrants, and data from independent surveys may well give different numbers.[7] However, these will be different numbers and different categories. Moreover, to assume that those who are moving from urban areas towards rural areas at this present junction necessarily belong to these alternative migrant classifications needs more than just independent estimates of the circulatory and floating migrants.

The issue was to ascertain the scale of persons moving out from urban areas. In the first wave, they are likely to have been casually employed, very poor and living in adverse accommodation arrangements. Undoubtedly, many of these persons are also likely to be working in the urban areas on a short-term basis. Where would they go? Many must have relatives in other parts of the country. They do not have money. They are desperate, and so they are walking. The overall number for this group is likely to be around 5 million in the first wave—persons who find themselves without shelter and have been mostly casually employed.

Depending on the speed of recovery, other affected groups like the self-employed may increasingly join a second wave. There is a possible confusion between the estimated scale of job losses, which are highly plausible, and alternative notions and estimates of migration. The two are not systematically linked.

Notes

1. The overall employment split between the rural and urban in India is around 71.3 per cent rural and 28.7 per cent urban, according to PLFS 2017–18. Thus, while it is true that a majority of the redundancies took place in urban areas, it is also the case that urban India has a minority of employment.
2. We estimate total urban employment to be around 129.36 million on UPS and 131.43 million on UPSS in 2017–18.
3. There are indeed short-term seasonal migrants to urban areas included in this group. It is likely that these persons also do casual work Many short-term seasonal migrants were also due to go back at that time of the lockdown to attend to duties in the rabi harvest season.
4. What we call the Housing Survey 2018 is technically unit-level data from the NSS 76th Round on Drinking Water, Sanitation, Hygiene and Housing Condition, July–December 2018.
5. There is likely to be a link between short-term residences, especially less than 1 year, and short-run migrants, who are the poorest of casual workers.
6. This number would go up a little (4.94 million) if we included those with written accommodation contracts.

7. For example, see 'Migrant Labour in the Shadow of the Pandemic', webinar hosted by Institute for Human Development (IHD) and Indian Society of Labour Economics (ISLE), 2 May 2020, available at https://www.youtube.com/watch?v=8y5MOaqN9SY (accessed 1 December 2020). For concepts linked to short-term circulatory migration, see Breman (1996).

References

Breman, Jan. 1996. *Footloose Labour: Working in India's Informal Economy*. New York: Cambridge University Press.

Centre for Sustainable Employment. 2020. 'COVID19: Analysis of Impact and Relief Measures'. Azim Premji University. Available at https://cse.azimpremjiuniversity.edu.in/covid19-analysis-of-impact-and-relief-measures/ (accessed 1 December 2020).

Vyas, Mahesh. 2020. 'The Jobs Bloodbath of April 2020'. Centre for Monitoring Indian Economy, 5 May. Available at https://www.cmie.com/kommon/bin/sr.php?kall=warticle&dt=2020-05-05%20 08:22:21&msec=776 (accessed 1 December 2020).

15

The Gig Economy in the Pandemic

*Outsourcing Risk, Privatising Gain?**

Gayatri Nair

On the Zomato page for raising funds for their 'delivery partners', the co-head of the food-delivery company, Deepinder Goyal (2020b), appeals to customers to contribute towards providing food, income support and insurance for workers in the time of the Covid-19 pandemic. He notes that due to the contractual nature of the work and low incomes, the workers have little to no savings to get them through the lockdown period. In the same breath, Goyal asks the question on everyone's mind: why doesn't Zomato itself take responsibility to offer these benefits to the workers? His response is succinct: 'It's beyond our financial viability.' Yet this is a company whose net worth was Rs 1,900 crore in September 2019 and which raised another Rs 353 crore in funding earlier this year (Abrar 2020; *Economic Times* 2019).

Some of the workers delivering food for Zomato were probably going hungry even before the lockdown, evidenced by the images from two years ago of a worker eating from a delivery parcel (*BBC* 2018). Goyal's point on workers' precarity therefore speaks not to the lockdown specifically but to the general conditions of low incomes in gig work.

Zomato is not the only defaulter here. Its rival Swiggy, or ride-hailing companies like Uber and Ola, all of whom depend on 'feet on the ground' work performed by people enduring high levels of

* First published in *The India Forum*, 5 June 2020.

risk, are all dependent on the 'generosity' of others. A curious system seems at work here. Companies that have continued to operate and even expand operations during the lockdown are enforcing conditions of work (including the mandatory use of Aarogya Setu), but are outsourcing responsibility for the risks that delivery workers endure to consumers, by asking them to contribute financially to support workers.

What makes this possible are the conditions of the gig economy: a form of work that has no recognisable employer or employee. While the debate on labour law suspensions rages on, there continues to operate in India a sizeable gig economy that never even had labour laws to begin with because it seemingly has no labouring class. In a situation of largely jobless growth, the gig economy's entry has been celebrated for providing new jobs and opportunities for work.

The world of work has seen significant shifts in the previous decade, with technology increasingly integrated into varying forms of work. These new technological interventions have been sold to us as 'disruptions' in the working of the old economy. Uber, Ola, Zomato and Swiggy represent this new gig economy, where tech corporates float platforms that are 'lean' without significant asset ownership—no cars, no restaurants (Woodcock and Graham 2020: 45)—and where there are no workers, only a world of self-employed, independent contractors who used these platforms to engage consumers. Although estimates of workers in the gig economy are notoriously hard to come by, they are estimated at over 70 million globally (ibid.: 1).

This gig economy had been celebrated by the Niti Aayog, which credited Uber and Ola alone for creating 22 lakh jobs in the wake of an unemployment crisis (*CNBC TV18* 2019). In their public offering last year, Uber reported 30 million cars attached to its platform in India (Salve and Paliath 2019), while in food delivery, the human resources firm Teamlease reported the creation of 8 lakh positions (Rao 2019). But the high and rotational attrition in the gig economy make these estimates sketchy at best, and the absence of regulations in the gig economy raises questions about the quality of these jobs.

The gig economy imagines that it is a world of equal stakeholders: tech corporates, service providers and consumers. But in reality, gig platforms are much more than just a point of connect between service providers and consumers. Gig platforms operate very much like employers in determining how work is to be conducted, seen, for instance, in Zomato making the Aarogya Setu app mandatory for its delivery workers. Companies in the gig economy are keen to distance themselves from the tag of being employers, because it allows them to limit expenses that would otherwise be incurred on workers: expenses that relate to mitigating and insuring against risks faced by workers.

Rather than representing a form of disruption, the gig economy extends capitalism: where one group owns property and assets necessary for production; and another, which does not, works for them. The gig economy imagines this with a slight difference. Tech corporates see themselves as providing aggregation services for independent service providers such as drivers or delivery personnel, who use the platform created by the company to connect with consumers. These service providers own some of the assets necessary for providing services like bikes, cars or smartphones. But given that the technology needed for building platforms is owned by corporates, this remains a system where one group owns while the other labours.

Much like industrial labour, gig workers who undertake the physical aspects of labour are at risk. In the app-based food delivery or in the transport network, this has been seen in the form of road accidents. Women beauty workers speak of the risk of sexual abuse as they enter unknown homes to work. In the time of Covid-19, delivery workers who continue to operate face an amplified risk. The nature of the work necessitates contact with numerous people, significantly raising the risk workers undertake. But because they are termed as independent contractors or 'delivery partners', and gig platforms are fashioned as 'aggregators', technology companies that own gig platforms can shirk legal responsibility for worker safety.

Terms of Employment

The sticky point legally has been to account for gig corporates as employers and those working for the platform as employees. This has been the subject of legal scrutiny and debate around the world. Most recently, California, the hub of tech corporates in the US, passed

Assembly Bill 5, legislating that drivers and delivery partners be classified as employees. The bill codifies a test to determine whether those hired in the gig economy constitute workers or not, a part of which rests on the notion that employees work in conditions determined by the employer. Under this test, gig economy workers were seen to be under the 'control and direction of their employer', as the California Supreme Court judgement stated (Dolan and Khouri 2018).

Carefully considered, in India too, there are a number of similar practices that gig platforms term as essential for the worker to perform. These include having to a wear a uniform bearing the signage and logo of the company, or use the delivery bags that the company mandates, with financial penalties imposed on workers who fail to comply. More significantly, workers have to adhere to price and incentive structures determined by the platform. Thus, even as gig work is supposed to be flexible, the income structure forces workers to work for more than 8 hours and even weekends in order to earn a living wage.

In the time of the pandemic, these essential practices have increased. Temperature checks, wearing of safety gear and cashless delivery are all part of this. Of course, these are necessary for the safety of the worker and the consumer, but there is no negotiation that takes place between these two stakeholders. Rather, gig platforms have taken the lead in determining and mediating on questions of risk and safety for the two parties, even as it claims to only operate as a point of contact between the parties. In other words, on close examination, gig platforms operate like employers: dictating and defining work practices, both prior to and in the times of Covid-19.

The problem here is not that these health practices are being made mandatory, but that the enforcement of these practices is immediately indicative of how implicated gig platforms actually are in the performance of gig work. This has only entered trickier terrain with the mandatory use of Aarogya Setu. If the gig firm is only a platform, and not an employer, does it have the authority to set in place such mandatory practices? And if it does, can they shirk responsibility for providing for the basic welfare and safety of their workers?

Risk for Whom? Safety for Whom?

The gig economy could always be understood as a disproportionate division of risk. It has taken a pandemic to realise just how serious the outcomes of this division are. For a world in lockdown, the shutdown in the gig economy has meant that platforms are under no obligation to provide financial remuneration to drivers or delivery professionals for the loss in pay they suffer.

Instead, many of these platforms have tried to outsource this responsibility to consumers, appealing for contributions to financial assistance funds (Medappa and Taduri 2020). Framed as appeals of compassion, rather than as obligations to workers, these take away from the vital political questions we ought to be raising: what is the responsibility of gig platforms to their workers? The question of welfare has been discussed in terms of state action. But there is also much to be gained from posing it to the gig economy, which has found a way to outsource risk to its workers and responsibility of welfare to its consumers.

In this world of temporary and often low-paying work that the gig economy creates, workers can only live and earn from gig to gig without a safety net to fall back on. The significance of legal recognition as a worker is that laws mandate some mitigation of risk and insecurity that workers are subject to by employers.

Minimum wages, paid leave, severance packages for loss of work, notice periods for job loss and contributions towards retirement were instituted keeping in mind the weaker position of workers. None of these can be availed of by gig workers who are seen as independent contractors. Shortfalls in incomes can only be met by undertaking higher risk, by logging in for longer to secure more work. Even with the minimal safety equipment provided to them currently, gig workers engaged in delivery put themselves—and by extension their families—at considerable risk. Insurance, for instance, is only available if workers test positive (Goyal 2020a), but there is little incentive to be tested at all. Apart from the increasing social stigma around Covid-19, the cost of testing is high and means loss of work for a day, if not more.

One can make the argument that in a stagnant economy the very availability of such jobs should be weighed against the risk that accompanies them. But this would only make sense if those creating these jobs took responsibility for the risk that arises from the work. This is particularly relevant when gig firms have found the pandemic an opportune moment to expand their operations, raise capital (Dash 2020), and enter into new domains, such as delivering groceries and other goods. This has been made possible not so much by technology but more by the availability of this at-risk labour force.

Had this relationship of employment been legally recognised as such, workers would be in a far more secure position to demand that they be protected financially and physically from the risks they endure. Instead, these workers have to now see if they qualify for receiving support—which firms such as Swiggy and Zomato have made clear will only come in the event that drivers test positive for Covid-19. How these funds are disbursed to workers remains unclear, and there have been reports of drivers who claim they have not received any assistance (Alawadhi 2020; Dedgaonkar 2020; Indian Federation of App-based Transport Workers 2020).

The Value of Work

In a recent piece, Pratap Bhanu Mehta (2020) makes the argument for why compassion is the dullest form of intervention we can seek. Soaked through with questions of morality instead of politics, compassion often limits possibilities of action. Instead of the focus on compassion, which gig corporates seek to build on, it would do us well to return to the firmly political terrain of examining the structure of the gig economy and indeed the world of work at large.

This political focus highlights that the new form of work embodied in the gig economy—of equal stakeholders coming together on virtual platforms—has never existed. Instead, this form of work is rooted in older forms of exploitative conditions. Insecurity for workers who are subject to conditions of contingent work are heightened, while any basic right that is made possible under labour laws is denied to them as they are classified not as workers but as independent contractors.

Capitalism has always been accompanied by negotiation and conflict between capitalists and the working classes. While the origin of capitalism is grounded in the belief that the capitalist and the labourer are equals entering into a contractual agreement of employment, given that capitalists as employers often set the terms of work, they have enjoyed an upper hand. Further, these terms often amplify risks associated with any kind of work: both the physical risks of the job, and the risk associated with inadequate wages or of losing a job suddenly. These risks have been the basis for early unionising and for working people to renegotiate their agreement with capitalists. Industrial accidents caused by the exploitative conditions of work have most significantly highlighted the power that capitalists wield against labour.[1] Through years of labour struggles, and by ensuring legal recognition that employers bear responsibility for their workers in the course of the working day, industrial workers were able to secure the most basic of rights: an eight-hour work day, health covers, and decent work conditions and contracts (McEvoy1995).

In looking at and considering life beyond Covid-19, an urgent task would be to return the question of gig workers to the political terrain of rights rather than the moral question of compassion. The halting of work and the looming recession should certainly not become the grounds to justify terrible forms of work that currently exist, something to especially consider when labour laws are being suspended by state governments. History has been replete with these mistakes. One can only hope that the pandemic shines a harsher light on what was always present: if equal stakeholders share existential risk so unequally, then perhaps it is time to rethink the gig economy.

Note

1. The infamous Triangle Shirtwaist Factory incident of 1911 in the US and the Tazreen Factory fire in Bangladesh in 2012 had significantly high death tolls caused by locked doors to ensure workers did not take unauthorised breaks. The Triangle Factory led to the rise of unionising in the US, notable also for women workers' participation in it. But this is predicated on a legal recognition of the employer and employee. A century after Triangle, the Tazreen Factory fire could still happen because the primary employers, including a number of global clothing brands, denied responsibility for work conditions.

References

'Niti Aayog Tries to Counter Bleak Unemployment Data, Says Ola and Uber Helped Create Over 2 Million Jobs'. 2019. *CNBC TV18*, 31 January. Available at https://www.cnbctv18.com/economy/niti-aayog-says-ola-and-uber-helped-create-over-2-million-new-jobs-pegs-total-new-jobs-at-8-million-2142841.htm (accessed 2 June 2020).

'Young and Rich: India's Wealthiest Startup Entrepreneurs'. 2019. *Economic Times*, 26 September. Available at https://economictimes.indiatimes.com/small-biz/startups/newsbuzz/young-rich-indias-wealthiest-startup-entrepreneurs/leading-the-way/slideshow/71305665.cms (accessed 2 June 2020).

'Zomato India Driver Sacked after Eating Customer's Takeaway'. 2018. *BBC*, 11 December. Available at https://www.bbc.com/news/world-asia-46522548 (accessed 2 June 2020).

Abrar, Peerzada. 2020. 'Food Delivery App Zomato Raises Rs 353 Crore from Antfin Singapore'. *Business Standard*, 17 January. Available at https://www.business-standard.com/article/companies/zomato-raises-rs-353-cr-from-ant-financial-in-series-j-funding-round-120011701425_1.html (accessed 4 June 2020).

Alawadhi, Neha. 2020. 'Uber Starts Disbursing Money to Drivers from Rs 25 Cr Dedicated Corpus'. *Business Standard*, 9 April. Available at https://www.business-standard.com/article/companies/uber-starts-disbursing-money-to-drivers-from-rs-25-cr-dedicated-corpus-120040901444_1.html (accessed 3 June 2020).

Dash, Sanchita. 2020. 'Zomato and Swiggy Both Raise Funds – But Swiggy Leads with a Higher Valuation'. *Business Insider*, 6 April. Available at https://www.businessinsider.in/business/startups/news/zomato-and-swiggy-both-get-raise-funds-but-swiggy-leads-with-a-higher-valuation/articleshow/75008445.cms (accessed 3 June 2020).

Dedgaonkar, Supriya. 2020. 'Ola, Uber Drivers Say No Help Received Yet'. *Pune Mirror*, 27 November. Available at https://punemirror.indiatimes.com/pune/civic/ola-uber-drivers-say-no-help-received-yet/articleshow/75331887.cms (accessed 3 June 2020).

Dolan, Maura and Andrew Khouri. 2018. 'California Supreme Court Deals a Blow to Uber'. *Governing*, 1 May. Available at https://www.governing.com/topics/transportation-infrastructure/gov-tns-california-court-independent-contractors-uber-ruling.html (accessed 4 June 2020).

Goyal, Deepinder. 2020a. 'Summary of All of Zomato's COVID-19 Related Initiatives'. *Zomato Blog*, 7 April. Available at https://www.zomato.com/blog/covid-19-initiatives (accessed 4 June 2020).

———. 2020b. 'Zomato Rider Relief Fund'. *Zomato Blog*, 12 April. Available at https://www.zomato.com/blog/rider-relief-fund (accessed 4 June 2020).

Indian Federation of App-based Transport Workers. 2020. 'Drivers/ Delivery Partners of App-based Companies on May Day 2020: COVID-19, #WeAreIFAT'. YouTube video, 30 April. Available at https://www.youtube.com/watch?v=kDQfGi14J98 (accessed 4 June 2020).

McEvoy, Arthur F. 1995. 'The Triangle Shirtwaist Factory Fire of 1911: Social Change, Industrial Accidents, and the Evolution of Common-sense Causality'. *Law and Social Inquiry* 20 (2): 621–51.

Medappa, Kaveri and Pradyumna Taduri. 2020. 'By Crowdfunding Benefits for Embattled Workers, App-based Services are Evading their Own Obligations'. *Scroll.in*, 22 April. Available at https://scroll.in/article/959766/by-crowdfunding-benefits-for-embattled-workers-app-based-services-are-evading-their-own-obligations (accessed 4 December 2020).

Mehta, Pratap Bhanu. 2020. 'Beyond Solidarity: The Migrant Labour and the Unemployed Will be Demanding Their Rights, Not Our Mercy'. *Indian Express*, 18 April. Available at https://indianexpress.com/article/opinion/columns/coronavirus-covid-19-india-lockdown-migrant-labourers-6367384/ (accessed 25 April 2020).

Rao, Mohit M. 2019. 'The "Gig" Economy is Creating Lakhs of Jobs, but Workers Don't See a Future'. *The Hindu*, 30 August. Available at https://www.thehindu.com/business/Economy/the-gig-economy-is-creating-lakhs-of-jobs-but-workers-dont-see-a-future/article29299673.ece (accessed 1 June 2020).

Salve, Prachi and Shreehari Paliath. 2019. 'Overworked and Underpaid, India's "Gig Workers" are Survivors of a Flawed Economy'. *Scroll.in*, 7 June. Available at https://scroll.in/article/926146/overworked-and-underpaid-indias-gig-workers-are-survivors-of-a-flawed-economy (accessed 1June 2020).

Woodcock, Jamie and Mark Graham. 2020. *The Gig Economy: A Critical Introduction*. Cambridge: Polity Press.

Section VI

Impact on the Economy

16

Understanding India's Economic Slowdown

*Need for Concerted Action**

R. Nagaraj

In 2019–20, the Indian economy grew by 4.2 per cent, adjusted for inflation, National Accounts Statistics (NAS) 2020 show. The growth rate got nearly halved in less than three years since 2016–17. Concurrently, the manufacturing growth rate collapsed to zero from 6.6 per cent. If the doubts raised about the official GDP's reliability have merit, the actual growth rate may be lower by 1–2 percentage points.[1]

The reality may be a lot grimmer, however, if one takes a longer view from when the economy had slumped after the boom of the 2000s—which I had called 'India's Dream Run' (Nagaraj 2013). In just a few years, India has gone from being one of the world's fastest growing, IT outsourcing–led, export-oriented economy to a protection-seeking laggard.

---

* First published in *The India Forum*, 24 January 2020.

This is an edited version of the I. G. Patel Memorial Lecture delivered on 4 January 2020, at the Gujarat Economic Association's Golden Jubilee Conference held at N. S. Patel Arts College, Anand. Permission to reproduce the lecture is gratefully acknowledged. The author thanks Atul Kohli and the Editor of *The India Forum* for their comments and suggestions on an earlier version of this chapter.

The postscript 'The Pandemic' is an edited excerpt from the author's chapter, 'Reviving Manufacturing and Employment', in *Beyond Covid's Shadow: Mapping India's Economic Resurgence*, ed. Sanjaya Baru, 223–41 (Delhi: Rupa, 2021). We thank the editor and the publisher of the volume for the permission granted to draw on that chapter.

What accounts for such a quick and sharp reversal of economic performance? Is it a mere perception problem, or hard reality, based on credible evidence? What would it take to restore the growth momentum of the first decade of the 2000s, with equity and inclusivity?

To answer these questions, one needs to have a consistent and quantitative account of economic performance in the last decade (the 2010s). As the government has changed many standard macroeconomic data series in recent years, the task is daunting. I narrate here a story of how the boom of the first decade of the 2000s turned into a sharp slowdown spanning most of the second decade of this century and how economic policy has failed to respond to the warning signals, a failure which has ended up in the current slump. I believe that a clear and credible narrative will help draw up policy options to get out of the present impasse.

A sub-theme here is on the recent changes in economic statistics which, I am afraid, have primarily contributed to a distorted picture of the economic reality that I will seek to correct.

The Boom and its Aftermath

The Dream Run

A decade ago, India was a rising star in the global economy, with its annual growth rate touching 8–9 per cent between 2003 and 2008, with price stability and modest fiscal and balance of payments deficits. It was hailed as one of the fastest growing large economies, nipping at China's heels and reckoned as the emerging global back-office, as against China being the world's factory.

That boom is associated with a sharp upturn in the investment rate peaking at 38 per cent of GDP in 2007–08, with the rising domestic saving rate financing (most) of this investment. Unprecedented foreign capital inflows—foreign direct investment (FDI), foreign portfolio investment (FPI) and external commercial borrowings (ECBs)—at close to 10 per cent of GDP supplemented domestic resources. A rising share of short-term financial inflows caused concerns about financial fragility. However, as the capital inflows were reportedly put to productive use, the criticisms against the inflows were muted. The 'dream run' was also a debt-led growth, with bank credit to the private corporate sector (PCS) burgeoning at an unprecedented pace; a large share of it accrued to big business and politically connected firms. These resources went into infrastructure projects such as roads, ports, and coal and thermal power plants (Nagaraj 2013). Public–private partnership (PPP) was the preferred mode of investment in infrastructure as the government cut down on public investment to adhere to fiscal orthodoxy in line with the Washington Consensus that was the guiding star of economic policy.

The global financial crisis in 2008 upended the boom, though it affected India only modestly for two reasons: (i) its stricter financial regulations and (ii) relatively large and closed domestic markets. After a brief dip in 2008–09, India, thanks to accommodative monetary and looser fiscal policies (a concerted effort by the Group of 20 countries), witnessed a V-shaped recovery that lasted until 2011–12. Quantitative easing (QE) by advanced economies meant renewed capital inflows into emerging markets in search of better yields (that is, higher returns), until the wake-up call of the 'Taper Tantrum' (in May 2013)—when the US Federal Reserve hinted at raising interest rates—took place, reminding India of the perils of fickle capital inflows.

For the protagonists of the reforms, the 'dream run' was a period of virtuous growth, with accelerating growth and poverty reduction. There were a fair number of sceptics, however. In 2006, at the height of the boom, political scientist Atul Kohli cautioned against the impact of the reforms that were not so much pro-market (as promised) but pro-business in reality, with the benefits accruing mostly to powerful business groups. Substantiating the idea, Kohli's 2012 book, *Poverty Amid Plenty in the New India*, demonstrated the unequal distribution of the fruits of market-oriented reforms and growth.

Amit Bhaduri (2008) argued how in the name of liberal reforms, rural land and forests were ravaged by powerful businesses, decimating the livelihoods of the poor and the marginalised in agriculture and the informal economy. He characterised the decade's economic boom as 'predatory growth'. Journalist James Crabtree's account,

The Billionaire Raj (2018), documented how India's super-rich (the 'Bollygarchs', as the author called them) quickly made their way into the *Forbes* list of global billionaires. And how the liberal economic policy era cemented the nexus between business people and politicians, substantiating the idea of crony capitalism operating under the guise of impersonal markets.[2]

As the boom petered out at the turn of the previous decade (2011–12), a revolt against cronyism and capitalist exploitation of land, labour and scarce natural resources came out into the open. The judiciary played its part in putting an end to these exploitative relations. There were massive protests across the country against land acquisition (in Nandigram, West Bengal, for instance), there were court cases against corrupt business houses for getting scarce natural resources at allegedly throwaway prices (2G, for example). Despite the credible record of economic progress, the perceptions of corruption and cronyism did the government in (*The Economist* 2014).

The Aftermath of the Boom

By the middle of the 2010s, the euphoria about reforms got muted with economic growth distinctly lower than in the previous decade; domestic saving, investment and capital inflows likewise trended downwards. IT exports were tapering off as the US imposed taxes on outsourcing and because of technological changes. Inflation, however, ruled high on account of international oil prices, and the balance of payments (BoP) deficit became precarious for a while.

Decelerating output growth affected the earnings of corporates and hence their ability to service the enormous debt they had accumulated during the boom. Corporate bad debts got translated into the banking sector's non-performing assets (NPAs) as firms could not repay loans, restricting the ability of banks to offer new loans.[3]

Wilted Outcomes since 2014–15

Points of Departure

Realising the deteriorating economic situation and the discontent with the previous political dispensation, the National Democratic Alliance

(NDA) government came to power on the agenda of development (modelled after Gujarat's supposed success), eradication of corruption and enforcement of the rule of law. The collapse of Kingfisher Airlines and then Vijay Mallya fleeing the country, leaving behind the public sector banks bleeding, were in the public imagination emblematic of everything that was wrong with the economic management of the previous regime. The incoming government vowed to use financial regulation (including enforcement of strict tax laws) to probe and punish financial wrongdoings. This was an agenda with a broad popular appeal.

In its political campaign, the new ruling coalition had also advanced the idea of 'minimum government and maximum governance', seemingly inspired by Margaret Thatcher and Ronald Reagan, to consciously promote free-market ideals. These views resonated well with global financial elites and the globalised Indian community. True to its beliefs, the government sought to adhere to fiscal orthodoxy, promoted inflation targeting and claimed to enforce the rule of law. To illustrate, the government devoted its considerable administrative capital to improving India's ranking in the World Bank's Ease of Doing Business (EDB) index to win over global investors. The ranking did move up to the 63rd position in 2019, from the 142nd position in 2014, a widely publicised accomplishment.

Yet, in parallel, the government nurtured nationalist projects such as Make in India to raise the manufacturing sector's share in GDP to 25 per cent by 2022 and create 100 million additional manufacturing sector jobs. And populist, targeted welfare programmes were promoted, such as the provision of free cooking-gas connections to women of below poverty line families (under the Pradhan Mantri Ujjwala Yojana), and no-collateral small bank loans for the poor and unemployed (called Mudra loans).

Policy Shocks

To eradicate black money and also to encourage greater use of digital transactions, in November 2016, the government demonetised the large-valued currency notes of Rs 1,000 and Rs 500, accounting for 86.4 per cent of the total value of the currency in circulation. It was indeed a macroeconomic shock, devastating the informal/unorganised sector (which mostly runs on cash transactions), employing up to 90 per cent of the workforce and contributing nearly half of the domestic output. There is near unanimity among economists about demonetisation's adverse effects (Ramakumar 2018). Many believe that it contributed to a contraction in economic activity. Nor has the policy shock led to reduced usage of cash: as a proportion of GDP, it is inching back to its pre-demonetisation level, as per the Reserve Bank of India (RBI) Annual Report of 2018–19.[4]

The Goods and Services Tax (GST) to replace various indirect taxes has been in the making for quite a while. However, its introduction in 2017 was the second shock in less than a year, welcomed in principle but widely criticised for its poor design and implementation. Besides adversely affecting small and informal enterprises (which find it hard and expensive to comply with GST's numerous computerised filings and procedures, thus leading to a severe shortfall in tax collection), it has hurt government finances and the sharing of revenue between the centre and the states.

Changes in Economic Statistics

Changing the base year of the national accounts every 7–10 years is a routine matter for statistical offices everywhere. The revision helps account for the changes in the economic structure and relative prices; and, it also allows for using better statistical methods and improved databases.

In early 2015, the then Central Statistical Office (CSO)—now the National Statistical Office (NSO)—introduced a new GDP series with the base year 2011–12, replacing the earlier one with the base year 2004–05. Surprisingly, the absolute GDP size for 2011–12 in the new series was marginally smaller (by 2.3 per cent) than that in the earlier series. But its annual growth rates in the following years were significantly and systematically higher than in the older series. As the new GDP growth rates were out of line with many economic correlates, there was widespread criticism that the new series seemed to systematically overestimate the GDP growth rate.[5] Two examples best illustrate this problem.

1. With the demonetisation in November 2016, output and employment contracted, especially in the unorganised or informal sector. Economists widely believe it to be so based on theory, empirical analysis and numerous field reports. Yet, the official GDP estimate for 2016–17 showed an 8.2 per cent growth, the highest in a decade![6]
2. For the same year, according to the actual tax returns filed by companies in the private corporate sector, the fixed investment to GDP ratio fell to 2.8 from 7.5 per cent in the previous year, as per the Ministry of Finance's Report on Income Tax Reforms for Building a New India (September 2018). The fall in the ratio seems understandable as demonetisation led to a contraction in economic activity. Surprisingly, however, the corresponding ratio according to the CSO's National Accounts rose to 12 per cent of GDP in 2016–17, compared to 11.7 per cent in the previous year. The divergence between the two sets of estimates (both the levels and the direction of the change) suggests that the National Accounts–based corporate investment estimates are out of line with reality.

Claiming that the National Sample Survey Organisation's (NSSO) five-yearly Employment and Unemployment Surveys (EUS)—conducted since 1972–73—were too infrequent and that they failed to capture the functioning of the urban labour market adequately, the government replaced the EUS with a redesigned PLFS. The decision was based on the recommendations of the report of the task force chaired by Arvind Panagariya (Ministry of Labour and Employment 2017).

Earlier, consumer expenditure surveys (CES) and EUS were conducted simultaneously with the same sample households. But with the introduction of the PLFS, a separate CES was conducted, also undertaken in 2017–18.

Regrettably, the PLFS and CES results for 2017–18 have failed to find favour with the government. The PLFS data, released after considerable controversy and delay, has been officially rejected as it is claimed to be not comparable with the 2011–12 EUS data, though most knowledgeable experts have dismissed the official objections.

Similarly, as the CES results for 2017–18 are at variance with the administrative data, the CES data has been scrapped and not released. However, many experts find the leaked CES data to be credible, and a few research reports with insightful findings are now available in the public domain.

Evidence on Output Performance

We now report economic outcomes during the 2010s, mostly using the official data sources, subject to the qualifications mentioned above.

Figure 16.1 plots the real annual growth rate, which shows GDP growth rising steadily from 5.5 per cent in 2012–13 to 8.2 per cent in 2016–17, declining after that to 5 per cent in the current year (2019–20), as per the official Advanced Estimates. If these estimates are correct, the economy has slowed down only after 2016–17, probably on account of the shocks of the demonetisation and shoddily implemented GST.

However, as already discussed, the GDP growth rates are overstated on account of the kind of methodological changes introduced, and the newer datasets that have been used. To illustrate, the annual GDP

Figure 16.1: Annual GDP Growth Rate (%), 2012–13 to 2019–20

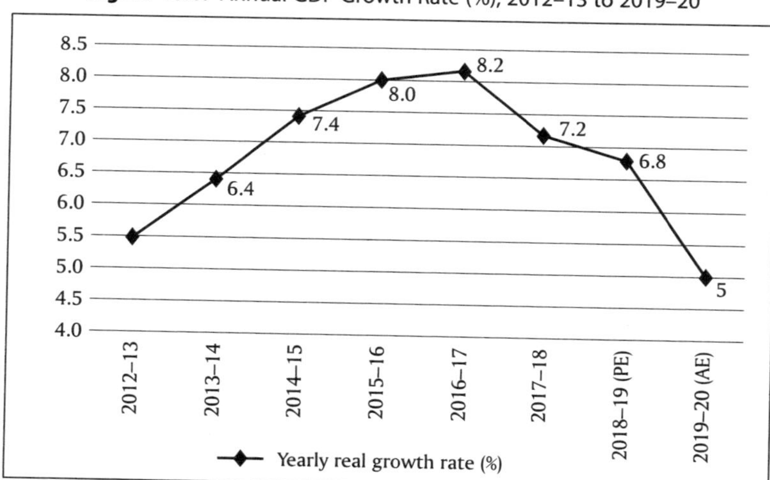

Source: National Accounts Statistics, various issues; and official press releases.

growth rate for 2013–14 went up sharply from 4.8 per cent in the old series to 6.2 per cent in the new series. Similarly, the manufacturing sector growth rate for same year swung from (–) 0.7 per cent in the old series to (+) 5.3 per cent in the new series.

Statistical exercises to validate the official GDP estimates have indicated a sizeable overestimation of the growth rates. Arvind Subramanian (2019), using cross-country growth regressions, inferred that '[o]fficial estimates place annual average GDP growth between 2011–12 and 2016–17 at about 7%. We estimate that actual growth may have been about 4.5%, with a 95% confidence interval of 3.5–5.5%.'

In a similar vein, in a time-series exercise for the period 2011–12 to 2017–18, Sebastian Morris has suggested, using official quarterly GDP data, that the actual growth rate may be between 5 and 5.5 per cent per year. To quote: 'We see that there is significant overestimation in the official series in the overall growth rates – on an average by about 1.3 percentage points over the period 2011–12 to 2017–18' (Morris 2019). Hence, we may infer the following:

- The GDP growth rates in the current decade (the 2010s) are distinctly lower than those recorded in the previous decade.
- Rising GDP growth rates from 2012–13 to 2016–17 are overstated by a margin of 1.5 to 2.5 percentage points in the new series.
- Therefore, the actual growth rates recorded for the six quarters from April 2019 to September 2020 may be far lower than the officially reported figures.

There is, though, a silver lining. The inflation rate, measured by the consumer price index (CPI), has declined sharply from 9.5 per cent in 2013–14 to 3.4 per cent in 2018–19, with an average annual rate of 5.3 per cent during the period (Figure 16.2). The fall largely mirrors a decline in international oil prices, an exogenous factor. As India imports nearly 80 per cent of its commercial energy requirements, oil prices perhaps remain the best predictor of the domestic inflation rate (besides food prices).

Figure 16.3 shows gross saving and investment rates from 2004–05 to 2017–18 (all at current prices).[7] The investment rate peaked at

Figure 16.2: Inflation Rate (%) and Oil Price ($/Barrel), 2012–13 to 2018–19

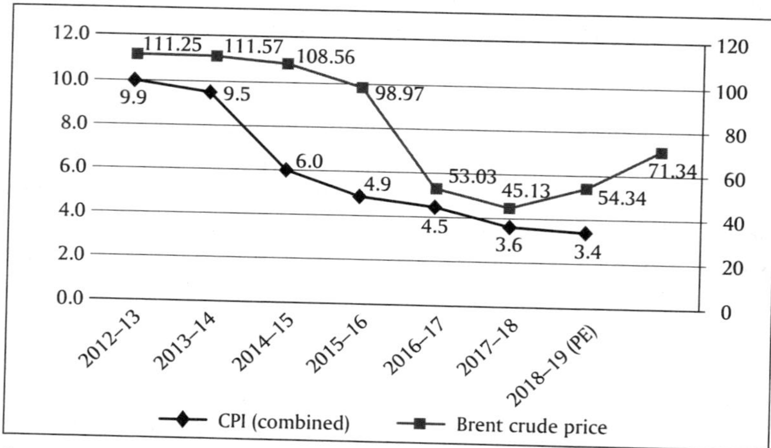

Source: RBI's Handbook of Statistics on Indian Economy, available at https://www.rbi.org.in/scripts/AnnualPublications.aspx?head=Handbook%20of%20Statistics%20on%20Indian%20Economy (accessed 8 December 2020); and Energy: Bloomberg, available at https://www.bloomberg.com/energy (accessed 8 December 2020).

Figure 16.3: Saving and Investment Ratios (% of GDP), 2005–06 to 2017–18

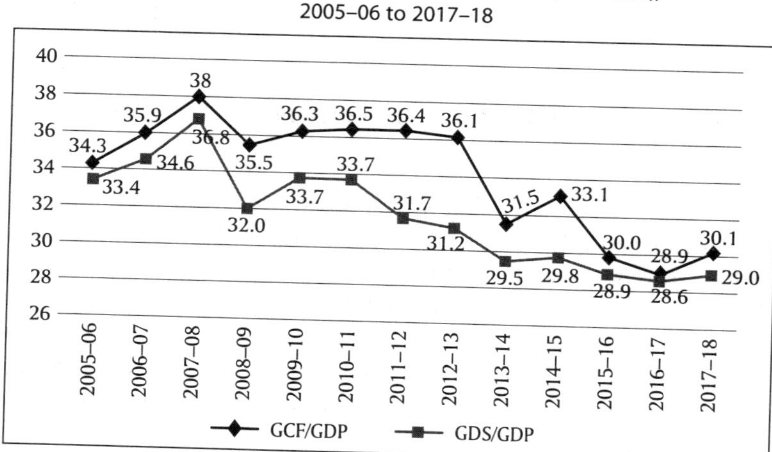

Note: GCF: gross capital formation; GDS: gross domestic savings.
Source: National Accounts Statistics, various issues.

38 per cent of GDP in 2007–08 (just before the global financial crash), and thereafter, steadily declined to 30 per cent of GDP a decade later in 2017–18. Corresponding figures for the saving rate are 36.4 and 29 per cent, respectively. Such a decline in saving and investment rates is unparalled in modern India, implying a deep dent in the economy's potential output growth. If one accepts the stylised fact of economics that a sustained rise in the domestic saving rate is a prerequisite for economic take-off (as happened in all of Asia in the twentieth century), the observed fall in India in the saving rate of such a magnitude portends ill for India's economic progress.

As mentioned earlier, a sharp rise in exports during the 2000s was the principal contributor to the incremental output growth. The global financial crisis followed by the Great Recession witnessed a reversal. India, too, has seen its exports, as a percentage of GDP, fall from 25 per cent in 2012–13, to about 19 per cent in 2017–18 (Figure 16.4). However, the reduction in oil prices contracted the import bill; hence the ratio of net exports to GDP has not changed much.

In 2015, the flagship initiative Make in India was launched, whose outcome shows the following dismal picture:

- A stagnation is evident, if not a slight decline, in the manufacturing sector's share in GDP (Figure 16.5).

Figure 16.4: Trade Ratios, 2011–12 to 2017–18

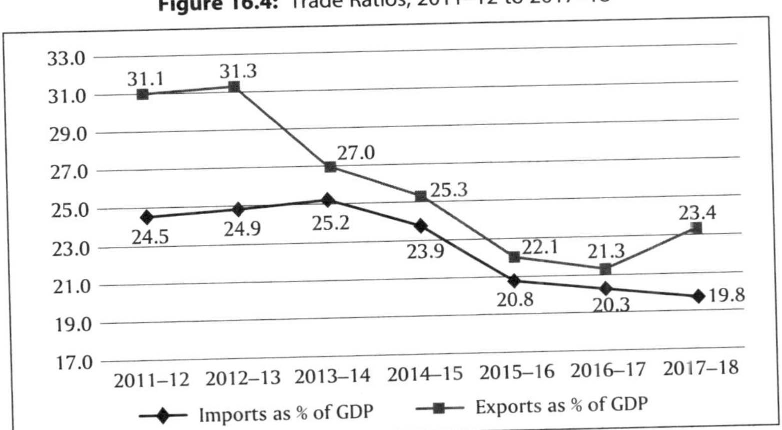

Source: RBI's Handbook of Statistics on Indian Economy.

Figure 16.5: Share of Manufacturing and Industry in GDP, 2013 and 2018

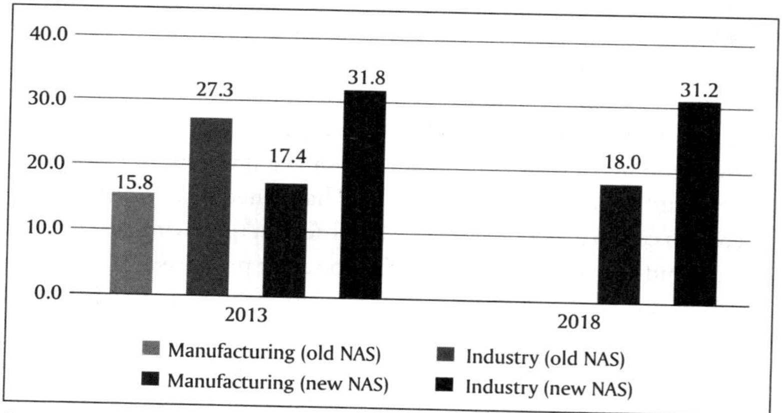

Source: National Accounts Statistics, various issues.

- The industrial sector lost 3.5 million manufacturing sector jobs between 2011–12 and 2017–18, according to the NSSO employment surveys (Mehrotra and Parida 2019).
- A secular decline is discernible in (i) industrial capacity utilisation since 2011, and (ii) a rise in the value of stalled investment projects, especially in the private sector since July 2015 (Figures 16.6 and 16.7).

Though a lot more disaggregated evidence can be adduced, suffice to say that the industrial sector has performed poorly since 2011–12 (Nagaraj 2019). Hence, contrary to the official view of a temporary setback, there has been a deep industrial slowdown spanning almost the entire decade of the 2010s.

An Aggregative Economic Account: Solving the Jigsaw Puzzle

The evidence of the weak domestic output growth naturally gets reflected in poor labour market outcomes. Table 16.1 describes some stark changes between 2011–12 and 2017–18—unprecedented since 1972–73—when the sample surveys began (Kannan and Ravindran 2019; Mehrotra and Parida 2019).

Figure 16.6: RBI Capacity Utilisation Index, 2008–09 to 2019–20

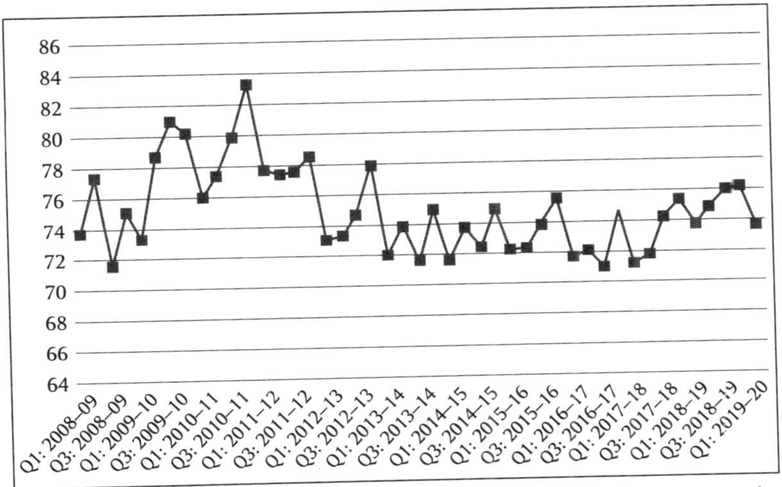

Source: RBI Survey of Industrial Capacity Utilisation, available at https://www.rbi.org.in/Scripts/QuarterlyPublications.aspx?head=Quarterly%20Order%20Books,%20Inventories%20and%20Capacity%20Utilisation%20Survey (accessed 8 December 2020).

Figure 16.7: Value of Stalled Projects as a Percentage of Total Projects under Implementation, 2012–19

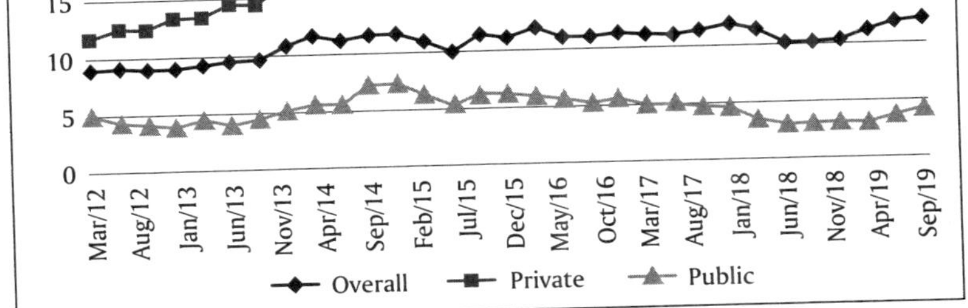

Source: CMIE data.

1. Job losses were in the range of 6.2–15.5 million, depending upon the population estimates used.[8] Rural India lost 21 million jobs, while urban India gained nearly 15 million. The most affected population and social groups were women, youth, Muslims and members of the OBCs. Job gains were primarily for men, members of the SCs, STs and the 'other' castes.[9]
2. Open unemployment—defined as those who did not find a job during the previous week as a proportion of workforce—rose from 3 to 8.8 per cent.
3. The labour force participation rate—that is, those working or looking for work as a proportion of the population in the age group 15–59 years—declined from 39.5 to 36.9 per cent. It means that discouraged workers have dropped out of the labour market due to a lack of employment opportunities (after accounting for those undergoing education).

Table 16.1: Total Employment, Labour Force, Unemployment Rates, 2004–05 to 2017–18

	2004–05	*2011–12*	*2017–18*
Total employment (million)	459.4	474.2	465.1
Labour force (million)	470.2	484.8	495.1
Workforce participation rate (%)	42.0	38.6	34.7
Labour force participation rate (%)	43.0	39.5	36.9
Unemployment rate as per usual status (%)	2.3	2.2	3.1
Unemployment rate as per weekly status (%)	3.4	3.0	8.8

Note: Labour force participation rate is the pecentage of working-age people who work or want work. The unemployment rate is the percentge of those in the labour force who want work but do not have it. Worker population ratio is defined as the proportion of working-age people who have work. Usual principal status is defined as having work for at least for six months during the year; subsidiary status employment refers to a person's employment status between one and six months of the year; weekly status refers to a person's employment status during the week prior to the survey.

Source: Mehrotra and Parida (2019).

More granular evidence can be added. But it would be right to categorise the current growth episode as one of 'job-loss growth' [to use Kannan and Ravindran's (2019) phrase], compared to the phenomenon of 'jobless growth' earlier, with most of the burden faced by socially and economically vulnerable groups. A rising unemployment rate and the decline in labour force participation rates, expectedly, have adversely affected wage growth in the rural economy.

Agricultural labourers—defined as those earning the majority of their income through wage work—represent the bottom of rural society. According to the 2011 Census, India has 107 million agriculture labourers constituting 26.5 per cent of the country's workers, and close to half of the agricultural workforce. Between December 2014 and December 2018 (Table 16.2), the real average wages of agriculture and rural workers grew at a rate of 0.5 per cent per year compared to a rise of 6.7 per cent per year during the previous five years from 2009 to 2013 (Damodaran 2019).

Table 16.2: Agriculture and Rural Wages (Year-on-year Wage Growth in %), 2014–18

Month and Year	*Rural Wages*	*Agriculture Wages*	*Skilled Worker Wages*	*Rural CPI Inflation (%)*
December 2014	4.58	5.13	6.16	4.16
December 2015	4.68	4.67	4.38	6.32
December 2016	6.07	6.77	5.50	3.83
December 2017	4.21	4.50	3.91	5.27
December 2018	3.84	4.64	4.06	1.50

Note: All figures for male workers. Rural: simple average for 25 occupations; agriculture: average for ploughing, sowing, harvesting, picking, horticulture, animal husbandary, general farm labour and plant protection; skilled worker: average for carpenter, blacksmith, mason, plumber, electrician and LMV/tractor driver.

Source: Damodaran (2019).

If domestic output growth has decelerated, millions have lost jobs and rural wages have practically stagnated, it is reasonable to expect a decline in personal consumption (unless, of course, workers can borrow to maintain their current level of living, an unlikely possibility). This is precisely what the leaked (but officially scrapped) NSO report finds. For all of India, between 2011–12 and 2017–18, the per capita personal consumption expenditure in real terms declined by

3.7 per cent. The decline was 8 per cent in rural India, but there was a 2 percentage point rise in urban India during those years.

Many have questioned the veracity of this decline in per capita consumption, arguing that the estimate does not match with a steep rise in consumption reported in the National Accounts (Felman et al. 2019; Rangarajan and Mahendra Dev 2019). These suspicions of the quality of CES data may not be valid for the following reasons:

1. There is no change in the methodology used between the two rounds of CES data (that is, 2011–12 and 2017–18); hence, the estimates based on the sample surveys are perfectly comparable.
2. For well-known reasons, many countries find a similar divergence between consumption survey estimates and the national accounts–based estimates; India is no exception (as the critics admit it).
3. In the Indian discourse on the national accounts, however, the non-comparability of CES and NAS consumer expenditure estimates is a well-researched issue, and conceptual and empirical differences between the two series are well understood but found not resolvable. We can do no better than to quote B. S. Minhas's highly regarded contribution on this question, which still holds, commended by Deaton and Kozel (2005):

> The independent data set (NAS), it would seem fair to conclude, is far short of the touchstone of quality expected of an independent validator dataset. A number of its components are based on such weak evidence and unverified assumptions as to seriously diminish its value in a cross-validation exercise, On the other hand, the NSS estimates of expenditure on such minor vices such as tobacco and intoxicants, and consumer durables and modern consumer services are of doubtful reliability. Nevertheless, despite these difficulties, which have to be overcome in both data sets, an overwhelming proportion of household consumer expenditure data of the NSS and independent private consumption estimates of the NAS do get cross-validation. (Minhas 1988, reproduced from Deaton and Kozel 2005: 91)

The observed decline in per capita personal consumption, expectedly, translated into a rise in absolute poverty. Figure 16.8 shows the

Figure 16.8: Poverty Rates in India (% of Population), 1993–94 to 2017–18

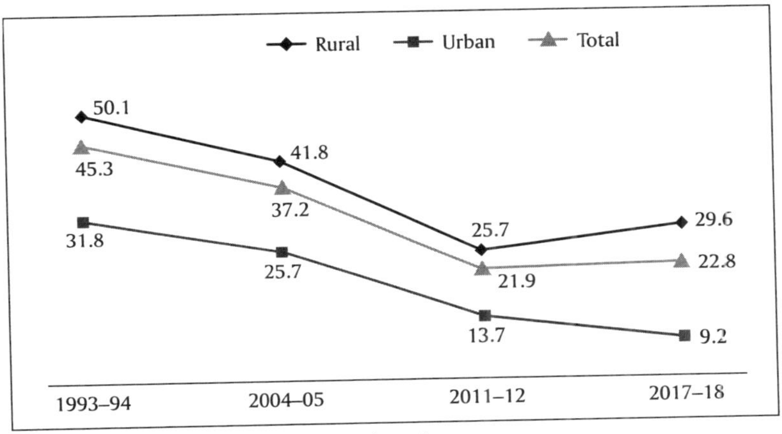

Source: Bhattacharya and Devulapalli (2019).

poverty trends since 1993–94 for all-India, separately for rural and urban areas. Evidently, for the first time in a quarter of a century, absolute poverty went up by nearly 1 percentage point, from 21.9 per cent in 2011–12 to 22.8 per cent in 2017–18. Though the rise in poverty rate is modest, shockingly, this represents a reversal of a long-term declining trend, translating into 30 million people falling back into the ranks of the poor in six years in the 2010s.[10] The poverty rate went up by 4 percentage points in rural India and declined by 5 percentage points in urban India. The states that have borne the brunt of the increase are mostly the poorer states like Bihar, Jharkhand, and Odisha, but (surprisingly) Maharashtra as well. The states showing a decline in poverty rates are the southern states and Gujarat (all figures from Bhattacharya and Devulapalli 2019).

A simple headcount ratio of poverty, as many an expert would argue, is an inadequate measure of social welfare. However, reporting the changes in various (theoretically sound) measures of poverty, Subramanian (2019), in his findings presented in Table 4 of his article, found an unambiguous deterioration in economic wellbeing in rural India (accounting for close to 70 per cent of India's population as per the 2011 Census).

So what is the picture that emerges by piecing together the available aggregate evidence? Sadly, the picture that emerges is sharp and scary: an unmistakeable story of an economy in distress. The suffering is not just about a declining growth rate in output compared to the previous decade. The lower output growth has translated into job losses, withdrawal of workers from the labour force (due to a lack of employment opportunities), a sharp rise in the open unemployment rate, and a stagnation in real wages in rural India. Weak output growth and poor labour market performance show up in a fall in per capita personal consumption and a rise in absolute poverty, and loss of social welfare (by all standard indicators). Hence, unambigiously, the 2010s have been a decade of an unheard of economic distress and a reversal of past outcomes.

Analysing the Slowdown and Policy Suggestions

What could possibly explain such a swift and sharp change in India's economic fortunes? There have been no major political threats or natural calamities disrupting normal commercial activities. The country has witnessed orderly changes in governments following national and regional elections. Globalisation is on the retreat closing many opportunities, but as India is a domestic-oriented economy the adverse fallout is relatively modest. The fall in international oil prices has kept the external balance under check.

Hence, the reasons for the economic regression during the 2010s are entirely domestic and policy-induced. That demonetisation in 2016 was a disaster is now widely acknowledged. As GST unravels, its glitches are coming to light with rising revenue shortfalls.

From a macroeconomic point of view, the slowdown in output growth is from the demand side. As Table 16.3 shows, between 2011–12 and 2017–18, the only item of aggregate demand which has fallen is gross capital formation. It fell from 36.2 to 32.5 per cent as a proportion of GDP (according to the new National Accounts series). If we measure the change from the peak of the boom in 2007–08, when it was 38 per cent of GDP, then the fall until 2016–17 was close to 7 percentage points. The fall is principally on account of the decline in the private corporate sector. But this fact is obsured by

Table 16.3: India's GDP by Items of Final Demand (%), 2011–12 to 2017–18

Year	*PFCE*	*GFCE*	*GCF*	*Net Exports*	*Total*
2011–12	56.2	11.1	36.7	–6.5	97.4
2012–13	56.2	10.6	36.3	–6.4	96.7
2013–14	56.7	10.0	33.9	–1.8	98.8
2014–15	56.2	10.0	33.7	–1.5	98.4
2015–16	56.1	10.0	32.8	–1.2	97.7
2016–17	56.1	9.7	31.8	–1.1	96.6
2017–18	56.3	10.5	32.5	–3.6	95.7

Note: The residual is on account of valuables and statistical discrepancies. PFCE: private final consumption expenditure; GFCE: government final consumption expenditure; GCF: gross capital formation. All figures are at current prices.

Source: National Accounts Statistics, 2019.

the overestimation of the sector's size and growth in the new GDP series—on account of the use of contested methodologies and the databases of questionable quality.

Admittedly, a collapse of investments when an economic boom unravels is understandable. But its secular decline for close to a decade is a sure sign of policy failure. How can this be explained? Policymakers defended the official growth record by claiming that India is a consumption-led success story and therefore the decline in investment will not matter for output growth. Government sources sought to dismiss the results of official nation-wide economic statistics (such as the Labour Bureau's employment surveys, NSSO/NSO surveys; see Jha 2019), claiming that they fail to capture the changing economic reality of growth in the newer platforms and the digital economy (such as Ola and Flipkart). One wonders how the narrative of a consumption-led growth success would square with the observed decline in per capita personal consumption in 2017–18, based on comparable NSSO consumer expenditure surveys.

Rhetoric aside, the narrative of a consumption-led success betrays a lack of an understanding of a simple stylised fact of economics: no country has secured sustained economic growth and acquired industrial maturity without stepping up the domestic investment rate to around 40 per cent of GDP for a few decades (with the domestic saving rate at 2–4 percentage points less than the investment rate). China is an extreme example of this with an investment to GDP ratio that has been sustained at over 50 per cent for three decades now, and private consumption has correspondingly reduced to one-third of GDP.

Realistically speaking, reviving private corporate investment was constrained by an unserviceable debt burden and, correspondingly, by rising bank NPAs as a proportion of total bank advances. However, the NPAs admittedly resulted mainly from an unexpected reversal of the economic boom (and changed economic conditions such as rising oil prices and high domestic inflation), and not on account of firm- or bank-specific reasons. In such a situation, a suitable policy package for specific sectors and industries would help reverse sagging fortunes.

Instead, policymakers viewed NPAs as an outcome of (i) the banking sector's inefficiency in loan screening and lending practices and (ii) deep-rooted crony capitalism. Such an understanding of economic reality echoed the anti-corruption agenda of the government. Following such a diagnosis, the RBI sought to rout out inefficiency in banks by making the rules for NPA recognition stricter, resulting in a sharp rise in the NPAs as a ratio of gross advances, from 4.3 per cent in 2014–15 to 11.2 per cent in 2017–18, as per RBI data (Figure 16.9).

On NPA Growth and Crony Capitalism

In the 2000s, when the economy was accelerating with rising investment and software exports, bank credit to the private corporate sector was also, naturally, galloping. Foreign capital was flowing in at an unheard of rate to supplement domestic saving, and foreign capital was also getting into infrastructure in PPP projects. These massive investments assumed the continuation of rapid output growth under benign macroeconomic conditions, following the well-known phenomenon of 'herd behaviour', common in investment and financial decisions. Policymakers, during the boom, urged banks to support the investment boom proactively.

The global financial crisis shattered expectations, though the investment cycle got prolonged until 2011–12 with the comfortable

Figure 16.9: Bank NPAs as a Percentage of Gross Advances, 2006–07 to 2017–18

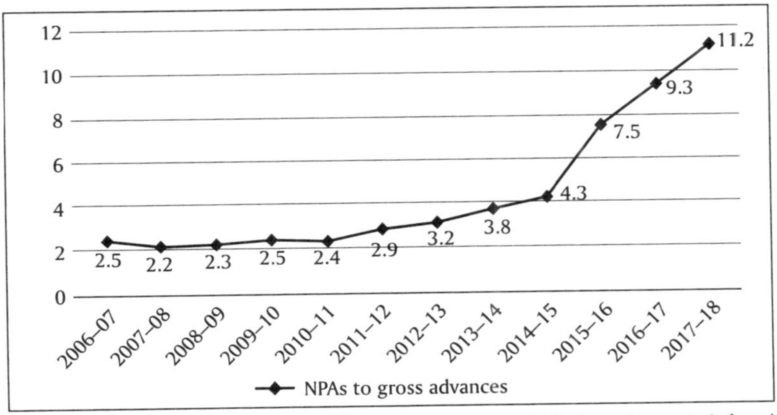

Source: RBI Annual Report 2018–19, available at https://rbidocs.rbi.org.in/rdocs/annualreport/pdfs/0annualreport2018193cb8cb2d3dee4efa8d6f0f6bd624cede.pdf (accessed 8 December 2020).

monetary and fiscal conditions maintained by the G-20 countries. As global growth stagnated and oil prices shot up, India's growth was hurt. Many projects in industry and infrastructure—accounting for the majority of investments—failed to generate adequate revenues to service their debt, thus increasing bank NPAs. And this, in turn, impaired the ability of banks to make new loans, setting in a mutually reinforcing downward spiral.

Admittedly, the banks lent generously to a few large politically connected business houses. Such (alleged) financial malpractices and malfeasance by public officials need to be dealt with strictly, as per the law. However, it would perhaps be erroneous to tar the entire debt-led investment boom with the same brush.

Hence, there can be two ways of looking at the problem of bank NPAs.

1. Diagnosing them as an outcome of a widely prevalent crony capitalism, the way to resolve the problem is by strict enforcement of the regulations and strengthening bank norms for NPAs. Such a drive would compel defaulting borrowers to pay up or face liquidation, as per the decisions of the bankruptcy courts.

2. Notwithstanding the deep-seated cronyism endemic to India's political economy, realistically speaking, a significant part of the NPAs was the result of slower output growth and changed macroeconomic conditions. Hence, they were beyond the control of enterprises. If such a view has merit, the recovery of growth would have melted away the NPAs with sales growth and expansion of domestic output. The solution to the problem of NPAs then would be to kickstart growth with (autonomous) public investment, at least until private investment recovers its lost momentum.

The second argument does in no way mean closing one's eyes to systemic corruption, cronyism, and banks' (alleged) inefficient screening and lending practices. These are long-term issues requiring long-term solutions, such as improving banking governance and supervision. What was needed when the investment boom ended was a boost from public investment to ensure that infrastructure spending was sustained at a high level, as China did (which bore far bigger brunt) to withstand the shocks of the global financial crisis (Nagaraj 2020a).

The financial problems got accentuated with the NDA government, with its zeal to root out corruption. It has apparently created 'tax terrorism'—a term reportedly coined by the entrepreneur Mohandas Pai—after V. G. Siddhartha, the promoter of Café Coffee Day, died by suicide in mid-2019 (Tejaswi 2019). Thus, an atmosphere of fear seems to have taken a toll on investment decisions—as suggested by Rahul Bajaj, an industrialist, in an event where senior ministers were present, and by Manmohan Singh (2019), the former prime minister, in an op-ed in the *The Hindu*.

The Insolvency and Bankruptcy Code (IBC) was agreed upon, but given the dysfunctional legal institutions and inordinate time the resolution proceedings take, it has had a minimal impact on resolving the bank debt problem—at least as yet.

Policy Suggestions

Reviving investment growth should now get priority. The private sector is not in a position to make new capital investment due to a lack of aggregate demand despite declining interest rates. High levels of debt in the private corporate sector, the banking crisis on account of NPAs and the collapse of large shadow banks [for example, of the Infrastructure Leasing and Financial Services (ILFS) and the HDIL-Punjab and Maharashtra Cooperative Bank crisis] have squeezed fresh lending for capital investment. Food price inflation is currently high, which I guess, is a seasonal and temporary problem apparently caused by weather factors.

Public investment can be expected to crowd-in private investment to boost the overall level of domestic demand, and hence revive output growth. Public expenditure can be on large infrastructure projects (highways and railways) and rural road connectivity. Even after 70 years of Independence, it is an appalling fact that a motorable road does not connect over 20 per cent of 6 lakh villages. The evidence reported earlier shows that rural unemployment and poverty have gone up. Hence, there is a crying need for public assistance. What better policy to address agrarian distress than a massive push to the National Rural Employment Guarantee Scheme (NREGS)?

These suggestions will face resistance as it goes against deeply ingrained fiscal conservatism. It is worth remembering that the obsession with controlling the fiscal deficit during 2010–15 in developed countries has left deep scars on their economies and politics, as Paul Krugman (2019) recently lamented. Such an orthodoxy surely has a place in times of inflation and external imbalances. But, for now, at a time of low real interest rates, an aggregate demand constraint and the private sector's inability to make new investments, public infrastructure investment can have a sizeable multiplier effect on output and employment growth. A temporary suspension of the fiscal deficit target and devising unorthodox means to turn around the economy are possible (subject to keeping inflation modest and stable). A rise in public debt in domestic currency, held by resident Indians, and used for productive purposes, is a sensible policy in such times, as many economists would endorse.

A few years ago, in the new context of weak growth in the US, despite interest rates being close to zero, Nobel Laureate Robert Solow (2013) said:

> ... *in bad times like now, Treasury bonds are not squeezing finance for investment out of the market.* On the contrary, debt-financed

> government spending adds to the demand for privately produced goods and services, and the bonds provide a home for excess savings. When employment returns to normal, we can return to debt reduction. (Ibid., emphasis as in the original.)

Conclusions

The current slowdown in India's economic growth is now widely acknowledged. It is not a mere cyclical (or short-term) decline, as the government would like us to believe. The economy has been underperforming for quite a while after the boom of the 2000s went bust. Regrettably, the current GDP series, like a faulty speedometer, has been overstating output growth. It probably helped policymakers propagate a false narrative of India as a consumption-led success story, ignoring warning signals of a decade-long decline in the economy's saving and investment rates (among other evidence). Such a reversal in the investment rate for so long has never happened since Independence.

Hence, our first task was to piece together the recent aggregate data to present a clear and credible account of the economy's performance. The picture that emerges is not pretty: it is one of unprecedented economic distress. The bold facts of distress are as follows: between 2011–12 and 2017–18, the country has witnessed job losses between 6.2 and 15.5 million, a rise in unemployment rate from 3.3 to 8.8 per cent of the workforce, a fall in labour force participation rates, stagnation in rural wages, a fall in per capita consumption, and an increase in absolute poverty by 30 million people. Never since the 1970s—if not earlier—for which definitive data is available, has the economy witnessed such a disastrous reversal of economic performance.

Overstated official GDP growth rates—on account of a faulty methodology and data of questionable quality being used in estimating GDP—seem to have obscured the reality and are likely to have misled policymakers. The gravity of the situation appears more realistically captured in GDP validation exercises, which knock-off 1.5 to 2.5 percentage points from the official growth estimates. The two economic shocks, namely the demonetisation of high valued currency in 2016 and the dodgy GST in 2017, have precipitated matters, as evident from the sharp fall in GDP growth rates during the last six quarters, from 8.1 per cent in January–March 2018 to 4.5 per cent in April–June 2019.

To analyse the reasons for the slowdown, one needs to start with the boom of the 2000s when there was a steep rise in domestic saving and investment rates, rising bank credit growth and a flood of foreign capital inflows (accruing mostly to the private corporate sector). As the boom went bust in the early 2010s, the un-fructified investments mounted, and new capital investment fell. Corporate bad debts turned into bank NPAs. It is reasonable to believe that a quick economic revival with public support could have melted way the NPAs earlier during the 2010s. But policymakers stuck to fiscal orthodoxy, inflation targeting and structural reforms to reduced policy-induced rigidities.

Policymakers have devoted their attention to cleaning up the banking sector as part of the anti-corruption drive and have sought to strike at the roots crony capitalism with a new corporate bankruptcy procedure that has not helped much—at least as yet—given the legal hurdles. A few large defaulters and high-profile corporate frauds made policymakers and the RBI view the NPAs as mostly representing inefficiencies and poor lending practices, and deep-seated crony capitalism. Corporate frauds need to be dealt with as such. But the poor lending practices of banks and the bank–corporate nexus are long-term issues of corporate governance and political economy, respectively, requiring sustained reforms in corporate and institutional governannce.

The way out of the slowdown now, in our view, is to step up public infrastructure investment as the real interest rate is low, and the private sector demand for credit is weak. Public investment in such a situation would help crowd-in (or, bring in) complementary private investment to create demand for the private sector to turn the economy around. Similarly, a substantial boost to the NREGS and bank credit in the rural economy would help mitigate agrarian distress, create jobs and add to rural public works.

These policy measures warrant setting aside fiscal orthodoxy for a while. For now, the infrastructure deficit and unemployment crisis are perhaps far more serious concerns than budgetary prudence. A rise in domestic public debt held domestically to create productive assets (within tolerable inflation rates) is sensible economic policy at a time of acute economic hardship.

Postscript

The Pandemic

What has changed during the last six months, after the Covid-19 pandemic and the economic lockdown? Uncertainties about the nation's health and economic conditions have bogged down everyone, especially the poor and the unemployed.

The lockdown imposed at the end of March, with just four hours' notice, considered the world's most severe, was indeed an economic shock. The government hoped to catch the virus by its neck to minimise its spread. But the sudden lockdown sharply dislocated production and transportation, retrenched output and employment, most acutely in the non-farm informal sector. Even after nearly six months, without work and shelter, the urban poor continue to suffer.

As there is an apprehension of a second wave of the pandemic emerging, we are indeed in it for a long haul. There are no quick fixes in sight, warranting more durable solutions. The pandemic has exposed India's long-term neglect of public health. Total government expenditure on health as a proportion of GDP, at about 1.3 per cent, is perhaps one of the lowest among countries with comparable development levels.

The health pandemic also revealed India's limited manufacturing capacities of critical items, significantly its rising dependence on Chinese imports for bulk drugs. The prime minister's call for 'Atmanirbhar Bharat' (self-reliant India) during the lockdown, reiterated in the 2020 Independence Day address, seems a tacit admission of the growing external economic threat.

Economic Effects of the Pandemic

India's quarterly GDP estimates for April–June 2020 showed a contraction of 24 per cent over the same quarter last year. It is the worst among G-20 countries, as per the IMF Chief Economist Gita Gopinath's tweeted data. The forecast for the full year 2020–21 suggests a decline in output level (or, a negative growth rate compared to the previous year), between 7 per cent by HSBC and 14.8 by Goldman Sachs.

To mitigate the economic crisis, in May, the government announced its most substantial relief and revival package, known as the Atmanirbhar Bharat, amounting to Rs 20 lakh crore, or about 10 per cent of GDP. However, the package mostly consisted of liquidity support and credit guarantees (conditional upon meeting reform criteria). Additional budgetary expenditure—as widely demanded—that would add to current spending is just about 1 percentage point of GDP.

What To Do Now?

Our suggestions have three parts:

- minimise the adverse health outcomes, restore jobs and livelihoods;
- double public health expenditure in three years on a mission mode; and
- revive fixed investment growth in industry and infrastructure.

As the health pandemic is here for a while (as experts indicate), the government needs to prepare a medium-term strategy to double public health expenditure to 2.6 per cent of GDP by 2024–25. India perhaps needs a public health revolution of the kind the advanced countries underwent during the late nineteenth and early twentieth centuries to control infectious diseases, as Monica Das Gupta (2005) showed. Such a strategic plan would call for investment in urban drainage, sanitation and drinking water. Since building such physical facilities are labour-intensive using local resources, they would boost employment of unskilled labour. Jean Drèze's (2020) idea of a decentralised urban employment and training (DUET) scheme could be operationalised for building public health infrastructure using an urban employment guarantee programme. The government could aggressively tap into the special lending windows now available with multilateral funding agencies, to cope with the pandemic.

They could provide low-cost budgetary resources, and also offer technical assistance for augmenting public health capabilities, which are now very poor at the state and local level.

Beyond restoration and rehabilitation, economic growth needs to revive urgently. During the last decade (that is, the 2010s), as discussed earlier, the most significant contributor to the economic slowdown was the fixed investment rate, as a proportion of GDP. India's investment rate, as a proportion of GDP, has declined by close to 10 percentage points from its peak of 38–39 per cent attained in 2008–09—an unprecedented collapse.

Export growth also fell, but net exports, as a proportion of GDP, declined marginally as the oil import bill came down precipitously. With global economic contraction and the cracks in the multilateral trading agreement, India cannot be hopeful about export revival anytime soon. The large domestic market is an advantage. *Atmanirbharta* (self-reliance) also calls for a rising share of local value addition, by firms owned and controlled by Indian nationals.

Growth should avoid—learning from the recent experience—predation of the rural and informal economy (by indiscriminate deregulation of mining and environmental laws, as seems likely from the recent regulatory reforms). Nor should it favour crony capitalists or Bollygarchs—to use Crabtree's picturesque phrase to allude to politically connected conglomerates. Moreover, India needs an ambitious investment plan if the government is still serious about the prime minister's aspirational target of a 5 trillion–dollar economy by 2024–25, announced last year.

The health pandemic, and the low-intensity border dispute with China since June 2020, is a rude reminder of how vulnerable India has become to imports (Dhar and Rao 2020). The Make in India initiative, therefore, needs a serious reimagination. It is worth recalling how Maruti in 1982 triggered the modernisation of India's automotive industry, or, how the Oil and Natural Gas Corporation (ONGC) helped overcome import dependence on oil by quickly developing the Bombay High offshore oilfield after the second Oil Shock in 1979—spurring an industrial revival in the 1980s.

Recent case studies of small firm clusters in manufacturing across the country have brought to light how the infrastructure and the state support at the ground level appeared frozen in times of the post-reform era, despite changes in definitions and terminology. Such clusters—mostly producing labour-intensive goods—seem to cry out for public support. There are compelling examples of how some clusters had stood up to the global competition when reasonable government assistance came forward (Nagaraj 2021, forthcoming).

If Make in India, and Atmanirbhar Bharat, are about overcoming technological stagnation, India has to step up research and development (R&D) expenditure. Here is a telling comparison with China. Figure 16.10 shows R&D expenditure as a proportion of GDP in India and China during 1996–2018, using comparable estimates drawn from the World Bank's World Development Indicators. Until 1999, the expenditure ratios in the two countries were identical, at 0.8 per cent of GDP. Over the next 20 years, for China, the proportion nearly trebled to 2.2 per cent of GDP. For India, the ratio declined to 0.6 per cent by 2018. The divergence is incredibly sharp after the 2008 global financial crisis. Considering that China's per capita income has grown at 3–5 times faster over this period, the gap in the absolute size of resources invested in scientific research is enormous.

Figure 16.10: R&D Expenditure as a Percentage of GDP, India and China, 1996–2018

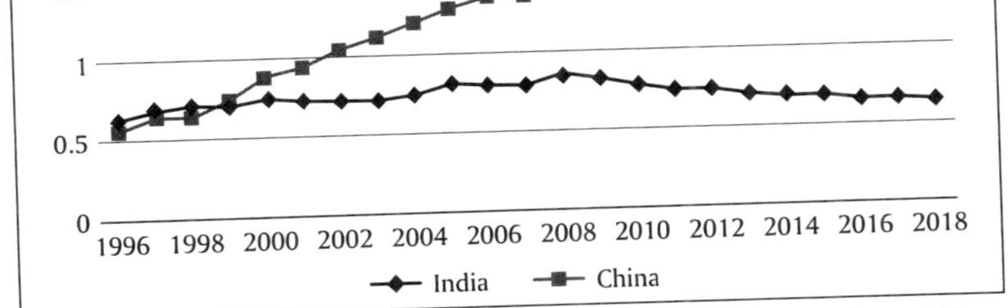

Source: World Bank's World Development Indicators, available at https://data.worldbank.org/indicator/gb.xpd.rsdv.gd.zs (accessed 8 December 2020).

To forge the above ideas into a credible and consistent strategy, India needs an industrial policy, with suitable instruments for execution. To finance it, reinvent development banks to provide long-term credit, that is, beyond the five-year term loans the commercial banks offer. No Asian economy has got industrialised—from Japan to China—without a state-led industrialisation strategy and development banks to support the plan, history shows. China, despite its rhetoric of globalisation and market reforms since Deng Xiaoping opened up the economy in 1978, never took its eyes off industrial policy—and the development banks underpinning the national goals.

Financing the growth plan

The preceding suggestions, indeed, appear like a wishlist. Many may endorse these ideas. The challenge though is to find real, that is, non-inflationary resources to finance the investments. Here are a few ideas, though detailed budgetary arithmetic is beyond the scope of this chapter.

The private corporate sector—the engine of the Dream Run during the 2000s—is not up to the task now, with mounting debt and declining profitability. The banking sector that fuelled the growth with copious credit is now neck deep in NPAs. With a fall in forecasted GDP (reported earlier), borrowers' revenue would shrink, reducing their ability to service the loans, thus raising bank NPAs. The RBI Financial Stability Report, July 2020, admitted it as much. To quote it, 'Macro stress tests for credit risk indicate that the GNPA [gross non-performing asset] ratio of all SCBs [scheduled commercial banks] may increase from 8.5 per cent in March 2020 to 12.5 per cent by March 2021 under the baseline scenario; the ratio may escalate to 14.7 per cent under a very severely stressed scenario.'

To expect foreign capital to fill in the investment gap is wishful thinking. To illustrate, at the peak of the boom of 2003–08, when the economy was ticking at close to 9 per cent annually, FDI inflow at best was 2–2.5 per cent of GDP. In China, FDI inflow never exceeded 5 per cent of GDP, most of which was anyway domestic capital round-tripped via Hong Kong, for securing better property rights.

History shows that economies that have successfully industrialised—without exception—have relied mostly on domestic savings. Foreign capital could be a catalyst bringing in technology, promoting 'learning by doing', and securing access to developed markets via global buying agents or supply chains. For attracting greenfield FDI, the host country needs to provide the complementary social and physical infrastructure, which, as known, is woefully lacking. Hence, India has to invest massively in infrastructure, of the kind noted above.

More seriously, history also demonstrates, no modern nation can hope to become atmanirbhar by relying mainly on foreign capital and technology, whose risk-adjusted costs tend to be high.

That leaves us with public investment and strategically significant public sector enterprises. Mobilising public expenditure in recessionary times, as a counter-cyclical policy, is a well-accepted principle in economics since Keynes. With little demand for credit forthcoming from the private sector, declining interest rates close to zero in real terms (known as the 'zero lower bound'), national development banks can be instruments for mobilising capital from the market. Such resources can be productively used in projects with a high rate of return, such as social and economic infrastructure. Such investments are unlikely 'crowding-out' private investment, and instead could bring in complementary private investment (Nagaraj 2017)—as recent experience indicates.

It is perhaps worth recollecting the NDA government's experience in 1999–2000. Faced with decelerating GDP and industrial production after the Asian Financial Crisis in 1997, the Atal Bihari Vajpayee government launched two major investment projects. One, the Golden Quadrilateral road reconstruction programme to connect the metro cities with high-quality roads, and two, the Pradhan Mantri Gram Sadak Yojana to construct all-weather roads to connect villages and hamlets with a population of 500 people or more. These public investments ushered in the automobile revolution, boosting output growth (Nagaraj 2013). Such massive labour-intensive projects offered alternative employment opportunities for rural workers, contributing to a rise in real rural wages—a first in post-Independence India.

However, in mainstream economic theory and popular media, such evidence goes against the tenets of fiscal virtue. Financial markets, it is argued, are expected to 'punish' such fiscal indulgence, triggering capital flight, potentially precipitating economic crises. The underlying reasoning is as follows: rising public expenditure could lead to breaching the fiscal deficit, increasing the public debt to GDP ratio. The rising fiscal deficit could stoke inflation fears, and widen the balance of payment deficit, potentially causing macroeconomic instability, downgrading of the credit rating, and raising the cost of external borrowing.

The preceding line of reasoning is possible when aggregate demand seriously overshoots aggregate supply, calling for stabilisation policies. The current situation is, however, different: it is one of inadequate aggregate demand as the economy is operating below the full-employment output. As the private sector is unable to use the additional credit at any interest rate due to the elevated debt burden, rising public spending is unlikely to pre-empt private investment. Government expenditure, on the contrary, could stimulate demand from the private sector and thus augment output growth. Further, if such public investments help relieve critical supply constraints—such as roads or ports or electricity—the chances of public expenditure leading to inflation and external imbalance are, in principle, remote. Hence, what matters is not the expansion of public spending per se, but its productive use.

Beyond borrowing from the bond market, the government could also borrow directly from RBI, which is known as debt monetisation, or deficit financing, or monetary financing. Operationally, it was earlier known as RBI's 'ways and means' advance to the central government. As deficit financing was reportedly the source of fiscal profligacy and inflation, in 1997 the practice ended, as per a formal agreement between the government and RBI.

However, given the current unprecedented situation of output contraction, there is a case for reviving the practice, if temporarily, to augment the government's resources. Extraordinary times call for such unconventional measures—just as the US Fed devised QE after the 2008 financial crisis. QE provided cash to Wall Street conglomerates by buying up government securities, to reduce interest rates to induce the banks to lend to the private sector. Likewise, now, one may argue, why not extend the same principle to put money in the hands of the government to boost public spending to save jobs and growth, or provide universal basic income by putting money directly in peoples' hands via employment-generating programmes (Coppola 2019).

Thus, there is now a case for monetisation of public debt, subject to inflation. If the preceding arguments are accepted in principle, preparing an action plan could follow, fleshing out many policy suggestions made in this chapter.

Notes

1. See Bhattacharya and Kwatra (2020) for an up-to-date summary of the GDP estimation debate.
2. For a close-up view of what the boom and bust was like and what crony capitalism meant, see the ground-level account of the iron ore mining town of Bellary in Karnataka in Srinivasaraju (2019).
3. Financial brokerage reports, 'House of Debt' by Credit Suisse (2012), and 'Strategy and Economy' by Ambit Capital (2013), offer detailed financial accounts of the debt held by large business houses, and politically connected companies, respectively.
4. The following example illustrates how demonetisation was a complete mockery. V. K. Sasikala (a close associate of the late J. Jayalalitha, former Tamil Nadu Chief Minister), jailed for alleged financial wrongdoing, has reportedly purchased real estate and industrial assets worth Rs 1,600 crore using the demonetised currency during the short window of time allowed to surrender the old currency for the new—as per an income tax filing with the Madras High Court (Imranullah S. 2019).
5. The current GDP revision has come under an intense scrutiny for the veracity of the estimates. For a non-technical introduction to the debate, see Nagaraj (2016); for a detailed stock-taking of the discussions as the debate progressed, see Nagaraj and Srinivasan (2017) and Nagaraj, Sapre and Sengupta (2019).
6. The Chief Economist of the IMF Gita Gopinath co-authored an academic research paper that confirmed an adverse effect of demonetisation on India's growth rate (see Chodorow-Reich et al. 2018).
7. The data shown in the graph is computed by splicing the estimates from older (2004–05 base year series) and the current National Accounts series, ignoring the underlying conceptual differences. The reported time-series data represents a fairly accurate approximation of the underlying trends.

8. There are three credible estimates of job losses by Himanshu (2019): 15.5 million; Mehrotra and Parida (2019): 9 million; and Kannan and Ravindran (2019): 6.2 million. They all use the comprehensive definition of employment, namely UPSS. However, as their population estimates vary, the corresponding job loss estimates are also different.
9. Amaresh Dubey and Lavesh Bhandari's reported study prepared for the Prime Minister's Economic Advisory Council arrives at an opposite estimate and conclusions. The reasons for the difference are as follows: (i) Dubey and Bhandari use the number of workers by their principal status only, leaving out the subsidiary status workers, and (ii) their population estimate is higher than in the other studies. The research paper does not seem to be yet available in the public domain, hence not commented upon here.
10. These estimates are based on the 2009 Tendulkar Committee report on poverty, which was officially accepted by the erstwhile Planning Commission, and for which comparable estimates are available since 1993–94.

References

'A Bad Boom: Fighting Corruption in India'. 2014. *The Economist*, 15 March. Available at https://www.economist.com/briefing/2014/03/15/a-bad-boom (accessed 8 December 2020).

Ambit Capital. 2013. 'Strategy and Economy: The One Report that Changed India', October. Available at https://www.scribd.com/document/451084445/Ambit-STRATEGY-ECONOMY-Theamatic-eRr-Group-The-one-report-that-changed-India (accessed 14 December 2020).

Bhaduri, Amit. 2008. 'Predatory Growth'. *Economic and Political Weekly* 43 (16), 19 April: 53–62.

Bhattacharya, Pramit and Sriharsha Devulapalli. 2019. 'Rural Poverty has Shot Up, NSO Data Shows'. *Livemint*, 3 December. Available at https://www.livemint.com/news/india/rural-poverty-has-shot-up-nso-data-shows-11575352445478.html (accessed 8 December 2020).

Bhattacharya, Pramit and Nikita Kwatra. 2020. 'Getting the GDP Measurement Right'. *Livemint*, 27 July.

Chodorow-Reich, Gita Gopinath, Prachi Mishra and Abhinav Narayanan. 2018. 'Cash and the Economy: Evidence from India's Demonetization'. NBER Working Paper No. 25370, issued in December 2018, revised in May 2019. Available at https://www.nber.org/papers/w25370 (accessed 8 December 2020).

Coppola, Frances. 2019. *The Case for People's Quantitative Easing*. UK: Polity Press.

Crabtree, James. 2018. *The Billionaire Raj*. New Delhi: HarperCollins.

Credit Suisse. 2012. 'House of Debt', 2 August. Available at https://research-doc.credit-suisse.com/docView?language=ENG&source=emfromsendlink&format=PDF&document_id=991849241&extdocid=991849241_1_eng_pdf&serialid=6D4Mc02hhUT0waPccTsATBcZQ%2bzXynsFIAQCD3qJ44E%3d (accessed 8 December 2020).

Das Gupta, Monica. 2005. 'Public Health in India: An Overview'. Policy Research Working Paper No. 3787, World Bank, Washington, D. C.

Damodaran, H. 2019. 'Rural Distress Deepens: Wage Growth Dips, Non-farm Jobs Hit'. *Indian Express*, 11 March. Availble at https://indianexpress.com/article/india/rural-distress-deepens-wage-growth-dips-non-farm-jobs-hit-5619766/ (accessed 8 December 2020).

Deaton, Angus and Valerie Kozel (eds). 2005. *The Great Indian Poverty Debate*. New Delhi: Macmillan.

Dhar, Biswajit and K. S. Chalapati Rao. 2020. 'India's Economic Dependence on China'. *The India Forum*, 7 August.

Drèze, Jean. 2020. 'An Indian Duet for Urban Jobs'. *Bloomberg*, 10 September. Available at https://www.bloombergquint.com/opinion/an-indian-duet-for-urban-jobs (accessed 8 December 2020).

Felman, Josh Justin Sandefur, Arvind Subramanian and Julian Duggan. 2019. 'Could Consumption Really have Fallen?'. *Business Standard*, 12 December. Available at https://www.business-standard.com/article/opinion/could-consumption-really-have-fallen-119121001527_1.html (accessed 8 December 2020).

Himanshu. 2019. 'The Seriousness of the Problem of Unemployment in India'. *Livemint*, 1 August. Available at https://www.livemint.com/opinion/columns/opinion-the-seriousness-of-the-problem-of-unemployment-in-india-1564679281965.html (accessed 8 December 2020).

Imranullah S., Mohamed. 2019. 'How Sasikala Bought Properties with Demonetised Currency Notes Worth Over ₹1,600 Crore'. *The Hindu*, 22 December. Available at https://www.thehindu.com/news/national/tamil-nadu/how-sasikala-bought-properties-with-demonetised-currency-notes/article30369359.ece?homepage=true (accessed 8 December 2020).

International Monetary Fund. 2020. World Economic Outlook Update, June 2020. Washington, D. C.

Jha, Somesh. 2019. 'Unemployment Rate at Four-decade High of 6.1% in 2017–18: NSSO Survey'. *Business Standard*, 6 February. Available at https://www.business-standard.com/article/economy-policy/unemployment-rate-at-five-decade-high-of-6-1-in-2017-18-nsso-survey-119013100053_1.html (accessed 8 December 2020).

Kannan, K. P., and G. Ravindran. 2019. 'From Jobless to Job-loss Growth: Gainers and Losers during 2012–18'. *Economic and Political Weekly* 54 (44), 9 November: 38–44.

Kohli, Atul. 2006. 'Politics of Economic Growth in India, 1980–2005'. *Economic and Political Weekly* 41 (13–14), 1–8 April.

———. 2012. *Poverty Amid Plenty in the New India*. New York: Cambridge University Press.

Krugman, Paul. 2019. 'The Legacy of Destructive Austerity: The Deficit Obsession of 2010–2015 did Permanent Damage'. *New York Times*, 30 December. Available at https://www.nytimes.com/2019/12/30/opinion/deficits-economy.html (accessed 8 December 2020).

Mehrotra, Santosh and Jajati K. Parida. 2019. 'India's Employment Crisis: Rising Education Levels and Falling Non-agricultural Job Growth'. Centre for Sustainable Employment, October. Available at https://cse.azimpremjiuniversity.edu.in/wp-content/uploads/2019/10/Mehrotra_Parida_India_Employment_Crisis.pdf (accessed 8 December 2020).

Ministry of Finance. 2018. 'Report on Income Tax Reforms for Building a New India'. Task Force for drafting the new Income Tax Law, September. Available at https://www.thehindu.com/news/resources/article29215092.ece/Binary/IncomeTaxReformsReport.pdf (accessed 4 December 2020).

Ministry of Labour and Employment. 2017. *Report of the Task Force on Improving Employment Data*. New Delhi: Government of India.

Morris, Sebastian. 2019. 'More Evidence of Overestimation of India's GDP Growth Rates'. *The India Forum*, 6 September. Available at https://www.theindiaforum.in/article/more-evidence-overestimation-india-s-gdp-growth-rates (accessed 8 December 2020).

Nagaraj, R. 2013. 'The Dream Run, 2003–08: Understanding the Recent Boom and its Aftermath'. *Economic and Political Weekly* 48 (20), 18 May: 39–51.

———. 2016. 'GDP Conundrum: A Synoptic View'. *Ideas for India* (online publication), 20 November. Available at https://www.ideasforindia.in/topics/macroeconomics/gdp-conundrum-a-synoptic-view.html (accessed 8 December 2020).

———. 2017. 'Economic Reforms and Manufacturing Sector Growth: Need for Reconfiguring the Industrialisation Model'. *Economic and Political Weekly* 52 (2), 14 January: 61–68.

———. 2019. '*Make in India*: Why Didn't the Lion Roar?'. *The India Forum*, 16 May. Available at https://www.theindiaforum.in/article/make-india-why-didnt-lion-roar (accessed 8 December 2020).

———. 2020a. 'China's and India's Economic Performance after the Financial Crisis: A Comparative Analysis'. In *The Political Economy of the BRICS Countries, Volume 1, BRICS: The Quest for Inclusive Growth*, ed. Biju Paul Abraham and Partha Ray, 39–60. Singapore: World Scientific.

———. 2020b. 'Understanding India's Economic Slowdown: Need for Concerted Action'. *The India Forum*, 7 February.

——— (ed.). 2021, forthcoming. *Industrialisation for Employment and Growth in India: Lessons from Small Firm Clusters and Beyond*. Cambridge: Cambridge University Press.

Nagaraj, R., and T. N. Srinivasan. 2017. 'Measuring India's GDP Growth: Unpacking the Analytical and Data Issues behind the Controversy that has Refused to Go Away'. *India Policy Forum 2016–17*: 73–128.

Nagaraj, R., Amey Sapre and Rajeswari Sengupta. 2019. 'Four Years after the Base-year Revision: Taking Stock of the Debate Surrounding India's National Income Estimates'. *India Policy Forum 2019*. Available at http://www.ncaer.org/IPF2019/IPF-Papers/Paper-II-IPF-2019-Nagaraj-Sapre-Conf-version.pdf (accessed 8 December 2020).

Ramakumar, R. (ed.). 2018. *Note-Bandi: Demonetisation and India's Elusive Chase for Black Money*. New Delhi: Oxford University Press.

Rangarajan, C., and S. Mahendra Dev. 2019. 'Mind the Statistics Gap'. *Indian Express*, 13 December. Available at https://indianexpress.com/article/opinion/columns/india-gdp-data-nso-survey-growth-6164226/ (accessed 8 December 2020).

Reserve Bank of India. 2020. 'RBI Releases the Financial Stability Report, July 2020'. Press release, 24 July. Available at https://www.rbi.org.in/Scripts/BS_PressReleaseDisplay.aspx?prid=50122 (accessed 4 December 2020).

Singh, Manmohan. 2019. 'The Fountainhead of India's Economic Malaise'. *The Hindu*, 18 November. Available at https://www.thehindu.com/opinion/lead/the-fountainhead-of-indias-economic-malaise/article30000546.ece (accessed 8 December 2020).

Solow, Robert. 2013. 'Our Debt, Ourselves', opinion. *New York Times*, 28 February. Available at https://www.nytimes.com/2013/02/28/opinion/our-debt-ourselves.html (accessed 8 December 2020).

Srinivasaraju, Sujata. 2019. 'How Bellary Went from Boom to Bust'. *Mint*, 23 December. Available at https://www.livemint.com/news/

india/how-bellary-went-from-boom-eto-bust-11577114594687.html (accessed 8 December 2020).

Subramanian, S. 2019. 'What is Happening to Rural Welfare, Poverty, and Inequality in India?'. *The India Forum*, 12 December. Available at https://www.theindiaforum.in/article/what-happened-rural-welfare-poverty-and-inequality-india-between-2011-12-and-2017-18 (accessed 8 December 2020).

Subramanian, Arvind. 2019. 'India's GDP Mis-estimation: Likelihood, Magnitudes, Mechanisms, and Implications'. CID Faculty Working Paper No. 354, Centre for International Development, Harvard University. Available at https://www.hks.harvard.edu/centers/cid/publications/faculty-working-papers/india-gdp-overestimate (accessed 8 December 2020).

Tejaswi, Mini. 2019. 'Ending Tax Terrorism was Part of BJP's Manifesto in 2014: Mohandas Pai'. *The Hindu*, 5 August. Available at https://www.thehindu.com/news/national/karnataka/ending-tax-terrorism-was-part-of-bjps-manifesto-in-2014-mohandas-pai/article28816168.ece (accessed 8 December 2020).

17

The Unequal Effects of the Covid-19 Crisis on the Labour Market*

Radhicka Kapoor

The widespread loss of jobs and incomes following the dual shocks of the pandemic and the lockdown has generated much concern. What is particularly worrying is that the impact of these shocks is not likely to have been uniform across the workforce.

Using data from the latest PLFS 2018–19, which captures the conditions of the labour market prior to the Covid-19 crisis, I argue here that the effects of the shocks would be particularly harsh on specific groups of workers. These would be the less-educated workers who are typically engaged in low-paying, precarious and unstable work arrangements in sectors that have been hardest hit by the shocks. Therefore, we can expect the crisis to accentuate the pre-existing inequalities in India's dualistic labour market, which has been characterised by stark disparities between, at one end, a small percentage of the workforce that is engaged in jobs that offer stability of income and social security benefits, and, at the other end, a disproportionately large proportion engaged in informal employment.

In 2018–19, the most recent year for which the labour force data is available, 52 per cent of the workforce was classified as self-

* First published in *The India Forum*, 17 July 2020.

I am extremely grateful to Professor Ajit Ghose, Dr Nomaan Majid and Srinivasan Iyer for their valuable comments and suggestions. I would like to express my sincere thanks to Abhishek Kumar for his help with the PLFS data.

employed. Over 95 per cent of the self-employed were either own-account workers (that is, those who operate enterprises without hired labour) or unpaid family workers. Less than 5 per cent of the self-employed were classified as employers (that is, those who operated enterprises with hired labour). Approximately 24 per cent of the workforce was employed as casual workers with no stability of income or security of tenure. And like the self-employed, they too were outside the ambit of employer–employee relationships that offered employment-linked benefits.

Regular wage salaried (RWS) workers constituted the remaining 24 per cent of the workforce. These workers received a salary on a regular basis and not on the basis of daily or periodic renewal of a work contract. This made them better off than casual workers, but not all of them had access to social security benefits or secure job contracts.

In 2018–19, the proportion of RWS workers who had access to at least one social security benefit (among provident fund/pension, gratuity, healthcare or maternity benefits) and therefore a minimal degree of social protection was 40.6 per cent. These workers—referred to as regular formal workers—accounted for 9.6 per cent of the total workforce. Of course, it should be noted that the definition of regular formal employment based on having access to just one social security benefit is a fairly relaxed one. If we adopt more stringent criteria, then only 17.7 per cent of RWS workers had access to all available forms of social security cover. This, in turn, means that a mere 4.2 per cent of the total workforce had jobs that offered them the maximum possible protection that would therefore fit the criteria of what is often described as a 'good job' or 'decent work'.

Regular formal jobs provide some degree of security; they also, on average, offer higher earnings than regular informal jobs (that is, RWS jobs that offer no social security benefits), casual work or self-employment. This is apparent from Table 17.1 that reports average earnings by employment status. Casual workers, who on an average earn Rs 209 a day, are clearly at the bottom of the pyramid. The financial vulnerability of casual workers is exacerbated by the fact that they are unlikely to get work every day and are therefore not likely to earn the bare minimum needed for the month. A sudden loss of income for those who have such low levels of earnings is likely to be devastating and will push them deeper into poverty. This may well be true of the self-employed as well, where 58 per cent reported monthly earnings below Rs 9,750 (the amount recommended in January 2019 as a national minimum wage by an expert committee constituted by Government of India).[1] In fact, 42 per cent of RWS workers too earned less than this amount.

Table 17.1A: Average Monthly Wage/Salary Earnings for RWS Workers in Current Weekly Status (Rs), 2018–19

	Rural	*Urban*	*Total*
Regular formal	20,429	28,664	25,866
Regular informal	8,314	10,399	9,487
All	12,574	18,623	16,220

17.1B: Average Earnings Per Day by Casual Labour Engaged in Works Other than Public Works (Rs), 2018–19

	Rural	*Urban*	*Total*
All	200	256	209

17.1C: Average Gross Earnings during the Last 30 Days from Self-employment Work in Current Weekly Status (Rs), 2018–19

	Rural	*Urban*	*Total*
All	6,587	14,549	8,363

Source: PLFS unit data, 2018–19.

On the basis of earnings and access to social security, the four basic forms of employment described above fall into a hierarchical order: regular formal employment, regular informal employment, self-employment and casual employment (Ghose 2019). That just a small proportion of workers is engaged in what is described as the best form of employment (and that too based on a very relaxed definition of formal employment) is reflective of the overall conditions of the quality of employment.

In previous employment–unemployment surveys too the share of regular formal workers was barely above 10 per cent. Regular formal jobs are a privilege for a limited few and are also typically held by those at the top of the education ladder. In 2018–19, more than

50 per cent of those in regular formal jobs were graduates or post-graduates (Table 17.2). In contrast, most self-employed and casual workers had low levels of education. For instance, 25.7 per cent of the self-employed were not literate and 80 per cent had secondary education or below. Amongst casual workers, the share of those who were not literate was 37 per cent and those who had secondary education or below was over 90 per cent. That it is the relatively less educated who are predominantly engaged in precarious work arrangements and therefore have a high probability of being rendered unemployed suggests that they stand to bear a disproportionate brunt of the Covid-19 shock.

Table 17.2: Distribution of Workers by Educational Qualifications within Each Category of Employment (%), 2018–19

Education Level	*Regular Formal*	*Regular Informal*	*Self-employed*	*Casual Workers*	*Total*
Not literate	2.29	11.79	25.70	37.41	24.30
Literate without formal education	0.04	0.19	0.43	0.50	0.38
Literate below primary	1.25	3.90	5.67	8.03	5.56
Primary	3.28	12.66	14.20	18.14	13.88
Middle	10.52	23.57	22.46	21.72	21.28
Secondary	10.99	15.00	12.99	8.90	12.09
Higher secondary	20.16	14.79	10.06	4.24	10.30
Graduate and above	51.48	18.09	8.51	1.06	12.22
Total	100.00	100.00	100.00	100.00	100.00

Source: Kapoor (2020), based on the PLFS 2018–19 unit data.

Furthermore, the less educated are typically employed in sectors where the first-order effects of the pandemic have been severe and the options for remote work are either limited or do not exist. Outside of the agricultural sector, which accounts for 42.2 per cent of total employment, the three sectors which cumulatively account for approximately 36 per cent of total employment are manufacturing, construction and trade, and hotels and restaurants. These sectors have been significantly affected by the pandemic, and the lockdown and other containment policies, due to both supply-side disruptions and a fall or collapse of demand. Adoption of physical distancing measures has not only adversely impacted production, but has also affected consumption patterns of the goods and services being provided by these industries. These sectors are a critical source of employment for the less educated (Table 17.3).

For instance, over 90 per cent of workers in construction have secondary education or below. In the manufacturing sector and the trade, hotels and restaurants sector, the corresponding statistics stood at 76 and 70 per cent, respectively. What is more, as the statistics in Table 17.4 suggest, these sectors are also dominated by informal and precarious work arrangements. This makes workers engaged in these sectors highly vulnerable to layoffs. In the construction sector, over 80 per cent of the workers are in casual employment and therefore can be fired easily. In the manufacturing sector too almost 85 per cent are in informal work arrangements. In the trade, hotels and restaurant segment, less than 5 per cent are in regular formal jobs.

In contrast, high-end services sectors (such as finance, business, real estate, and public administration, health and education) are more amenable to remote work and have a higher share of regular formal employment. As Table 17.4 shows, the share of casual workers in these sectors is less than 5 per cent. These sectors offer more secure terms of employment and they also pay higher wages. This gives workers greater financial wherewithal to cope with any loss of earnings or periods of unemployment. However, the contribution of these sectors to total employment is low (approximately 14 per cent). Furthermore, these sectors largely generate employment opportunities for those at the top end of the education ladder (Table 17.3).

That the impact of the Covid-19 crisis on workers varies and depends on the nature of the employment arrangement and the sector of employment suggests that we are likely to see increasing inequality in India's labour markets. There are the more educated workers who are engaged in work arrangements that offer a steady source of income and some degree of social security, and who are able to shift their work online. Then there are those who have low levels of education and are engaged in precarious and low-paying work of the kind that does not offer them the luxury of working from home. It would not

Table 17.3: Distribution of Workers across Sectors by Educational Qualifications, 2018–19

Classification (NIC 2008)	*Not Literate*	*Literate without Formal Education*	*Literate Below Primary*	*Primary*	*Middle*	*Secondary*	*Higher Secondary*	*Graduate and Above*	*Total*
Agriculture	37.50	0.42	6.80	15.21	19.77	9.96	6.64	3.71	100
Mining and quarrying	20.91	0.07	10.31	12.02	21.33	12.54	10.66	12.15	100
Manufacturing	14.00	0.33	5.70	15.79	25.71	14.62	13.89	9.96	100
Electricity, gas and water supply	13.33	0.35	3.00	8.15	18.29	15.08	20.29	21.53	100
Construction	27.72	0.62	6.60	18.35	25.86	11.25	6.51	3.10	100
Trade, hotel and restaurants	11.13	0.30	4.55	11.98	24.73	17.09	15.86	14.35	100
Transport, storage and communication	9.94	0.33	3.85	12.97	25.58	15.05	12.30	19.99	100
Finance, business and real estate	3.00	0.12	1.35	4.61	11.71	10.41	16.08	52.73	100
Health, education and public administration	10.30	0.21	2.68	7.31	13.67	11.45	15.11	39.28	100
Total	24.30	0.38	5.56	13.88	21.28	12.09	10.30	12.22	100

Source: Kapoor (2020), based on the PLFS 2018–19 unit data.

Table 17.4: Sectoral Breakdown of Employment by Employment Category (%), 2018–19

Sectors	*Share of Employment in Total Employment*	*Regular Formal*	*Regular Informal*	*Self-employed*	*Casual Workers*	*Total*
Agriculture	42.43	0.08	1.12	74.13	24.67	100
Mining and quarrying	0.42	28.56	23.66	9.25	38.52	100
Manufacturing	12.03	16.49	27.17	42.95	13.38	100
Electricity, gas and water supply	0.56	45.27	31.51	19.44	3.78	100
Construction	12.14	1.60	3.88	10.83	83.68	100
Trade, hotel and restaurants	12.63	4.69	23.02	67.72	4.57	100
Transport, storage and communication	5.95	20.37	29.76	38.39	11.47	100
Finance, business and real estate	3.37	41.53	26.55	30.08	1.85	100
Public administration, health and education	10.48	36.98	38.82	20.15	4.04	100
Total	100.00	9.66	14.13	52.04	24.16	

Source: Kapoor (2020), based on the PLFS 2018–19 unit data.

be unreasonable to expect the latter to account for a disproportionate share of the pandemic-related job losses.

Estimates from CMIE pegged job losses at 122 million in April 2020, with most of these losses accounted for by small traders, hawkers and daily wage–earning labourers (90 million) who fall in the category of casual workers and self-employed (Vyas 2020). Given the low and volatile earnings of this cohort, they are at risk of falling into poverty. Their financial inability to cope with the ongoing economic distress is evident from several recent surveys.

For instance, a survey conducted by economists from Azim Premji University after the announcement of the lockdown in March 2020 found that the share of households without enough money to buy even a week's worth of essentials stood at 64 per cent in urban areas and 35 per cent in rural areas (Lahoti et al. 2020). In a separate study, Bertrand, Krishnan and Schofield (2020) analysed data collected by CMIE and found that only 66 per cent of households reported having the resources to go on for more than another week before facing distress. The ILO (2020) estimated that in India, about 400 million workers in the informal economy were at risk of falling deeper into poverty.

Estimates from the World Bank suggest that the Covid-19 shock will push 12 million people in India into extreme poverty, that is, those living on less than $1.90 per day (Mahler et al. 2020). Significantly, these estimates are based on the poverty data available from CES (2011–12). More recent data from CES (2017–18), leaked to and published by *Business Standard* (Jha 2019), indicates that there was a decline in real consumption expenditure of around 4 per cent per annum between 2011–12 and 2017–18, and that poverty in India may have started rising even before the Covid-19 crisis. This suggests that the estimate of those at risk of falling into extreme poverty based on CES (2011–12) may well be on the lower side.

Even at the best of times, the poor and uneducated do not have the financial wherewithal to remain unemployed in developing countries such as India where there is no unemployment insurance. This is reflected in their low unemployment rates. In 2018–19, the unemployment rate of the illiterate was 1.08 per cent, whilst the rate for those with secondary education and above was 11.03 per cent.

In the current crisis, where there is considerable uncertainty about the duration and intensity of the pandemic and an absence of direct income support, the poor and illiterate certainly do not have the luxury of waiting for a good job. In rural areas, MGNREGA has emerged as a critical safety net. It involves hard physical labour and is likely to have provided employment for the unskilled and low-skilled. In June 2020, 32.2 million households were employed under the programme, a 50 per cent increase from the number of households employed in June 2019 (People's Action for Employment Guarantee 2020). However, in urban areas where there is no fall-back employment option such as MGNREGA and the costs of living are higher than in rural areas, many of those rendered unemployed will be compelled to do any low-paying and low-productivity work that comes their way in order to eke out a subsistence living. They are likely to create self-employment or seek casual employment, even if the remuneration offered is lowered or the terms of employment are more precarious than before the shock of the pandemic.

Against this backdrop, it is perhaps not surprising that we are already witnessing a decline in the unemployment rate from the estimate of 23 per cent reported for April and May. For June, the CMIE estimates the unemployment rate at 10.99 per cent. In rural and urban areas, the rate stood at 10.52 and 12.02 per cent, respectively. The lower unemployment rate in rural areas is not just a consequence of employment generated under MGNREGA, but also of the uptick in agricultural activities during the kharif sowing season. The overall decline in the unemployment rate may give the illusion that the effects of the pandemic and lockdown on the labour market are not longlasting and persistent. However, it is important to note that the decline in open unemployment rate masks the problem of underemployment. This problem is not just of reduced working hours but also of a deterioration in the quality of employment in terms of earnings, job security and access to social security, in particular in urban areas.

Recent evidence suggests that by adversely affecting the prospects for market work, pandemics have driven more activity into precarious work. Furceri et al. (2020) find that there is a statistically significant increase in the share of self-employment for about three years following an epidemic. Whether laid off regular formal workers, particularly the more educated ones, too opted for self-employment or other informal work arrangements is unclear at this point. They may have even chosen to withdraw from the labour force for the short term, given the bleak prospects of finding new regular formal work in the midst of the pandemic and the contraction of the economy.[2] Whilst a detailed analysis of the issue will be possible only once data on the labour force participation and employment rates is available, the recent decline in the unemployment rate is potentially a consequence of two factors: one, the fact that the poor and the uneducated do not have the luxury of remaining unemployed; two, the educated and the better off, who typically have a high unemployment rate, may have withdrawn from the labour force. Of course, the former is likely to be the more dominant factor in a developing country.

Therefore, despite the recent decline in unemployment rates estimated by the CMIE, the employment situation remains dismal. Prior to the Covid-19 crisis, much of the workforce was already engaged in unstable work arrangements that offered no social security benefits and provided low earnings, which left them with little or no financial buffer to protect themselves from any shock. The pandemic and lockdown have worsened the situation by pushing even more people into a dire position.

Addressing the deteriorating conditions of employment and the widening disparities in the job market requires a strengthening and rebuilding of the labour market from the bottom up. In the immediate term, this calls for an expansion of social assistance and public workfare programmes to provide relief and protection to the most vulnerable and disadvantaged. However, this alone is not enough. In the long run, there is a need to expand earnings, job opportunities and give security to those at the lower end of the education and skills ladder. This will require a serious rethinking of our growth and development strategy.

Notes

1. The expert committee set the national minimum wage (NMW) for India at Rs 375 per day (or Rs 9,750 per month) as of July 2018, irrespective of

sectors, skills, occupations or rural-urban locations. It also introduced an additional house rent allowance (city compensatory allowance), averaging up to Rs 55 per day (Rs 1,430 per month) for urban workers over and above the NMW. It also established the NMW for five different regions with diverse socio-economic and labour market situations, ranging from a low of Rs 342 per day (Rs 8,892 per month) in Region I to a high of Rs 447 per day (Rs 11,622 per month) in Region IV (Ministry of Labour and Employment 2019).

2. Estimates from CMIE suggest that even five months after the lockdown, the labour force participation rate in September 2020 stood at 40.7 per cent, 200 basis points lower than it was in 2019–20.

References

Bertrand, Marianne, Kaushik Krishnan and Heather Schofield. 2020. 'How are Indian Households Coping under the COVID-19 Lockdown?: 8 Key Findings'. Rustandy Center for Social Sector Innovation Blog, 11 May. Available at https://www.chicagobooth.edu/research/rustandy/blog/2020/how-are-indian-households-coping-under-the-covid19-lockdown (accessed 14 July 2020).

Furceri, David, Prakash Loungani, Jonathan D. Ostry and Pietro Pizzuto. 2020. 'Pandemics and Inequality: Assessing the Impact of COVID-19'. In *COVID-19 in Developing Economies*, ed. Simeon Djankov and Ugo Panizza, 200–13. London: VoxEU/CEPR Press. Available at https://voxeu.org/content/covid-19-developing-economies (accessed 14 July 2020).

Ghose, Ajit. 2019. *Employment in India* (Oxford India Short Introductions). New Delhi: Oxford University Press.

International Labour Organisation. 2020. 'ILO Monitor: COVID-19 and the World of Work'. Second edition, briefing note, 7 April. Available at https://www.ilo.org/wcmsp5/groups/public/---dgreports/---dcomm/documents/briefingnote/wcms_740877.pdf (accessed 14 July 2020).

Jha, Somesh. 2019. 'Consumer Spend Sees First Fall in 4 Decades on Weak Rural Demand: NSO Data'. *Business Standard*, 14 November.

Kapoor, Radhicka. 2020. 'COVID-19 and the State of India's Labour Market'. ICRIER Policy Series No. 18, June. Available at http://icrier.org/pdf/Policy_Series_18.pdf (accessed 14 July 2020).

Lahoti, Rahul, Amit Basole, Rosa Abraham, Surbhi Kesar and Paaritosh Nath. 2020. 'Hunger Grows as India's Lockdown Kills Jobs: Results of a Survey from 12 States'. *The India Forum*, 5 June. Available at https://

www.theindiaforum.in/article/hunger-grows-india-s-lockdown-kills-jobs (accessed 14 July 2020).

Mahler, Daniel Gerszon, Christoph Lakner, R. Andres Castaneda Aguilar and Haoyu Wu. 2020. 'The Impact of COVID-19 (Coronavirus) on Global Poverty: Why Sub-Saharan Africa Might be the Region Hardest Hit'. World Bank Data Blog, 20 April. Available at https://blogs.worldbank.org/opendata/impact-covid-19-coronavirus-global-poverty-why-sub-saharan-africa-might-be-region-hardest (accessed 14 July 2020).

Ministry of Labour and Employment. 2019. 'Report of the Expert Committee on Determining the Methodology for Fixing the National Minimum Wage'. Government of India, January. Available at https://labour.gov.in/sites/default/files/Commitee_on_Determination_of_Methodology.pdf (accessed 14 July 2020).

People's Action for Employment Guarantee. 2020. 'National Rural Employment Guarantee Act Implementation Tracker by PAEG'. Available at https://drive.google.com/file/d/1_k1S7AuTexoMGDlYAEL9d2fWPzxhcyns/view (accessed 14 July 2020).

Vyas, Mahesh. 2020. 'India Has a Jobs Bloodbath as Unemployment Rate Shoots up to 27.1%'. *Business Standard*, 4 May. Available at https://www.business-standard.com/article/opinion/the-jobs-bloodbath-of-april-2020-120050400524_1.html (accessed 14 July 2020).

18

States' Loss of Fiscal Autonomy in a Centralised Federal System*

M. Govinda Rao

The response to Covid-19 has brought out the fragility of the Indian federal system. A tendency towards extreme centralisation during the pandemic and the absence of checks and balances to correct this centralisation is a matter of concern.

The process of concentration that happens when a country is at war with another comes from a patriotic zeal to empower the government to fight the war. However, the pandemic has to be fought by both the centre and the states as both have stakes in protecting lives and livelihoods—in fact, the states more so since they are at the forefront. But they do not have the fiscal strength to do so. In such a scenario, the centre is using the states' distress situation to force them to adopt its economic and institutional agenda.

Pandemic and Centralised Decision-making

The Constitution places 'public order' and 'public health' in the State List (Entries 1 and 6), and 'prevention of the extension from one State to another of infectious or contagious diseases or pests affecting men, animals or plants' as a joint responsibility in the Concurrent List (Entry 29). The common interest in mitigating the pandemic should normally have led to decisions by the centre on broad policy matters relating to inter-state movements and by the

* First published in *The India Forum*, 29 May 2020. The author alone is responsible for the views in this chapter.

states on policies and implementation of the lockdown and on public health interventions.

Instead, what we have seen are decisions by the Union government that have reduced the states' role to being merely agents to implement decisions handed down to them.

Considering the poor financial situation of the states, the centre should have empowered them fiscally to fight the pandemic effectively. But the Union government has completely centralised decision-making by invoking the Disaster Management Act, 2005, for reasons of 'consistency in the application and implementation of various measures across the country'.

The decisions on the lockdown were taken by the centre and so too, until mid-May, were the risk classification of districts and listing of permissible activities. The first video conference by the prime minister with the chief ministers that took place on 20 March 2020 did not have a proposal for a lockdown on the agenda, but the centre decided on its own on 24 March to impose a nation-wide lockdown. The subsequent video conference discussions have been mostly in the nature of a formality.

Faced with loss of employment, uncertainty about the length of the lockdown, little reserves in hand and the fear of contacting the virus in the cities, there has been an exodus of migrant labour, creating a humanitarian crisis which the states are having to confront. There is little coordination between the centre and the states, leading to avoidable hardship and misery to millions of vulnerable people.

Being closer to the people, the states have a larger responsibility for waging this war. They have had to immediately ramp up their public health infrastructure, deal with the humanitarian crisis arising from the exodus of migrant labour, and meet the basic requirements of the vulnerable sections facing adversity during the lockdown. Kerala unveiled a Rs 20,000 crore financial package immediately to tide over the crisis and decided to go to the market to borrow Rs 6,000 crore at a high cost of 8.9 per cent. Karnataka too unveiled a package to reduce the suffering of various sections of society that have suffered a serious loss of incomes due to the lockdown and loss of employment.

Fiscal Vulnerability of States: Erosion of Revenues

The lockdown has completely eroded the states' revenue from the meagre sources of revenue at their disposal. Even the promised GST compensation has not been forthcoming. The constitutionally mandated tax transfers from the centre too are in a precarious situation.

As the GDP is expected to contract during the year, tax revenues will fall and the divisible pool of central tax revenue is therefore likely to shrink substantially. Even if GDP remains at the same level as in the previous year (2019–20), the tax devolution to the states will be lower by Rs 2.5 lakh crore than the budget estimate of the Union government, which the states took into account while formulating their budgets. If the economy contracts and the tax revenue of the Union government is lower than the 2019–20 revenues, the loss to the states will be even higher.

In this distressed financial situation, the states had hoped that the centre would help them with a Covid-19 grant that would at least partially cover the loss of revenue in their share of central taxes. They had hoped that the centre would settle their pending dues, particularly the GST compensation. Unlike the centre, neither do the states have broad-based tax handles, nor do they have the autonomy to borrow to tide over their difficulties.

The states had agreed to surrender the right to levy domestic trade taxes in order to implement the GST, based on the undertaking that the centre would compensate for the loss of revenue if actual collections fell short of the projected revenue from the subsumed taxes (calculated as the 2015–16 collections with a growth of 14 per cent every year until 2022). Actual collections have fallen short, but the compensation has been paid only up to November 2019. This is a clear abrogation of the agreement. Releasing the pending compensation at this juncture would have fiscally empowered the states.

Similarly, low international crude oil prices presented an opportunity for the states to levy additional value-added tax (VAT) on high speed diesel and motor spirit, which would have helped them to garner some additional revenue. However, with the central government levying additional excise duty on petroleum products to collect Rs 1.4 lakh crore of non-shareable revenue, very little space was left to the states for an increase in taxation of petroleum products.

Facing a severe financial crunch and the need to release funds to save livelihoods and prevent starvation, many states have had to take extreme steps like postponing all payments to contractors and cutting salaries and pensions of their employees. Most states have kept large bills pending. A number of states like Andhra Pradesh, Maharashtra, Odisha, Rajasthan and Telangana have deferred payment of salaries of the ministers by 60–75 per cent and of bureaucrats by 20–50 per cent. Even CPM-ruled Kerala has deferred the salaries of employees by six days in a month for up to five months. States like Punjab and Tamil Nadu have deferred increases in dearness allowance payments.

Additional Borrowing Space: Conditions Apply

In such a dire situation, the states were hoping that the announcements made by the Union finance minister in May would include a Covid-19 grant and permit additional borrowing to help them tide over their fiscal difficulties.

The central government's measures, as part of the Atmanirbhar Bharat Abhiyan package, do not address the issue of additional grants but allow the states to borrow an additional 2 per cent of their GDP from the market, up from the current limit of 3 per cent of GDP.

However, there will be a graded increase in borrowing and much of it will be dependent on meeting certain conditions. The states have been allowed to increase their borrowing from 3 to 3.5 per cent of GDP without any conditions.

But they can borrow an additional 1 per cent of GDP only by fulfilling four reform conditions—meeting each condition will allow the states to borrow an additional 0.25 per cent of GDP for each reform. The four reforms are:

1. introduction of the 'one nation, one ration card' scheme for all, which will require linking Aadhaar with ration cards and installing point-of-sale machines in all fair-price shops;
2. improvement in ease of doing business, which requires (a) district level assessment of ease of doing business according

to the Department of Promotion for Industry and Internal Trade (DPIIT) norms, (b) automatic renewal of state industrial and commercial licences to businesses, and (c) making randomised inspections with prior notice and full transparency;

3. implementation of power sector reforms, which would entail reducing aggregate technical and commercial losses, direct benefit transfers to farmers instead of charging them lower power tariffs, and reducing the gap between average cost and average revenues; and
4. urban local body reforms requiring the states to notify property tax floor rates according to circle property values and to notify water and sewage charges.

Finally, if at least three of these four reform conditions are satisfied, the states can borrow another 0.5 per cent of GDP as well, with the new ceiling yielding a total of an additional 2 per cent of GDP.

The additional borrowing space for states does come as a relief, but the imposition of conditions raises important questions of the appropriateness of using the distress situation to force the states to implement an agenda set by the Union government.

To be sure, Article 293(3) of the Constitution requires the Union government to permit the states to borrow when they are indebted to it, and Article 293(4) enables that, 'A consent to borrow may be granted subject to such conditions, if any, as the Government of India may think it appropriate.' Also, the reform conditions now stipulated by the centre may not be inherently undesirable. However, there is no precedence to putting conditions on market borrowing. Never in the history of independent India has there been any occasion when the Union government has put conditions on market borrowings of the states. In 2008, there were no conditions imposed by the Union government when, in the wake of the Global Financial Crisis, it allowed the states to borrow an additional 1.5 per cent of GDP.

It appears that the Union government seems to have been thinking about putting conditions on states' borrowing for quite some time, but was apprehensive about doing so as there is no precedence to this. In fact, the terms of reference of the Fifteenth Finance Commission asked it to consider '[t]he conditions that [the government of India] may impose on the states while providing consent under Article 293(3) of the Constitution'. The first report of the commission, covering 2020–21, was silent on the matter and it is possible that the commission had decided to make recommendations on these terms of reference in its second report, which will cover 2021–22 to 2024–25.

In the meantime, considering the fiscal distress the states are now faced with, the centre seems to have found it opportune to impose conditions on borrowing. Once this precedence is set, it opens up a pandora's box. The Union government can in the future impose on the states conditions that it deems fit, irrespective of their merits.

There may not be anything wrong with the conditions themselves. Linking of ration cards with Aadhaar and enabling the ration shops to have point-of-sale machines is certainly desirable to ensure nation-wide portability of the cards. However, this does not solve the problem of not having the ration card itself.

It is also important to resolve the issue of the losses of power distribution companies, which despite repeated attempts has persisted. The problem, however, is not the same for all states. West Bengal and Gujarat have solved the distribution problems in different ways and do not have large deficits in their power utilities, whereas the distribution companies in Andhra Pradesh, Madhya Pradesh, Punjab, Rajasthan and Tamil Nadu continue to suffer large losses. Again, the problem could be obsolete infrastructure that requires fresh investments, or overemployment in distribution companies, or a failure to raise tariffs, or unmetred supply. The 'one size fits all' reform then may not yield the desired results.

It may be easy to levy charges on water and sewerage, but property taxation may not be easy to implement. There are states like Maharashtra where the implementation of property tax reform is constrained by the Rent Control Act. Moreover, the first report of the Fifteenth Finance Commission has already mandated that property tax reform must be undertaken to avail urban local body grants. Finally, promoting competition to achieve ease of doing business may achieve the outcomes better than micromanaging policies and their implementation through district-level assessment according to the DPIIT norms, automatic renewal of industrial and commercial licences, etc.

The Union government need not have thrust these reform conditions on the states by taking advantage of their current financial difficulties. These reforms could have been discussed with the states and each state could have implemented them in a manner best suited to it. In any case, it may be difficult to measure the outcome of these reforms within a year. The Union government will have to go by the initiatives taken, which may not necessarily ensure the desired outcomes. Moreover, it is not possible to ensure that the reforms undertaken will remain. There are not once-for-all reforms but require periodic changes. Revision of power tariffs has to be done periodically. Property tax rates and the base will have to be changed at regular intervals. There is no guarantee that the inspections of manufacturing units will remain randomised and transparent.

What could be the outcome of stipulating these conditions? The states will weigh these conditions and carry out the reforms they think would be easy to implement. Most of the states have already linked Aadhaar to ration cards and it may not be difficult to install point-of-sale machines in the shops. Hopefully, there will be attempts to ensure adequate supply of the rations.

Similarly, most states may work, at least on paper, on the ease of doing businesses. There may also be attempts to reform urban property taxes, but to what extent it will increase revenue will have to be seen. As mentioned earlier, this has also to be done to avail the Fifteenth Finance Commission's urban local body grants. Power sector reform will perhaps be the most difficult as reform in the sector is stuck due to strong special interest groups.

Clearly, the states will implement only those reforms that are politically easy. If they are not able to fulfil the three conditions, they may even decide to forgo the borrowings and instead prefer to cut expenditure. At a time when it is important to stimulate demand, the conditions stipulated for borrowing could lead to the unintended result of compressing capital expenditure.

Need for an Institution for Bargaining and Conflict Resolution

The experience of dealing with Covid-19 has underlined the need for an institutional mechanism to enable inter-governmental bargaining, foster inter-governmental cooperation, conflict resolution and promote non-predatory competition. The absence of such a mechanism is a major institutional vacuum in Indian federalism. This has shown that in emergencies like the current pandemic, the states can be prevented from playing the legitimate role envisaged in the Constitution and be relegated to being mere agencies of the Union government. We should have seen the Union and the states working in unison in the spirit of cooperative federalism to mitigate the adverse economic consequences of the lockdown, especially in giving relief to the vulnerable.

The National Development Council is no longer effective and the Inter-state Council, having been made a part of Union home ministry, is not an independent institution. The states do not have a remedy when the Union government simply abrogates the agreement to pay compensation for the loss of revenue from GST. The states have to simply take orders when the centre invokes the Disaster Management Act to deal with events like Covid-19 and when the centre treats the states not as partners but as agents.

Having created a precedence of imposing conditions for borrowing, the Union government will now use the instrument to further its agenda by imposing conditions irrespective of whether or not they are in the interest of the states. In fact, in a situation of asymmetric power distribution and in the absence of an independent institution to oversee bargaining, coordinate actions and resolve conflicts, excessive centralisation is a natural outcome. This could lead to disharmony and divisions according to political allegiances, and it does not bode well either for democracy or for federalism.

19

Knowns and Unknowns in the Covid-19–triggered Global Economic Crisis*

C. P. Chandrasekhar

The novel coronavirus or Covid-19 pandemic has put the world's economic decision-makers and their advisors in no man's land. The challenge they must address is visible and obvious, but the means to do so effectively are almost an unknown.

It is clear that in the first quarter of 2020, the economies of most of the world's nations would have contracted, some to a significant degree. Whether that contraction will continue and, if it does, for how long is anybody's guess. Speculative forays into estimating the degree of contraction in the GDP and where collapsing stock markets would settle are mere games that can yield the right numbers only by accident.

These conjectures only serve to divert attention from the more crucial questions that must be confronted.

The fundamental problem today is that while the policy establishment must act to mitigate and overcome an inevitable crisis, the known instruments of economic policy hold out no promise of being effective, at least in the near future.

This situation is the result of the nature of the crisis at hand. The virus, which quickly moved across frontiers from the first epicentre of infection in China, the world's manufacturing hub, to new epicentres in developed country locations in Europe and the US, has overwhelmed underfunded and/or unprepared health systems. This has made national isolation through closures of borders and

* First published in *The India Forum*, 3 April 2020.

aggressive intra-border physical distancing, culminating in lockdowns, the main means of trying to control the spread of the pandemic.

As expected, this has meant a sudden stop to economic activity. Even before the lockdowns, the disruptions in trade and global value chains had adversely affected production because of a loss of market access and/or shortage of raw materials. With flights banned and even domestic transportation restricted, the travel and tourism businesses were crippled. Full-scale lockdowns then shut down production and closed a host of businesses. Masses of workers lost their jobs, especially since across the world there has been a rise in the share of casual and precarious employment in recent decades.

These developments have affected both supply and demand. With production chains broken, factories shut down and businesses forced to close, the supply of a range of goods and services, barring those considered essential, was suddenly blocked. This has had its spin-off effects on upstream and downstream sectors. Even suppliers of essential goods, facing problems in transportation and distribution, have had to curtail production.

The supply shocks soon translated into demand compression for most goods. With incomes and earnings curtailed or wiped out, demand has fallen for consumption goods. The halt in production cut demand for intermediates as well. And with capacity idle and economic activity disrupted, investment froze.

Since supply was independently disrupted, the magnitude of the demand compression (driven in part by the supply shock) cannot be easily estimated. But the collapse in energy demand that led to the unwinding of the production-limiting agreement between the Organisation for Petroleum Exporting Countries (OPEC) and non-OPEC oil-exporting countries like Russia which, in turn, resulted in a collapse of oil prices to less than $20 a barrel reflects the grim situation.

In the past, exogenous supply-side shocks that reduced production and availability, such as the effects of adverse weather conditions on monsoon-dependent agriculture, were limited to a few sectors and one or a few countries. Where national reserves could not address such shocks, trade came to the rescue. National availability was enhanced by imports from abroad. In this crisis there is much less flexibility, with Covid-19 infections reported from more than 100 countries and cases of disease approaching a million worldwide.

With stringent lockdowns in place and almost half the world's population confined to their homes, production shortfalls are now globally widespread. These shortages have been amplified by their transmission through global value chains. Moreover, trade is limited as transportation links have been cut or weakened. This has led to a synchronised reduction in production and supply of most goods and services other than of essentials. Essential commodities too are flying off the shelves in many locations.

Given the virus-induced and exogenous nature of this shock, throwing money into the system to ramp up production cannot immediately help. Capacity shortages are not the problem in most areas. The difficulty in keeping economic activity running is the problem. Where there is a shortage of capacity, the problem is that fresh investment cannot be made immediately.

Production can be sustained only where the state steps in and ring-fences production on the grounds of the activity concerned being crucial, for example, to address a medical emergency or to produce essentials. In other areas, a slow return to normal production levels must await an environment- or immunity-induced reduction in the intensity of the pandemic. Physical distancing and lockdowns are interim means of reducing the number of cases or 'flattening the curve' of rising infections and mitigating damage till factors that help the pandemic subside become operative. That increases the uncertainty about the period for which the supply shock is likely to be in play.

Given this supply shock, addressing the other aspect of the crisis, which is demand compression, becomes difficult too. Wages, earnings and profits have shrunk or have been wiped out. However, a Keynesian-style fiscal stimulus or monetary measures to fuel credit-financed spending are both likely to run up against exogenously generated supply bottlenecks, triggering inflation. They would create a new problem without resolving the old one.

These features of the Covid-19-induced economic seizure make this an unusual conjuncture, which is what leaves policymakers without any sense of direction.

Monetary policy measures, the policymaker's favoured instrument for a few decades now, cannot work at this point of time. These measures have been pursued with limited effect since the 2008 global financial crisis and during the global recession that followed. Once the banks were bailed out and the financial system was stabilised, central banks in the rich countries went on a bond-buying spree with the express purpose of infusing liquidity into the system. The motivation was to trigger credit-financed consumption and investment, thereby spurring demand and a recovery.

To encourage the clients of banks and non-bank financial companies to borrow, policy rates were reduced to near zero or even allowed to go negative in the hope that the benefit would be passed on to private borrowers. This worked only partially, as the 'new normal' of low growth that has characterised much of the world for over a decade makes clear.

Banks were not too keen to lend to clients burdened with past debt, and many borrowers were reluctant to take on more debt. Credit did grow significantly in this period. But this was used in substantial measure for investment in asset markets that experienced unwarranted price inflation driven by speculation. Even over-leveraged corporates that managed to access credit used a lot of it for financial investments.

Despite the ineffectiveness of the currently favoured monetary tools for macroeconomic management, confused policymakers have returned to the same toolbox in the current crisis. In Europe, Christine Lagarde, the president of the European Central Bank, while recognising that the virus attack was 'a major shock to the growth prospects of the global and euro area economies', initially argued that saving the Eurozone is not the sole responsibility of the European Central Bank, but also that of member governments. In response to demands that the European Central Bank should cut interest rates to reduce borrowing costs for highly indebted Eurozone countries that are faced with interest rates much higher than German bonds, for example, Lagarde declared: 'We are not here to close [bond] spreads, there are other tools and other actors to deal with these issues' (*Financial Times* 2020). She, in fact, felt that a region-wide fiscal stimulus coordinate by governments was the need of the hour.

The reaction to these views was aggressively negative, forcing Lagarde to backtrack. Within a week the European Central Bank announced a huge and additional €750 billion bond-buying programme, covering sovereign and corporate debt, to be completed within the year (D'Souza 2020). Lagarde also said: 'There are no limits to our (ECB's) commitment to the euro. We are determined to use the full potential of our tools, within our mandate.'

In the US too, the Federal Reserve decided to opt for another dose of the same medicine that had been used in 2008 to save the banks. It decided to reduce interest rates to near zero and buy $700 billion worth of Treasuries and mortgage-backed securities, and in the process feed liquidity to the banking system. Ben Bernanke and Janet Yellen (2020), two former chairpersons of the Federal Reserve, noted in the *Financial Times* that this was unlikely to work because while in 2008 a financial collapse had frozen credit and spending, currently financial markets were 'only reflecting underlying concerns about the potential damage caused by the coronavirus pandemic, which of course monetary policy cannot influence'.

Essentially, any attempt to pour cheap liquidity into the system and force cash into the hands of anyone who can spend it cannot help, because the money will not move from the financial system to needy borrowers. If yet governments and central banks are returning to discredited monetary instruments, it is for two reasons. One, to provide banks, financial institutions and big corporates the liquidity needed to meet commitments when business is slack or stalled. Small firms and vulnerable citizens are unlikely to directly benefit much. Two, to facilitate borrowing by the government because at the least as Bernanke and Yellen admit, fiscal policymakers must 'fund the public health response while providing critical aid to people whose lives and livelihoods have been shattered by the virus and its effects', and 'do more as the size of the hit to economic activity becomes apparent' (ibid.).

On the surface, the pandemic seems to have increased the acceptance of proactive fiscal policy measures, though references to remaining within the 'available fiscal headroom' persist. In Europe, the European Commission appears willing to relax its unjustifiable fiscal rules (D'Souza 2020), and governments in France, Germany,

Italy and Spain have announced higher than conventionally supported fiscal packages. In the US, President Donald Trump and the Congress have negotiated a $2 trillion stimulus package, which is touted as the 'largest of its kind in modern American history'.

This appears surprising since unprecedented spending may not yield expected results when there are, as noted earlier, supply constraints. But these packages, large and small, merely fund what governments think they can do. Besides working hard (and competently) to contain the spread of the pandemic and mitigate its effects, there are only a few things they can immediately do, such as ramping up spending on protection of medical staff, testing and treatment.

Not all the things that have to be done can be anticipated straight away. There are some required actions that are obvious. One, for example, is to reach relief to those devastated by the sudden stop in economic activity. This would include covering those who are vulnerable for the simple reason that their jobs are not regular or are precarious and they therefore now find themselves without a job or income. Relief should also cover those who cannot help themselves and are severely affected when the people or systems on whom they depend are themselves helpless. Massive transfers in cash and kind to these sections are imperative, combined with an emergency drive to ensure that the essentials of daily living are produced and distributed.

Putting cash in the hands of people when what they need is not available would only trigger price increases, benefit hoarders and speculators, and erode the real value of the relief provided. In many areas, public provisioning of essential goods and services may be the better solution.

A second obvious action is to ensure that the huge informal sector and small business entities that do not have the reserves and the wherewithal to restart business as and when normalcy returns must be provided the support needed to survive. This would involve not just provision of credit, but subsidies and transfers as well, so that whenever the time comes, individuals and businesses would be in a position to return to managing their economic lives.

The problem is that when designing emergency programmes to address an exogenously triggered crisis, governments may go wrong or even misuse the opportunity. This is partly reflected in the US's mammoth Coronavirus Aid, Relief and Economic Security (CARES) Act that provides for a $2 trillion package. It was essential that transfers be provided to those whose incomes are under threat. So, around $300 billion of the $2 trillion package is likely to be devoted to such transfers. Direct payments of $1,200 would be made to tax-paying individuals earning up to $75,000 a year.

There is much that is problematic in this design. With the average hourly minimum wage in the US at around $8 an hour, the minimum wage for a 40-hour working week would stand at $320. This would mean that the maximum transfer per person would not cover even four weeks' earnings at the minimum wage. The effects of the crisis, on the other hand, are likely to be felt for much more than a four-week period.

The transfer scheme is, however, combined with enhanced unemployment benefits. A sum of $250 billion has been allocated to an extended unemployment insurance programme, which widens eligibility and provides workers an additional $600 per week for four months, in addition to what states provide. This programme applies to the self-employed, independent contractors and gig economy workers.

But compare these outlays with the support big business gets. A sum of $500 billion is to be devoted to providing loans and loan guarantees, at near-zero interest of course, for a period not exceeding five years to the big players (Snell 2020). Airlines are to receive $50 billion of that money for passenger air carriers and $8 billion for cargo air carriers. One-fourth of the US package is devoted to salvaging that section of corporate America that in the past was in a position to build reserves to face a crisis of this kind. Add to this the Federal Reserve's contribution to save the banks and financial institutions, and it is clear that much money would flow to the narrow top of an unequal structure.

On paper, the motivation underlying the large fiscal spend in response to the crisis is not to directly spur demand but to provide relief and support to selected sections and sectors. But as is inevitable, power relations determine allocations in ways that do spell inequality. Since the impact of the underlying virus-induced economic crisis is more severe on the poor and the vulnerable, an intensification of inequality will be the outcome.

Such inadequacies in relief packages are to be found elsewhere as well. In India the Pradhan Mantri Garib Kalyan Yojana is woefully inadequate in the current circumstances. The Yojana has two main components. One is a set of measures aimed at reaching essential food to those who cannot access it or would find it difficult to access it through the open market. The second is to quickly put money into the pockets of chosen sets among the poor so that they can meet essential expenditures.

On the first component, the government has declared that it would provide, free of cost, to the 800 million beneficiaries of the National Food Security Scheme (NFSS), 5 kg of rice/wheat per person per month and 1 kg of pulses for a household for the next three months (Ministry of Finance 2020). This would be in addition to the 5 kg they are already provided against payment. However, restricting access to only those covered by the NFSS would not only deprive those groups such as migrant workers who are known to be excluded from the scheme, but also those who may not be eligible usually but have now been pushed into a dire situation. Some way of including such sections, or universalising access should have been found.

The second main component of the package includes an *ex gratia* payment of Rs 1,000 per individual to poor senior citizens, widows and the disabled, and transferring an even smaller sum of Rs 500 to 200 million Jan Dhan accounts held by women. This is indeed niggardly. When a crisis of unprecedented proportions throws a large number out of work and leaves them without an income, the obvious solution is a direct income transfer that protects them as best as they can.

In a city like Delhi, where even the official minimum wage for unskilled workers is close to Rs 15,000, a transfer should aim to cover at least half that sum. What we have instead is a one-time Rs 1,000 *ex gratia* payment for the most disadvantaged and a one-time transfer of Rs 500 to poor women with Jan Dhan accounts. That definitely is little more than tokenism.

Globally, the crisis would accentuate existing inequalities. In fact, the global crisis is likely to hit developing countries particularly adversely, with their own internal Covid-19 crisis aggravated, one, by steep declines in commodity prices and, two, by an outflow of capital. Given the uncertainties generated by the crisis, the footloose capital that had been accumulated during the many years when accommodative monetary policies had injected large volumes of cheap liquidity into these countries has already begun to exit in large volumes.

The United Nations Conference on Trade and Development (UNCTAD) reports that portfolio capital outflows (both debt and equity) from nine emerging markets (Brazil, India, Indonesia, Philippines, Republic of Korea, South Africa, Thailand and Turkey) in the month after the Covid-19 crisis went global (21 February to 20 March) was $59 million—more than double the outflow over a similar period starting 19 September 2008 during the global financial crisis. One consequence has been a sharp depreciation in the value of the currencies in these countries. This will naturally have an impact on the cost of servicing external commercial borrowing by the corporate and financial sectors, borrowing that had risen steeply during the years of access to cheap dollar credit.

With the local currency cost of servicing hard currency debt rising, defaults and bankruptcies are unavoidable. The poor in the developing countries, devastated by lockdowns and the sudden stop, would also experience the adverse effects of this larger crisis and the harsh ways in which governments respond to the situation.

Altogether, a crisis of huge proportions is overwhelming the world economy and its most vulnerable regions and populations. The problem is that given the exogenous nature of the prime driver of this crisis and the inability of most governments to restrain the force of that influence with means other than isolation and harsh lockdowns, it is not clear when the crisis would abate.

Till the Covid-19 pandemic loses much of its momentum, to pull economies out of the economic crisis they are experiencing seems difficult. The only certainty now is that how and when the crisis will bottom out remains unclear.

References

'Introductory Statement'. 2020. European Central Bank Press Conference by Christine Lagarde, President, and Luis de Guindos, Vice-President,

12 March, Frankfurt. Available at https://www.ecb.europa.eu/press/pressconf/2020/html/ecb.is200312~f857a21b6c.en.html (accessed 8 December 2020).

'Lagarde Triggers Investor Jitters as ECB Launches Virus Response'. 2020. *Financial Times,* 13 March. Available at https://www.ft.com/content/11ab8f84-6452-11ea-b3f3-fe4680ea68b5 (accessed 8 December 2020).

Bernanke, Ben and Janet Yellen. 2020. 'The Federal Reserve Must Reduce Long-term Damage from Coronavirus'. *Financial Times,* 18 March. Available at https://www.ft.com/content/01f267a2-686c-11ea-a3c9-1fe6fedcca75 (accessed 8 December 2020).

D'Souza, Deborah. 2020. 'ECB Announces €750 Billion Stimulus, Declares No Limits on Policy'. *Investopedia,* 19 March. Available at https://www.investopedia.com/ecb-announces-eur750-billion-stimulus-declares-no-limits-on-policy-4800196 (accessed 8 December 2020).

Ministry of Finance. 2020. 'Finance Minister Announces Rs 1.70 Lakh Crore Relief Package under Pradhan Mantri Garib Kalyan Yojana for the Poor to Help them Fight the Battle against Corona Virus'. PIB Release, 26 March. Available at https://pib.gov.in/PressReleaseIframePage.aspx?PRID=1608345 (accessed 8 December 2020).

Snell, Kelsey. 2020. 'What's Inside the Senate's $2trillion Coronavirus Aid Package'. *NPR,* 26 March. Available at https://www.npr.org/2020/03/26/821457551/whats-inside-the-senate-s-2-trillion-coronavirus-aid-package (accessed 8 December 2020).

Section VII

Impact on Society

20

Psychosocial Challenges in the Midst of the Coronavirus*

Honey Oberoi Vahali

The Covid-19 pandemic is likely to have biopsychosocial, economic and political consequences, little of which we are able to fully cognise, leave alone respond to effectively. It is unlikely that any aspect of our lives will be left unaffected for long after the actual medical concerns posed by the virus are over. Media representations and news of the growing number of infections and deaths are invading and entrapping our minds. This chapter outlines a few psychosocial challenges of this historical moment and their possible translation into long-term issues.

Every crisis carries the possibility of reactivating older issues with a new energy. Whenever humankind has been confronted with the outbreak of contagious diseases and epidemics, states and societies have—with some exceptions—responded by blaming, shaming, shunning, humiliating and practising untouchability against patients. The disease becomes a marker of identity enveloping the individual, family and the extended community within its folds. This has been true in the case of leprosy, plague, tuberculosis, AIDS, and even for mental illnesses where there is no evidence of any form of biological spread by contamination.

In all such instances, the suffering individual with a distinctive past disappears. Instead we have a stigmatising label that subsumes the entirety of the person's identity and existence. The ill person, who is seen to be a transmitter of disease and someone who can flood us

* First published in *The India Forum*, 22 May 2020.

with biological and/or psychological vulnerability, is cruelly ostracised and alienated. In all cases, the actual transmission of the illness is outweighed by a far greater intensity of anxieties.

The novel coronavirus grips us with fears of an impending catastrophe. It is very difficult to grapple with the fact that there are very few barriers to restrict the invisible virus' invasion of the human body. The long incubation period during which one can be an asymptomatic carrier and transmitter of the disease transforms the virus into a power to reckon with in the real as well as psychological sense.

The psychic fear is compounded by the fact that the asymptomatic transmitter of the coronavirus—unlike a person with leprosy or tuberculosis—carries very few external signs of the disease on their body. This can evoke powerful and intense anxieties of contagion from almost anyone and everyone.

Regressing from Covid-19

Explorations and insights into individual and group psychology tell us that the most basic dread of human beings is that of death and annihilation. This dread shadows us everywhere.

In ordinary contexts, we are able to 'defend' ourselves by repressing this dread or by using our psychic repertoire to consciously live our lives by distancing ourselves from a moment-to-moment awareness of our impending mortality. But the everyday maintenance of psychological equilibrium through defences such as repression and dissociation comes at its own cost.[1] This is compounded in situations where humans perceive a threat to their survival, such as the outbreak of an epidemic.

In times such as these, the usual unconscious dynamics and means of protecting the personal or group self may be experienced as grossly inadequate. As the mind gets flooded with looming threats invoking annihilatory anxieties, a fusion of primitive unconscious aggressive and destructive forces in the individual with those in the social and collective psyche may take place. This coming together can then be exploited by the stated and unstated agendas of authoritarian and fascist states. The complex merger of psychic and hegemonic political drives can easily acquire a life of its own.

The crisis set off by the epidemic might end up becoming an occasion for the multiplication of structural injustice, mob violence and harsher forms of discrimination. For, at the heart of the fear of contagion and of practices such as untouchability is the threat of being contaminated, invaded or annihilated. In situations where our survival feels at stake, we may end up hating, externalising blame, succumbing to authority and venting out our totalitarian instincts by joining authoritarian forces to find an enemy to exterminate.

In the grip of the coronavirus, we already seem to be giving way to strong regressive impulses. In Delhi and Mumbai there have been instances of spitting at and hurling abuse at people of the North Eastern states and their being denied access to shops. With the virus originating in China, people have been stigmatising the citizens of the North East for no reason other than their facial similarities with the Chinese. These instances of targeting the people of the North East are a part of a long history of them being mocked and slighted by 'mainland Indians'.

Similarly, it is tragic to note how a biological calamity is being used in our country for purposes of consolidating hatred against Indian Muslims. There seems to be an active tendency and a powerful need to shift blame for the spread of coronavirus in India onto Muslims. As the print, electronic and digital media irresponsibly create psychological hype by repeatedly flashing provocative news and statements against Muslims, a fresh wave of anti-Muslim sentiments has been unleashed.

The intensity with which hatred is being whipped against them reeks of a defensive agenda. Is it that by transferring blame onto them for the spread of the disease, we are trying to conveniently forget and wipe out from our collective conscience and memory the manner in which carnage and large-scale destruction of property were unleashed on them in the city of Delhi in February 2020? The divisive forces within our society are working up a fresh wave of Islamophobia, preparing a fresh ground through which future violence against them can be justified. One shudders to think of what lies ahead once the lockdown is over.

Beyond India too, there is news from other parts of the world, including America, of ways in which racism against Black and

Asian communities is on the rise. Instead of being a 'leveller', the pandemic is turning out to be a 'multiplier' of structural discrimination (Kendi 2020).

A Split Psyche

The insidious manner in which the invisible virus can survive on surfaces and within the human body is liable to bring us face-to-face with many other psychosocial challenges too. If every other surface and person is indeed a potential carrier, then we have to avoid almost everyone: those with travel histories, doctors, nurses and hospital staff, vegetable vendors, shopkeepers, sanitation workers and domestic helpers. We must also avoid touching parts of our body, railings, door knobs, light switches and so on. The list is endless indeed!

While today precautionary habits of maintaining cleanliness are necessary, in times to come these same habits are likely to invoke an unwitting participation in heightened obsessive-compulsive practices, leading to a form of collective suspiciousness and paranoia. Before we know, we may end up rekindling untouchability with a renewed ferocity. As the virus hits harder, our fears are possibly going to intermingle with the dread of contamination and be directed towards Dalits, the working classes and economically marginalised people, the same groups that have been worst affected by the unplanned lockdown.

There lies a thin line between adhering to the mantra of physical distancing and its conversion into a powerful projective force of othering and discrimination against the most marginalised members of society. Blue-collar workers, migrant workers, slum and street dwellers, and all those existing on socio-economic peripheries are liable to be easily considered *the* agents spreading the virus.

We are already face-to-face with a telling psychic split as doctors, nurses and other hospital staff are being pushed out of their homes and localities by neighbours who fear being infected by frontline health workers. It is instructive to recognise the workings of the psyche here. On the one hand, medical professionals are being applauded for their work and are being looked upon as gods. They are also the ones from whom we seek care and on whom we will be fully dependent if we or our family members contract the virus. On the other hand, they are treated as the 'untouchable other' or the 'contaminating agent' and are being evicted. This is a clear instance of how survival is maintained, by denying and splitting off complex aspects of an all-pervasive, multidimensional threatening reality.

Processes of othering are intrinsic to human history. At different junctures they become the impetus to justify targeted hatred and violence. The usual unconscious psychological defences deployed by humans in creating an 'other' include dissociation, projection, projective identification, and the deployment of paranoid-schizoid defence.[2] These might constitute the bedrock on which prejudice, stereotyping, scapegoating, and the splitting up the world into good and bad thrive. Such splitting may ultimately give way to identifying supposed sources and embodiments of badness, which can then be wiped up and eliminated by morally self-righteous forces and by collective aggression. In times of heighted stress, these may become our habitual ways of countering the full impact of any crisis that involves us as humans.

A Flight towards Authoritarianism

Adding to the complexity enumerated so far is also the deep-seated propensity in humans to succumb to authoritarianism and authority figures. This is liable to be on the rise whenever we are faced with circumstances that challenge our sense of continuing existence.

Among several other works, a famous study by American social psychologist Stanley Milgran demonstrated that there exists a deep and unconscious trait in us to obey orders even when they go against our personal conscience and usual ethical considerations (Cherry 2019). During the Nuremberg trials, several perpetrators of Nazi violence justified their participation in killings as being innocent. They believed that they were killing others as this was part of acting in a dutiful, moral and 'pure' manner. Throughout human history, we have many examples of people going against their personal sense of ethics and fusing their identity with forms of totalitarian power couched in morally pure forms, and demanding their unwavering allegiance.

The Covid-19 epidemic, which is capable of arousing fears of total collapse, can become a trigger intensifying human tendencies to submit to fascism, hyper-masculine nationalism and other forms of authoritarian regimes. We can see only too clearly how the present occasion will be used by undemocratic authoritarian governments to their advantage by demanding from their citizens unquestioned submission under the garb of maintaining regulations and enforcing discipline so as to ensure and maintain safety. Large segments of society are most likely to align their 'inner' proclivities for fascism with 'outer' socio-political forces, and actively seek shelter in anti-democratic regimes.

Long after the virus' actual biological force has disappeared, it can make us give in to subservience, surveillance, violence, hatred and the legitimacy of controlling structures and forces. The recognition of the enormity of a situation and its multi-layered actuality demands a deep contact with our sources of insecurities and fears, without allowing them to take over our capacity for rational judgement.

The Possibility of Rejuvenation

The thousands of deaths related to Covid-19 taking place everyday is a tragedy gripping the entirety of humankind. Painful as this is, the moment promises an authentic encounter with what it means to be a mortal human being. It is thus crucial at this juncture to resist giving in to fundamental forces and instead retain an awareness of our destructive proclivities.

This awareness can redirect attention to the 'voice of our conscience'. Retaining a connection with this voice can make us resist the tendency to align with projections fuelling hatred and othering. It can also help us take accountability for our collective actions and/or complicit silence in exacerbating the myriad forms of discrimination.

Several studies in collective psychology show that individuals and groups who mourn loss and suffering, rather than give in to othering or finding an enemy to destroy, are more likely to work towards justice, self-renewal and self-transformation (Erikson 1968; Vahali 2008). To be in awareness of the other's pain and to allow oneself to be touched by it can, at times, make us uncomfortable with our tendency of giving in blindly to unjust power and authoritarianism.

There are important lessons to be learnt from this historical moment. Today we are starkly confronting the limits of our power (indeed all power) and claims to hasty development and greed-driven advancement. The moment presents us with recovering forgotten lessons about our reality as vulnerable, fragile and impermanent embodied beings, forever existing under uncertain and unpredictable circumstances. It is hitting us hard. Our belief in the omnipotence of science, technology and the state; our desire to capture and subjugate other humans, animals and nature; and to create a world of endless needs and consumable desires, all are so easily shaken—by a microscopic virus.

In recognising the limits of power and in expanding our emotional life to be touched by the suffering around and inside the self, we can reach a different appreciation of mutual interdependence and a healthy acknowledgement of the fragile nature of our existence. The awareness of impending death can change us deeply. Perhaps a transformation awaits us here. This might make us capable of reaching out with empathy instead of by giving in to the instinct of aggressing against and hating those who are vulnerable or affected. In small quarters of the world this is already happening.

In this chapter, we have remained preoccupied with the darker shades of the psychological challenges confronting us; it would take us an equal amount of effort to document and expand on the innumerable compassionate actions, sacrifices of health workers and civil society initiatives across the world to feed, offer shelter and save others from Covid-19.

In this sobering time, the virus is indeed beholding a possibility that can make us reflectively pause as a species. However, it all depends on whether we will let the ongoing crisis touch us authentically or will we once again lose the opportunity and meet it with our usual defensive rigidity.

Notes

1. Repression is a basic psychological defence mechanism by way of which the human psyche pushes out of consciousness unbearable feelings,

experiences and memories. That which is pushed outside the realm of awareness nonetheless continues to exist in the unconscious mind, and also exert pressure as an active force, propelling our actions and life choices.

Dissociation is a psychological defence of reducing or making bearable the impact of traumatic, extremely uncomfortable or painful realities by denying, minimising, disconnecting feelings from thoughts and/or making them unknowable to the self through a number of ways. One type of dissociation is depersonalisation: the feeling that one is not in one's body and is disconnected from one's sense of self. Another type of dissociation is derealisation: the world and environment feel unreal to the individual.

2. Projection is an unconscious process through which we disown the negative and unacceptable parts of personal or group self/identity and then attribute the same to the 'other'. For instance, by disowning propensities for violence and hatred in the 'majoritarian Hindu consciousness', Muslims are looked at as 'terrorists' and 'repositories of all kinds of badness'. Or for instance, in the European and American racial context, Black and Jewish people have had to bear the burden of the disavowed violence, greed, sexuality and criminality of the White people/consciousness.

   In projective identification, we retain an emotional connection with the disavowed part and by the force of our feelings and/or actions 'unconsciously force' the 'other' to embody and enact the negative projections which have been thrown at them. The paranoid-schizoid defence is a basic primitive unconscious defence against self-annihilation in which inner sources of insecurity and hatred are projected on to external individuals or groups. Those on the receiving end are then looked at with suspicion and attacks against them are considered appropriate and justified.

References

Cherry, Kendra. 2019. 'Milgram's Experiments and the Perils of Obedience'. *VeryWellMind*, 16 September. Available at https://www.verywellmind.com/the-milgram-obedience-experiment-2795243 (accessed 18 April 2020).

Erikson, E. H. 1968. *Life History and the Historical Moment*. New York: Norton.

Kendi, Ibram X. 2020. 'Stop Blaming Black People for Dying of the Coronavirus'. *The Atlantic*, 14 April. Available at https://www.theatlantic.com/ideas/archive/2020/04/race-and-blame/609946/ (accessed 28 April 2020).

Milgram, Stanley. 1974. *Obedience to Authority: An Experimental View*. New York: Harper and Row.

Vahali, H. O. 2008. *Lives in Exile: Exploring the Inner World of Tibetan Refugees*. London: Routledge.

21

A Novel Virus, a New Racial Slur*

Naorem Pushparani Chanu and Gorky Chakraborty

The North East has historically been associated with in-migration from 'mainland' India and beyond. Since 1991, this has changed, and the difference between in- and out-migration has narrowed significantly.[1] In absolute terms, the Census indicates that between 1991 and 2011, approximately 2.3 million people have migrated from the North East to different locations in mainland India. West Bengal, Maharashtra, Delhi and Karnataka have been the main locations, largely due to the presence of urban metropolises.

Work is the principal reason for out-migration. The migrants, particularly the youth, are employed in service sectors like business process outsourcing (BPOs), restaurants, shopping malls, nursing or spas, in cities like Delhi, Mumbai, Bangalore and Kolkata. Bengt Karlsson and Dolly Kikon (2017) suggest they are recruited for their 'exotic Asian' appearance. Their 'oriental' looks, proficiency in English and good dressing sense enable them to secure jobs, according to Tiplut Nogbri and A. S. Shimreiwung (2017). Ironically these also become the reasons for their indictment of being 'un-Indian' by the locals.

Chinky-Momo-Corona!

The ongoing Covid-19 pandemic brought to the fore a novel racial epithet for those with Mongoloid phenotypes in India, affecting the

* First published in *The India Forum*, 3 July 2020.

migrants from North East India. Many of them who were already used to the racial slurs 'chinki', 'momo' or 'Chinese', now became 'corona'. Incidents of stigmatising hapless citizens appeared in the press and on social media.

This could take the shape of physical intimidation in excluding the perceived 'carriers'. A female Mizo out-migrant student residing in Delhi spoke to us over the phone and shared her experience during the initial days of the pandemic:

> It was before the lockdown during March when I went to my university to submit my assignment. Three men in a bike constantly followed me shouting "corona, corona" and they were teasing and laughing at me. They were scary and I preferred not to respond although [I] felt like making a video. But they could have easily snatched my phone. I had to constantly avoid them by walking fast, taking a different lane.

The student further reflected how calling names has been part of the daily lived experience of North Easterners in Delhi:

> You may find [it] strange but it's nothing different when they call me "corona". [I] feel, they are just using a different slur instead of "chinki". Actually, we were never respected by them [mainstream Indians]. They are now associating us with some "germ" or "virus" which only shows how they really feel about us. Before Corona, North East women were seen as "walking prostitute chinkies" and now we are "walking deadly virus". Either way, we need to be purged or eliminated from their society.

Venturing out appears to be full of dangers in an environment of the reactivated *us* and *them*. A male student migrant from Manipur residing in Gujarat narrated his experience over the phone:

> I went out of my apartment to a nearby vegetable vendor. There in the way, some guys called me "corona", and said why don't I just go back to China? I ignored because these are dangerous times ... I feel scared even when I am staying inside my apartment. For the first time, I have become desperate to go back home. This place no more seems to be safe.

This sense of desperation to return home was common. Another student from Nagaland residing in Delhi expressed similar fears when we called her:

> I have stopped going out of my flat even for essentials. News about increasing racial attacks against North Eastern people in various parts of the country not only makes me scared but my parents too at home. They remain worried about my well-being and have asked me not to go out at all. I do online shopping now which I find comparatively expensive, but it's okay since spending a little more money is better than becoming a victim of a racial attack. People have become crazy here. I would go back once the special trains are finalised ... I want to reach home.

A male from Manipur, currently employed in a private firm in Delhi, voiced his frustration over the phone regarding his identity, especially in times of the pandemic:

> The outbreak of Coronavirus brings out the hostile attitude of the locals against the North Eastern people in the city. This feeling was already there ... Coronavirus brought out the worst out of them [mainstream Indian society]. We have been called "chinkies", "Nepalis" or "Chinese" before, but now we are "corona". They never consider us Indians. Why do we need to tell people that we are "Indian"? Why do we need to prove our identity when a Bengali, Panjabi or Malayali doesn't? They also look different like us. Don't they realise that Indians comprise different phenotypes ... ascribing one face to all Indians may itself lead to racism.

Such racism has been all too common. The shuttler, Jwala Gutta was savagely trolled as *'half Corona'* because her mother is from China (*News18* 2020). On the pretext of keeping the 'virus' at bay, a 21-year-old Ladakhi student was shouted down by a man in a local market in Jammu, *'chal hatt, aap logon ki wajah se coronavirus aaya hai'* (get lost; it is because of you people the coronavirus has come [to India]) (*Deccan Herald* 2012).

Such thought processes also 'infect' healthcare providers. A 24-year-old woman from Sikkim narrated how she visited three different hospitals to treat herself for intense abdominal pain from a pre-diagnosed urinary tract infection in Kolkata (Colney 2020). She neither exhibited symptoms of viral infection nor did she have any travel history, but was asked to undergo screening for Covid-19. On her visit to the third hospital, where eventually the treatment was initiated, the woman was sent to an isolation ward. The next morning when the doctor came to check on her, the first question was: 'Are you from China?'

Similarly, a group of students hailing from Darjeeling, studying in Kolkata were addressed as 'coronavirus' by fellow passengers on a bus. One of the students was quoted as saying: 'I have never faced such a situation in my three years of stay in Kolkata. The bus was crowded, but no one sat beside me. They gawked at me. They know we are from the Hills … why such behaviour … I felt so bad' (Bhattacharya 2020).

It seems that 'otherisation' is not enough, they should also be taught a lesson or two. In Delhi, a middle-aged man spat on a Manipuri girl and called her 'corona', which became the first highlighted case of racial discrimination during the ongoing pandemic. Students in Kolkata were allegedly beaten by their neighbours who forced them to vacate their premises (Sirur 2020). As the students were leaving, the crowds chanted, 'Go corona go!'

Similar incidents have been reported from Bengaluru, where female North Eastern out-migrants were not only threatened by male neighbours at midnight and asked to move out of their premises, but the act was also videographed to exhibit how 'patriotic' they have been in their act of kicking out the 'virus' (Menezes 2020). The local police, however, did not stop this. In a similar instance, in May, a 20-year-old girl in Gurugram was brutally attacked by local residents, after she was called 'corona' and was told the police would be called, whom the locals said 'are on our side' (Das 2020). After she fell unconscious the police intervened, but instead of filing a complaint against the perpetrators, they asked her to 'compromise'.

These incidents pin-point how the police officials, instead of acting as enforcers of the law, become the 'carriers' of racial evils that afflict society and in the process create an *us* and *them* division. Has institutional racism, thereby, not become a part of the system?

When a 20-year-old student hailing from Nagaland went to buy groceries in Mysore with friends, they were prevented from entering the store on the presumptive understanding that they were not 'Indian' but 'Chinese' (Kidwai 2020). They produced their Aadhaar cards as proof of their Indian nationality, but were still refused service. In another bizarre incident, six young women from Nagaland working in a BPO in Ahmedabad were 'mistaken' as Chinese and taken to a hospital, tested for the coronavirus and not released even after testing negative (Mazumdar 2020). This incident occurred after a complaint that these women were infected with the virus. One of the victims exclaimed 'how looking different may lead one to be treated differently'.

Being a woman in a patriarchal social order has several underpinnings. More so, if she bears a Mongoloid phenotype: the vulnerabilities of victimisation in public become glaring. The return to the North East of a large number of nurses after quitting their jobs from several care-providing institutions in Kolkata reinforces such an impression (*New Indian Express* 2020). For these hapless nurses, stigmatisation and victimisation lay at the intersection of race, gender and profession that made them vulnerable to any eventuality.

On Racial Discrimination

The large-scale exodus of North Eastern migrants in 2012 from different cities stands as a watershed which is worth reflecting on. Rumours of attacks on them in retaliation for the killings of Muslims in Assam generated a fear psychosis. To 'escape' the fear, migration back to the North East appeared to be the only option. The stabbing of a 22-year-old Tibetan student, Tenzin Dhargiyial in Mysore, who 'looked' like someone from the North East further added fuel to the exodus (*Deccan Herald* 2012). It is noteworthy that the perceived fear of the migrants lay in their different phenotypes and, second, the cause of the murder of the Tibetan student also lay in his phenotype, irrespective of the fact that he had no link with the North East. Prejudices and stereotypes rooted in the ideology of racism led to the exodus of panic-stricken North Easterners from urban centres.

The underlying phenomenon of racial discrimination and stigmatisation has been around for a while and has manifested on many occasions in violence. The killing of 19-year-old Loitam Richard from Manipur in Bengaluru in 2012 (Mondal 2012); the mysterious murder of 21-year-old Reingamphy Awungshi from Manipur in Delhi in 2013 (Nishtha 2013); and the brutal killing of 20-year-old Nido Taniam from Arunachal Pradesh in Delhi in 2014 (Colney 2020) are a few incidents pointing in such a direction. It was only after large-scale protests both within the North East and outside that the home ministry was forced to constitute the Bezbaruah Committee (2014) to look into the matter of discrimination and violence against North Eastern people in various urban centres in India. Despite recommendations of this committee to bring in changes to the provisions of the Indian Penal Code to sternly deal with racial attacks, not much progress has been made in this regard.

Why the 'Other'

Epidemics, otherwise biological processes, can carry cultural overtones which often generate racial prejudices by constructing the perceived carrier individuals and communities as the 'other' who are to be excluded from 'sanitised' spaces. For various reasons, othering becomes a potent tool during pandemics in calibrating relations amongst individuals and communities within a society.

First, it provides an *alibi* for identifying scapegoats. David Arnold (1986), writing on cholera epidemics in colonial India, noted that the scapegoat was often 'a low caste or a tribal woman, or a prostitute, who was driven out of the village to symbolise the expulsion of the disease from its boundaries'. Second, it provides a semblance of (false) knowledge of understanding the novel virus by analysing the 'other' as the perceived carrier.

Third, it enables communities to shift the blame on to the 'other' and their 'unnatural' way of life by associating them with the disease, while the sanitised 'rest', who do not adhere to 'unnatural' ways, potentially remain at a lower risk. Fourth, a novel virus and accompanying epidemics come as a shock as we attempt to adjust to the changed 'normal', and adjustment strains the fault lines of the pre-epidemic social order. As Henri Lefebvre (1991) reminds us, 'in space what came earlier continues to underpin what follows', racism, communalism and other forms of 'otherisation' get reactivated until a known aetiology emerges.

It began in India by stigmatising those bearing Mongoloid phenotypes, along with their food, lifestyles and manners. The absence of the Mongoloid phenotypes in Indian imaginaries even necessitates a mainland Indian face to play the lead role in a biopic on the Manipuri boxer Mary Kom because North Eastern people 'don't look Indian enough'.

Lack of cultural understanding among a major section of the Indian mainland's mainstream societies makes them interpret any difference—phenotypes, attire, hairstyle, food habits and lifestyles of the migrants—through a racial lens. This ultimately manifests in racial slurs: 'chinki', 'momo'.

As migrants from the North East reach new destinations in mainland India, they are exposed to newer social spaces. Adjustment and adaptation become buzz words for coexistence, a complex process dependent on both the migrants and locals in the host societies. Since the migrants are culturally and racially distinct, they are more exposed to social challenges in terms of language, food habits, attire and life styles vis-à-vis others in the host societies. These differences along with their Mongoloid phenotypes attract unwanted gaze, often leading to prejudices, stereotypes and presumptions about their personalities. These create *unseen* borders, which are more *felt* than visualised, often embedded in racial undertones.

Note

1. The 1991 Census showed that out of the total migration, out-migrants accounted for 39 per cent, rising to 52 per cent in 2001 before declining to 45 per cent in 2011. Individual states have shown fluctuating patterns, except Manipur, which consistently had a higher out-migration during this period.

References

'After Pune, Tibetan Student in Mysore Stabbed on Suspicion He's from North East'. 2012. *Deccan Herald,* 15 August. Available at https://

www.deccanherald.com/state/after-pune-tibetan-student-in-mysore-stabbed-on-suspicion-hes-from-north-east-263702.html (accessed 10 March 2020).

'COVID-19: 185 Manipuri Nurses Quit Private Hospital Jobs in Kolkata, Health Worker Kills Self in Jalpaiguri'. 2020. *New Indian Express*, 16 May. Available at https://www.newindianexpress.com/cities/kolkata/2020/may/16/covid-19-185-manipuri-nurses-quit-private-hospital-jobs-in-kolkata-health-worker-kills-self-in-jal-2143894.html (accessed 18 May 2020).

'People Call Me "Half-corona" Now: Jwala Gutta on Racism Amid Coronavirus Pandemic'. 2020. *News18*, 6 April. Available at https://www.news18.com/news/badminton/people-call-me-half-corona-now-jwala-gutta-on-racism-amid-coronavirus-pandemic-2566505.html (accessed 8 May 2020).

Arnold, David. 1986. 'Cholera and Colonialism in British India'. *Past and Present* 113: 118–51.

Bhattacharya, Ravik. 2020. 'On Kolkata Streets, Students from Darjeeling Face Racial Slurs Linked to Coronavirus'. *Indian Express*, 17 March. Available at https://indianexpress.com/article/education/on-kolkata-streets-students-from-darjeeling-face-racial-slurs-linked-to-coronavirus-6317822/ (accessed 10 May 2020).

Colney, Kimi. 2020. 'Indians from the Northeast Face Intensified Racism as Coronavirus Fears Grow'. *Caravan*, 3 April. Available at https://caravanmagazine.in/communities/coronavirus-increases-racism-against-indians-from-northeast (accessed 7 May 2020).

Das, Amlan Jyoti. 2020. 'Manipur Girl Racially Abused, Assaulted by Locals in Gurugram'. *EastMojo*, 12 May. Available at https://www.eastmojo.com/manipur/2020/05/12/manipur-girl-racially-abused-assaulted-by-locals-in-gurugram (accessed 17 May 2020).

Karlsson, Bengt G., and Dolly Kikon. 2017. 'Wayfinding: Indigenous Migrants in the Service Sector of Metropolitan India'. *South Asia: Journal of South Asian Studies* 40 (3): 447–62.

Kidwai, Nehal. 2020. '2 Men from Nagaland Denied Entry to Mysuru Store Amid COVID-19 Scare'. *NDTV*, 29 March. Available at https://www.ndtv.com/karnataka-news/coronavirus-2-men-from-nagaland-denied-entry-to-mysuru-store-amid-covid-19-scare-2202617 (accessed 10 May 2020).

Lefebvre, Henri. 1991. *The Production of Space*. Oxford: Basil Blackwell.

Mazumdar, Prasanta. 2020. 'For Young Nagas in Ahmedabad, Racial Virus More Horrific than COVID-19'. *New Indian Express*, 23 March.

Available at https://www.newindianexpress.com/nation/2020/mar/23/for-young-nagas-in-ahmedabad-racial-virus-more-horrific-than-covid-19-2120542.html (accessed 7 May 2020).

Menezes, Naveen. 2020. 'Neighbour Barges into Women's Flat in Koramangala and Calls then Covid Carriers'. *Bangalore Mirror,* 13 May. Available at https://bangaloremirror.indiatimes.com/bangalore/others/neighbour-barges-into-womens-flat-in-koramangala-and-calls-them-covid-carriers/articleshow/75705103.cms (accessed 15 May 2020).

Mondal, Sudipto. 2012. '"The Loitam Case was Just a Trigger"'. *The Hindu,* 8 May. Available at https://www.thehindu.com/news/cities/bangalore/the-loitam-case-was-just-a-trigger/article3396513.ece (accessed 8 May 2020).

Nishtha. 2013. 'Cry for "Fair" Probe into Death of 21-year-old'. *Hindustan Times,* 2 June. Available at https://www.hindustantimes.com/delhi/cry-for-fair-probe-into-death-of-21-year-old/story-aWo5a32PLRegcWMtrkwKdP.html (accessed 10 May 2020).

Nongbri, Tiplut and A. S. Shimreiwung. 2017. *Migration, Identity and Conflict: Lived Experience of Northeasterners in Delhi*. New Delhi: Rawat Publications.

Sirur, Simrin. 2020. '"Beaten, Abused, Spat On": People from Northeast Endure Racist Slurs Amid Coronavirus Panic'. *The Print,* 25 March. Available at https://theprint.in/india/beaten-abused-spat-on-people-from-northeast-endure-racist-slurs-amid-coronavirus-panic/387716/ (accessed 9 May 2020).

Section VIII
The Future

22

Extreme Events in Nature

*An Ecological History of the Present**

Ramprasad Sengupta

Humanity is currently facing an existential crisis due to the pandemic caused by the highly infectious novel coronavirus. Apart from the pandemic, the world in recent times has experienced other extreme natural events like super-cyclones, heavy rainfall, floods and forest fires.

In this chapter, I point out that the common driving factor behind many of these events is the unfolding of an imbalance between the human appropriation of natural resources of the earth's eco-systems (the ecological footprint) and the carrying-capacity of the biosphere (the biocapacity). If we are to arrive at a long-term solution, we need to first situate today's challenge with Covid-19 within a perspective of such imbalances in the ecological history of humankind.

Coincidence of Extreme Events and Covid-19

In October 2020, the world is still in the midst of the Covid-19 pandemic and we cannot, as yet, make a total assessment of what its

* First published in *The India Forum*, 30 October 2020.

I would first of all thank Professor Mihir Deb, retired Professor of Geology at Delhi University, for useful discussions and comments on a draft. I would also like to thank Chetana Chaudhuri of the Public Health Foundation of India, and Sovik Mukherjee of St Xavier's University, Kolkata, for assisting me with data and the development of the figures. However, the burden of all assertions made in this chapter is mine.

complete impact will be. All countries have already been affected by the pandemic in a manner that their normal socio-economic life has been derailed. As will be seen in my narrative about the development of this disease, the extreme damage caused to the health of humans has in fact an ecological linkage. It is a message from nature pointing to the dangerous consequence of a growing imbalance between the human system and the carrying capacity of the biosphere of the earth (see Figure 22.1).

Extreme Events

It is noticeable that apart from Covid-19, India has also faced several cyclonic storms in the recent past that have caused catastrophic damage. The frequency of such extreme events has been growing.

Already in 2020, India has experienced one super-cyclone hitting the eastern coast of India in West Bengal and Odisha on 20 May, which saw wind speeds and devastation that had not been experienced in the region since 1737. A second severe cyclone hit the west coast near Mumbai on 2 June, an unusual event of a cyclone crossing the west coast. The increasing frequency of cyclones, their extreme severity,

Figure 22.1: Total World-wide Number of Natural Disaster Events Recorded, 1970–2019

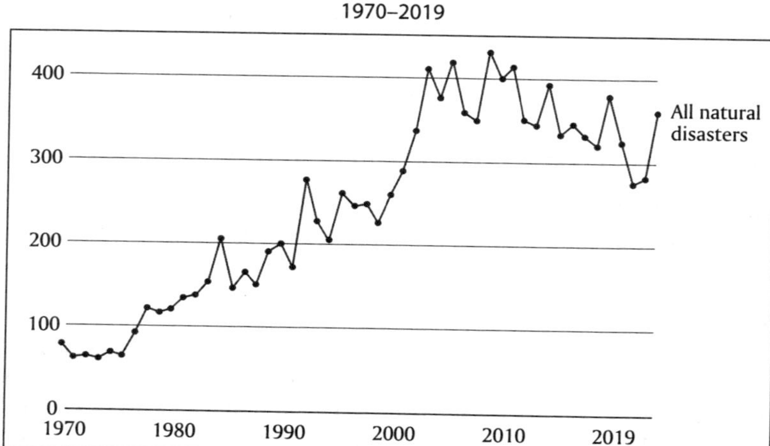

Source: EM–Dat (2019) CRED International Disaster Database, available at ourworlddata.org (accessed 10 May 2020).

and the rising frequency of incidents of extreme rainfall arise mainly because of changes in temperature on land and sea. Such extreme events render millions of people homeless, destroy standing crops and wipe away the infrastructure built over the past many years; causing huge damage and wasting our environmental and human-made capital.

Global satellite data shows that the frequency and scale of forest fires have also been increasing over time in recent years. Vast tracts in Brazil, Russia, Indonesia and Africa have been burning for quite some years. Apart from others, the Amazon rainforest—one of the wettest places on earth and a major carbon sink of the planet—and the very biodiverse forests of Indonesia, are both burning at several places, causing a huge erosion of both biodiversity and the environmental capital stock of the planet. India too has been witnessing forest fires in Uttarakhand over years. There were 1,000 fires in 2019. These are attributable to the exceptionally dry nature of the region caused by unusually low rainfall. The number of fires, however, came down in 2020 because of action undertaken by the forest department and by local communities (Pinto 2020).

Is there any underlying common causal or driving factor of these disparate extreme events as experienced in India and elsewhere? Or is it just coincidental? The coincidence itself sends us a message from nature, warning us about a deep malady that can have a dangerous and devastating impact in the contingent event of such a coincidence. What is common among the driving factors of all such events is that they are all caused by human interventions in the form of an overuse of resources or a running down of the biocapacity of the local and global ecosystems. The destruction of the habitat of wildlife and ongoing climate change are both hurting humanity, Covid-19 being a 'clear warning shot' (Carrington 2020).

Essentially, what has happened is that global warming, climate change and the destruction of the natural world for farming, mining and construction of infrastructure have driven wildlife into contact with humans. According to the United Nations, a huge natural forest area of 290 million hectares was lost in the world between 1990 and 2015. This deprived billions of large or small animals, birds, insects and other micro-organism of their habitats.

The rate of loss of biodiversity on land in this age of the Anthropocene is estimated to be 100 to 1,000 times faster than during any preceding geological age, before the arrival of *Homo sapiens*. According to the 2020 Global Assessment of the Intergovernmental Science Policy Platform on Biodiversity and Ecosystem Services (IPBES):

> around 1 million animal and plant species are now threatened with extinction, many within decades, more than ever before in human history. The average abundance of native species in most major land-based habitats has fallen by at least 20%, mostly since 1900. More than 40% of amphibian species, almost 33% of reef forming corals and more than a third of all marine mammals are threatened. The picture is less clear for insect species, but available evidence supports a tentative estimate of 10% being threatened.

Apart from deforestation, climate change has also destroyed the habitats of wildlife and has forced animals to come close to humans, which created opportunities for pathogens in animal bodies to get new hosts in the human body (Carrington 2020; United Nations 2020).

Since the turn of the century many new diseases have emerged, all linked to the transmission of microbes from animals, birds and other life forms to human beings. MERS, SARS, Covid-19, Avian flu, Swine flu, Ebola, ZIKA fever, West Nile fever, are all zoonotic diseases caused by pathogens of various kinds jumping from animals to humans (Wong et al. 2020; Ye et al. 2020). The fundamental problem is that we do not as yet have an adequate understanding of the origin of these viruses, the nature of their mutation and fatality rates in humans. It is like the throw of a dice to get the answer to any question. The phenomenon is not only random in nature but possibly so uncertain that it cannot be modelled using the calculus of probability to make predictive simulations.

Human Interventions and Non-linear Behaviour of the Ecosystem

As humans are an integral part of the biosphere, one may ask, how is it then that human behaviour can so evolve that it may be held responsible for biodiversity loss? This can happen because of two reasons: (i) human intervention to change the land-use pattern of the ecosystem for economic development; and (ii) non-linearity of the functioning of the ecosystem (Dasgupta 2020).

Most human activities that result in an appropriation of resources—particularly those involving land-use changes—cause fragmentation of ecosystems, both on land and water. The sum of the productivities of such fragmented ecosystems would, in fact, be less than that of an undivided productivity. This contributes to the erosion of the biosphere and causes non-linear complex behaviour of its ecosystems (that is, a disproportionate change in the final outcome as compared with the size of an initial disturbance to the ecosystem). It fundamentally weakens their resilience, making them vulnerable to exogenous shocks.

Moreover, the processes driving the spread of an infectious disease like Covid-19 are also non-linear. With globalisation, human beings' ability to intrude into any ecological niche that is occupied by various organisms with whom we have not evolved has exposed us to unfamiliar pathogens. Biodiversity loss creates niches for pathogens that are waiting in the wings in small numbers to explode into a large population, creating conditions for new pathogens to evolve through mutations as part of a non-linear process. The non-linearity of the behaviour of Covid-19 is such that one cannot be certain about how it will evolve if a vaccine is invented, and then how to control the spread and treat the disease. Besides, quantitative studies on the transmission of the infectious disease point to the fact that large-scale movement of people and goods have made the socio-ecological system quite fragile. This mobility in human economies in the era of global integration has eroded the modularity of our socio-economic system. It has facilitated the invasion of the coronavirus from zoonotic sources into cells of the human body in one part of the world, the disturbance soon reverberating across the world.

How is it that humanity has ended up in the twenty-first century with such a deep problem of sustainability of human existence? For a perspective of how the present state has emerged, we need here to reflect on the history of the emergence of the imbalance between the ecological footprint of humans and the biocapacity of our planet, an imbalance that is fundamentally responsible for the present crisis.

History of the Struggle between Humans and the Ecosystems of the Biosphere

Earth was formed as a planet in the solar system about 4.5 billion years ago. According to the theory of evolutionary biology, life emerged on earth at least 3.7 billion years ago. There exist now on earth 1 trillion different species, out of which only 1.8 million have been named. These currently living species constitute only 1 per cent of all species that have ever lived on this planet.

Modern intelligent humans, *Homo sapiens*, the only extant species of the hominid group, who now dominate earth, emerged in the evolutionary process about 300,000 to 500,000 years ago in east Africa (near Ethiopia) and south Africa (near the pinnacle point).

Other than in the last 10,000 to 12,000 years, in their long history on earth, humans have obtained their subsistence through a combination of food-gathering and hunting animals. Ninety-nine per cent of human history is one of humans as hunter-gatherers. To begin with, they used to move in small mobile groups and followed the most successful and flexible way of life that caused the least harm and damage to ecosystems. It enabled them to spread across the face of the globe and every terrestrial ecosystem in various continents from the Arctic of the north polar regions to the dry lands of Australia and South Africa and both the American continents (Ponting 2011).

Ice Age and Early Human Migration

How was such migration possible for the early humans? Such migration started soon after humans learnt about the controlled use of fire and to make tools out of stone (the Palaeolithic and Neolithic ages). It is during the period of the last glaciation and the Ice Age that a large part of the earth's surface was covered with ice due to a fall of surface temperature in many parts of the planet below zero degree Celsius. As a result, the polar ice sheet got extended and the seas were frozen and became shallow, enabling nomadic tribes to cross the straits at places to reach other continents of the earth's land mass.

Milankovitch Theory of Cycles and Climate on Earth

The Ice Age is a cyclical phenomenon; a period of glaciation is followed by an interglacial warm period. The phenomenon is explained by Milankovitch's theory (see Figure 22.2) of cycles and climate, according to which once every 96,000 years, the earth's orbit around the sun changes from the circular to the elliptical and again returns to the circular position (Buis 2020). It happens because of the stronger combined gravitational pull of Jupiter and Saturn on Earth, both of which planets have a much larger mass than Earth or any other planet of the solar system. The climate and the Ice Ages—their timing and intensity—depend on this cycle along with the two other astronomical phenomena of the axial precession[1] and axial tilt (nutation).[2]

Figure 22.2: Milankovitch Cycles

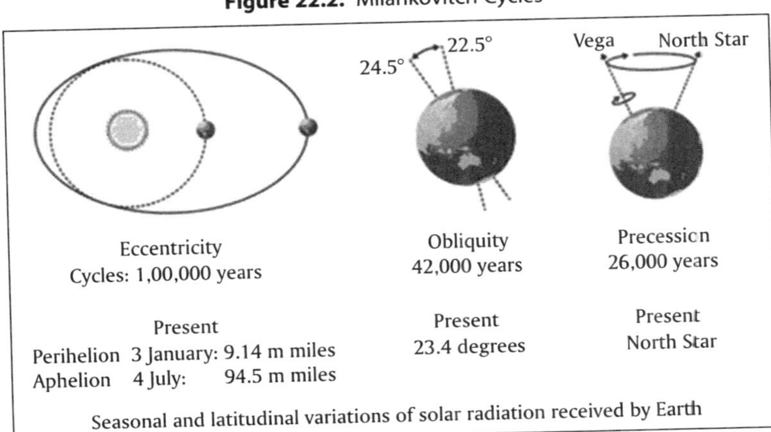

Source: Author's own compilation and design.

The climate on our planet is influenced by the impact of these three cycles on solar radiation as received by the earth. The glaciation of the earth occurs when for several millennia, the earth is at a distant location from the sun on the elongated elliptical path with eccentricity (the degree of elongation of an ellipse that is oval shaped as compared with the circle which has zero eccentricity) on the higher side. The duration of glaciation is several millennia because of the long duration of the cycle of 96,000 years. These astronomical phenomena have relevance in today's debate on the imminence of climate change.

First Great Transition in Human History

After the end of the last glaciation 11,700 years ago, the landscape that emerged of continents, lakes, rivers and seas, hills and boulders, forests and grassland, etc., formed the contours of the natural map of our known world. The deposition of huge biotic masses of plants and animals under the ice sheets over hundreds and thousands of years contributed to the formation of the humus content of soil and its build-up.

Humankind invented agriculture by domesticating plants and animals, cultivating land for an intensive system of production of food and fibre, and by rearing cattle for milk, meat and animal energy. Humans developed tools and implements like the plough and the wheel for such agricultural activities. These developments revolutionised the productivity of both land and labour, generating a surplus over the subsistence requirement for the tiller of the soil. There now emerged settled societies with all their hierarchies and complexities. The surplus of agriculture was mobilised by the ruler (king) of the society who redistributed it among the different socio-economic groups of the ruling classes, priests and soldiers, artisans and traders (when exchange started), builders of monuments, etc. The early civilisations of Babylonia, Egypt, Indus Valley, China and the Mayan civilisation of central America (Guatemala) are illustrative of such developments (Ponting 2011).

This first great transition of human history was accompanied by the beginning of interference of humans in the ecosystems of the biosphere, marking the onset of its degradation. According to the classical economists of the eighteenth and nineteenth centuries, the emergence of a surplus output over subsistence due to the higher carrying capacity of land led to the growth of the human population.

Thomas Malthus, the British classical economist, thought this growth would be in geometric proportion while food production would grow at a lower rate of arithmetic progression due to the fixed amount of land available. As a result, there would ensue a long period of struggle in human history over several millennia between the human population and food production, one chasing the other.

This struggle resulted in a history of degradation of the ecosystems of the earth. The degradation took the following forms:

1. Conversion of forest land into crop land for cultivation as or into pasture. This triggered a huge biodiversity loss and the emergence of zoonotic diseases of various kinds from time to time.
2. Intensification of cultivation by the use of irrigation and fertilisers, which was often carried out without proper drainage, resulting in water-logging and salinisation of soil, and desertification.
3. Overgrazing by animals of pasture denuded the land of vegetation. Degradation due to these two processes is illustrated by the fact that the seat of the Babylonian civilisation of ancient times is now one of the deserts of the Middle East. Stories of desertification of north Africa and Sahara would be similar.
4. Migration of population and wars for occupying land and natural resources. Illustrations of the impact of migrations and war abound in history, for example, the fall of the Roman empire due to the barbarian invasion, fall of the Byzantine empire due to the invasion by Arabs, Turks, Slavs, Bulgars, Normans, etc., invasion of Mongols in eastern Europe and India, development of the huge empire of Genghis Khan, among many others. And many other migrations and wars took place in human history essentially for capturing land and natural resources.

As humans migrated and trade took place, knowledge, technology and culture got propagated and benefited humanity at large through the early forms of trade imperialism. At the same time, germs and diseases also spread across countries and continents. These often resulted in extreme events of epidemics or pandemics as we are experiencing today. There was the Bubonic plague (black death) in the thirteenth and fourteenth centuries in Europe that depopulated

40 per cent of the European population. The plague had in fact devastated many parts of the world since the days before the common era (Ponting 2011).

The imbalance in history between the human demand for basic necessities of food and the capacity of the ecosystem has largely expressed itself in the form of hunger and famine in years of droughts and unfavourable climate. An accentuating factor of the impact of such calamities has often been the inequality in the distribution of food and necessities in society, which has been determined largely by hierarchies and power structures ever since the emergence of agrarian settlements in different parts of the world. One may, however, point out that the imbalance between human numbers and food was corrected by Malthusian checks like the pestilence of the bubonic plague—a zoonotic disease—in medieval Europe.

History has also shown that humans finally circumvented or tided over crises by the development of technology, augmenting the productivity of land and labour, and by the discovery of medicines, vaccines and medical treatment. All these proved Malthus's prediction wrong. The inventions of the wheel for grinding cereals, making pottery, spinning fibre and of the driving cart for transportation were landmark developments in early stages of human civilisation. The later innovations of machines (by application of the principle of generating kinetic energy by circular rotation), initially driven by renewable energy (watermills and windmills), greatly facilitated the productivity of labour and of natural resources to yield a social product during the long eras of feudalism in the agrarian societies of medieval Europe and Asia.

The Second Great Transition: The Industrial Revolution

A second great revolution or transition, if we want to call it that, took place in human history 250 years ago, when the use of non-renewable fossil fuel–based energy was introduced to drive machines and transport vehicles.

The first industrial revolution was based on coal-based steam power that greatly increased the efficiency of driving machines and transportation. The steam locomotive engine and rail transport came as great inventions. Steam-powered printing presses facilitated human communication. These led to the development of a division of labour in industrial activity that revolutionised productivity.

The second wave of the industrial revolution came with the use of hydrocarbons and internal combustion engines for road transportation and for electricity. The latter was the most clean and efficient energy form for end use. It provided the most efficient way of obtaining end-use energy at the burner tip, from basic energy resources.

However, as in the case of the agricultural revolution, this second great transition in the form of the industrial revolution, which began in western Europe, involved significant costs in the form of (i) a depletion of non-renewable fossil fuels; and (ii) emission of carbon dioxide and other greenhouse gases causing heating up of the planet.

In terms of the ecological footprint created, the carbon footprint from carbon dioxide emissions has contributed to more than half of the total ecological stress on earth caused by humans. The carbon footprint is measured in terms of the forest land area required to absorb the carbon dioxide emissions from fossil fuels, in excess of that absorbed by the carbon cycle of photosynthesis and by the oceans. This would be at least half of the total ecological footprint of human land use to meet the entire demand for crops, animal products, industrial goods, infrastructural and urban development, and waste absorption. This is measured in units of use or diversion of photosynthetic land area, normalised to units of equivalent cropland area with average global crop productivity per unit area. Today, we need 1.7 units of earth to ensure a balance between the ecological footprint and biocapacity of our planet, according to the Global Footprint Network, using the data of 2016.[3]

If there were no carbon dioxide or other greenhouse gas emissions from anthropogenic sources in the coming years, the earth might well cycle back again into the Ice Age in 50,000 years from now. However, we are unlikely to see the next Ice Age for another 100,000 years because of the carbon dioxide emissions we are putting into the atmosphere at the current rate, according to the Potsdam Institute of Research on Climate Impact (2016). This finding indicates the profound impact of human interference with the ecosystems of the planet. But does this postponement of the next Ice Age give us any sense of comfort? There are, in fact, problems of uncertainty of whether the impact of such carbon dioxide emissions on the Milankovitch Cycle can last so long in the current geological time scale. This is a non-issue, as what matters to us are happenings on the human time scale. Even if the carbon dioxide concentration is kept elevated over hundreds and thousands of years and the Ice Age gets postponed, the damage that would be caused in the coming decades and centuries due to super-cyclones, floods, rise in the sea level, droughts, desertification and forest fires would threaten the very existence of the present civilisation on earth.

The issue now is how to meet the challenge of sustainability of humanity at the present juncture. Dasgupta (2020), in his interim report on the Economics of Biodiversity for the UK government, points to the ecological footprint as having exceeded the biocapacity since the 1960s. He considers the ecological deficit (that is, the shortfall of biocapacity from the ecological footprint) in terms of land use as responsible for the enormous biodiversity loss of the planet. The emergence and alarming rate of spread of Covid-19 is a warning signal of humanity crossing the safe operational limits of the functioning of the biosphere.

The sustainable development goal of the United Nations requires that an economy should operate within such safe operational limits. Since the GDP of a country or the world is determined by the actual use of biocapacity and the productivity of its use to yield GDP, the delimiting of the ecological footprint to ensure sustainable development would require reducing the growth rate of GDP and raising the productivity of biotic resources (biocapacity) of the earth. The rise of the productivity of environmental resources also has to offset the secular decline of the biocapacity of the earth, a decline that is being experienced over time because of the degradation of the ecosystem in terms of its ability to reproduce natural resources.

In the long term, to prevent the onset of pandemic diseases like Covid-19, it is important that we attain the goal of sustainable development. If we assume that the United Nations Sustainable Development Goal is to be attained by 2030, Dasgupta's report points out that given the growth rate of global GDP per capita at 3.4 per cent per annum and the rate of decline of global natural capital stock at 0.3 per cent per annum, as experienced during the period 1992–2014, the productivity of bioresources in terms of GDP would have to grow at 9.1 per cent per annum. This is going to be too tall an order, given the fact that the historic rate of growth of such economic productivity of bioresources has been 2.5 per cent per annum.

Now, if the productivity of natural resources cannot grow at such a high rate, the only other option is to make serious efforts to reduce the size of the footprint by reducing the growth of both population and that of per capita income. Is that feasible?

Conclusions

The root of the Covid-19 pandemic and of the other extreme natural events that the world is experiencing is the disruption of the ecological balance between the human appropriation of resources of the biosphere and the biocapacity of our ecosystem. This has expressed itself in forms of biodiversity loss and climate change, which again affect each other. We are confronted with a tough choice today between lives and livelihoods (because the Covid-19 pandemic is devastating our fellow beings), and between economic growth and halting the erosion of the environmental capital stock of the biosphere.

This takes us to the fundamental question: how do we reduce the requirement of growth of the global economy that is essentially driven on one side by the capitalist forces of indefinite accumulation of wealth and growth of economic power in the Organisation for Economic Cooperation and Development (OECD) countries, and on the other side by the requirement of a rapid removal of poverty of Afro-Asia in the non-OECD countries?

The reduction of the size of an economy and its growth would call for a change in the preference structure of society and a redistribution of income and wealth so that the new total demand can limit use of the biosphere's resources within the regenerative capacity of the biosphere. The feasibility of such a change would depend on our sense of values and ethics about growth, well-being and sustenance of other species. These would require *a change in our ways of thought* and our long-run policies. This is necessary to reduce the scale of our consumption demand, on the one hand, by changing our value system and preference structure and, on the other, by making scientific advances and innovating new technologies and social organisation of production to raise the productivity of biocapacity.

All these ultimately lead to the need for setting up two goals of equal importance:

1. control our greed and demand by developing an enlightened set of preferences of the structure and level of consumption; and
2. cooperation of people at the global and local level for an equitable sharing of the benefits from the use of natural resources.

All religions and faiths of the world have preached the values of empathy, sharing, charity and compassion so that society does not collapse due to chaos in times of environmental crisis. For meeting today's existential crisis, we are now facing the issues of a conflict between growth and saving nature, and between lives and livelihoods. To meet this challenge, we need to sustain our march of progress in science and technology, especially in the domain of genome and biomedical research, to ensure food and health security. This development of knowledge has to be translated into that of social well-being through the choice of appropriate strategies and policies of development. Finally, all these initiatives and actions need to be combined with our intellectual and emotional commitment to humanity, for the universal and equitable sharing of global resources for the development of all.

Notes

1. The axis of the earth, which is rotating like a wobbling top, again rotates, making a conical shape completing one conical cycle in 26,000 years. This causes the astronomical phenomenon of the axial precession.
2. The axis of the earth makes an angle with its orbital plane around the sun (called ecliptic), which varies between 22 and 24 degrees, one such cycle of variation from and back to 22 degrees taking 40,000 years. This causes the astronomical phenomenon of the axial tilt.
3. See Global Footprint Network, available at https://www.footprintnetwork.org/our-work/ecological-footprint/ (accessed 4 July 2020).

References

Buis, Alan. 2020. 'Milankovitch Cycles and their Role in Earth Climate'. NASA Global Climate Change Features, 27 February. Available at https://climate.nasa.gov/news/2948/milankovitch-orbital-cycles-and-their-role-in-earths-climate/ (accessed 8 December 2020).

Carrington, D. 2020. 'Coronavirus: "Nature is Sending Us a Message", Says UN Environment Chief'. *The Guardian*, 25 March. Available at https://www.theguardian.com/world/2020/mar/25/coronavirus-nature-is-sending-us-a-message-says-un-environment-chief (accessed 8 December 2020).

Dasgupta, P. 2020. *The Dasgupta Review: Independent Review on the Economics of Biodiversity*. Interim report, April. Available at https://www.gov.uk/government/publications/interim-report-the-dasgupta-review-independent-review-on-the-economics-of-biodiversity (accessed 8 December 2020).

Harari, Y. N. 2014. *A Brief History of Humankind*. New York: Penguin Random House.

Intergovernmental Science Policy Platform on Biodiversity and Ecosystem Services (IPBES). 2020. 'Media Release: Nature's Dangerous Decline "Unprecedented"; Species Extinction Rates "Accelerating"'. Available at https://ipbes.net/news/Media-Release-Global-Assessment (accessed 8 December 2020).

Ponting, Clive. 2011. *A Green History of the World: The Environment and the Collapse of Great Civilizations*. New York: Penguin Books.

Pinto, Deekshith Nevil. 2020. 'Fact Check: Experts Say Uttarakhand Forest Fires at Record Low as Cries to #SaveTheHimalayas Trend'. *The Weather Channel*, 27 May. Available at https://weather.com/en-IN/india/news/news/2020-05-27-uttarakhand-forest-fires-record-low-cries-savethehimalayas-trend-experts (accessed 8 December 2020).

Potsdam Institute of Research on Climate Impact. 2016. 'Human-made Climate Change Suppresses the Next Ice Age', 13 January. Available at https://www.pik-potsdam.de/en/news/latest-news/human-made-climate-change-suppresses-the-next-ice-age (accessed 8 December 2020).

United Nations. 2020. 'Nature's Dangerous Decline "Unprecedented"; Species Extinction Rates "Accelerating"', 6 May. Available at https://www.un.org/sustainabledevelopment/blog/2019/05/nature-decline-unprecedented-report/ (accessed 8 December 2020).

Wong, G., Y. H. Bi, Q. H. Wang, X. W. Chen, Z. G. Zhang and Y. G. Yao. 2020. 'Zoonotic Origins of Human Coronavirus 2019 (HCoV-19/ SARS-CoV-2): Why Is This Work Important?'. *Zoological Research* 41 (3): 213.

Ye, Z. W., S. Yuan, K. S. Yuen, S. Y. Fung, C. P. Chan and D. Y. Jin. 2020. 'Zoonotic Origins of Human Coronaviruses'. *International Journal of Biological Sciences* 16 (10): 1686.

23

Four Future Scenarios, or, What's Different about the Covid-19 Crisis?*

Itty Abraham

What does the novel coronavirus pandemic mean for our collective futures? No one can be quite sure as the pandemic is far from over, but the variation among those offering answers to this question is striking. The starkest difference can be seen between those who see this moment as a turning point of the kind that will be discussed in the future in terms of 'before and after' Covid-19, and those who do not.

Turning Point or Not?

There have been remarkably few truly *global* turning points in the last century and a half, so calling the Covid-19 coronavirus pandemic a historic turning point is no small matter. In my view, the World Wars and the Great Depression meet that high standard, while the 'End of the Cold War' does not. At the risk of considerable simplification, and focusing particularly on the intersection of geopolitics and biopolitics, I propose that analysts of this crisis can be divided into four largely discrete but inevitably overlapping groups. Two kinds of optimists and two kinds of pessimists can be identified, all of whom see this moment as a critical time, but whose assumptions, evidence and prognostications differ considerably.

* First published in *The India Forum*, 24 April 2020.

Optimists and Pessimists

Within the set of those who argue for this moment as an irreversible world-historic turning point, there are two positions: one more hopeful, the other less so.

Progressive voices are confident that given the lessons learned from this crisis, we have seen the end of the so-called Washington Consensus that promoted the ideology of neoliberalism. Neoliberalism, in essence, was a dominant elite view that looked to the private sector for answers and recommended reducing state activities to an absolute minimum. Evidence offered in support of this position includes how the virus has shown that there is no substitute for a well-resourced and responsive state. It has also offered unequivocal proof that universal and inclusive public health systems are a necessary public good, the absence of which puts us all at risk. Progressives see a more inclusive and just social contract in the future, a 'new' New Deal.

Others, more pessimistically, see this moment as marking the end of the current era of globalisation and prefiguring a return to increased inter-state competition. In this view, our highly interconnected world has acted as an unwitting vector of the pandemic by furthering and multiplying the spread of the virus; the crisis has shown the limits of international cooperation and multilateral institutions; dependence on international supply chains and just-in-time logistical systems have left countries more vulnerable than they would be otherwise. These, pessimists argue, are the main lessons national governments will take away from the crisis and augur a moment of relative international autarky.

For those who do not see much real change coming (even as they view the current moment as a major crisis), again two positions are discernible. Pessimists read the pandemic in terms of disaster capitalism, to borrow Naomi Klein's (2007) term, a moment which powerful private interests will exploit to further strengthen themselves. They look to the outcomes of previous crises, especially the 2008 financial crisis and 9/11. These antecedents show that due to their material resources and privileged access to information, entrenched vested interests are more able than others to take advantage of the disruptions caused by a crisis. The top 1 per cent will emerge from the pandemic strengthened, they predict, reinforcing what is already a deeply unequal world, with all its resultant tensions and contradictions.

There is another group that also does not see this crisis as a turning point, albeit for a very different reason. They see this moment instead as the latest challenge to the power of human ingenuity. For them, innovation materialised as technology is the answer. This group is the most optimistic of all, viewing this moment as only a temporary setback in the long struggle of humans over their environment. If, in the past, we have found answers to deadly diseases such as polio and smallpox, sent men to the moon and beyond, and explored the deepest depths of the ocean, why will we not do so again? The only limit to human imagination for these optimists is a lack of confidence and faith in the ability of humans to overcome all problems. In short, this crisis will be weathered by a technological fix, something far easier to imagine and implement than the social upheavals implicit in other visions of the future.

What we have are four future scenarios offered by, respectively, pro-state progressive optimists, end-of-globalisation pessimists, disaster capitalism pessimists and techno-optimists. Stepping back, we can see that each of these positions has its strong points; indeed, all of them may well turn out to be correct in some settings and to some extent.

These views must, however, be set against what we know about the pandemic, which, to be honest, is still very little. At best we can say confidently that, first, the Covid-19 pandemic is not a 'black swan' event; it is better characterised as a 'known unknown' that experts knew was coming but did not know when or how it would manifest itself. Second, this pandemic is not a natural disaster, it is a man-made event for two primary reasons. These are, first, the enforced proximity of wild animals to humans for commercial purposes in the now-notorious Wuhan 'wet market', and second, the mismanagement of the situation once it was realised that a new virus had 'crossed over' to infect human populations. Third, the pandemic constitutes a crisis that has no discernable end. Hence, rather than calling it a moment, it should be considered an ongoing historical *process*. Finally, while the pandemic is indifferent to our usual fault lines of national origin, class, ethnicity, religion and sexuality (but not age and gender), its effects are felt unevenly around the world due to existing social fault lines and prior resource endowments. Given these minimalist starting points, what can be said about these four scenarios?

Progressive Optimists

That a trusted, well-functioning and inclusive public health system can save lives is evident from the South Korean and Taiwanese experiences. Both cases join a highly responsive state apparatus with a population long disciplined to follow public health mandates. But this desirable outcome was far from inevitable. Korea's current system is the result of decades of popular struggle wearing down the infrastructure of an authoritarian state, repeatedly calling governments to account, including most recently jailing a former president for corruption.

The missing piece in the predictions of progressive optimists, in other words, is the necessity for popular mobilisation around a message of universal inclusion. This call needs to be combined with constant vigilance from an empowered civil society that holds governments of all political leanings to account when they fail to deliver social goods at a high level of efficiency. Countries with a politically engaged middle class, *weak* political party systems, and a state apparatus that can reach across the 'last mile' are more likely to succeed in this task than others. Given these (relatively rare) conditions, the likelihood of these very desirable changes is low. Actual outcomes are likely to vary enormously around the world.

End-of-globalisation Pessimists

The end-of-globalisation pessimists predict a rolling back of global interconnectedness and the promotion of national self-sufficiency as a result of lessons learned from this crisis. The ongoing competition between a declining US and a rising China is only likely to be exacerbated following the reduced virulence of the pandemic, suggesting that the prospects of greater (and much needed) international cooperation and coordination at the global level are less likely.

Faced with the intensification of international competition, countries will feel the need to diversify their international supply chains and to promote domestic capacities and national champions. Costs of goods will rise as a result, while global remittances are likely to decline alongside international trade and tourism. National resource monopolies will become useful points of leverage. Few countries, however, have the population size, resource base or depth of human capital to implement an autarkic strategy on a national scale.

Some countries will choose—or be forced—to align with the US, others with China, in return for privileged access to markets and aid. Others may opt for a strategy of greater *regionalisation* to compensate for limited national resource endowments. The tensions between pressures for alignment and regionalisation are most likely to be visible in regions that have long been associated with one or another hegemon while also having an established history of cooperation with their neighbours, namely South America and Southeast Asia.

With the passage of time, a new era of globalisation will undoubtedly emerge, yet without resolving the question that obsesses the geopolitically minded: who's on top? Rather, we are in for what Antonio Gramsci called the interregnum, a moment when the old is dying and the new not yet born. This is a period of turmoil without recourse to stable norms and standards, exhibiting a variety of what he called 'morbid symptoms'.

Disaster Capitalism Pessimists

Disaster capitalism pessimists particularly have in mind the United States. The US might well be the most extreme example of a rich country that consigns those on the bottom end of the social scale to an entirely different morbidity profile than those at the top, but this trend is visible wherever the ideology of neoliberalism has taken root. This pessimistic projection relies heavily on conclusions drawn from the experience of recent economic crises and the 9/11 attacks. In 2008, for example, those who were most responsible for the economic crisis saw private losses bailed out by public funds, with few individual sanctions and little structural change. In the case of 9/11, an elite cabal was able to seize the opportunity to carry out a programme of massive geopolitical transformation based on an empirically flawed, ideologically grounded set of beliefs. In both examples, the instigators and the deadly aftermath of their actions are still with us, decades later. Could this moment inaugurate instead another New Deal, rather than more of the same?

In the US, the critical moment will be the elections scheduled for November 2020. If the American people can be induced to vote their interests rather than their fears and aspirations, for Congress as well as the presidency, elite capture of the crisis may well be averted. However, it must be remembered that this pandemic is not a 'one-off' crisis, similar to the historical antecedents already mentioned. The pandemic has no obvious end-point, *even after a vaccine is successfully tested and made available universally.*

We have few modern precedents for how the world will come to terms with this novel condition of a crisis with no end. The closest analogy might be the threat of total nuclear annihilation that characterised the Cold War. While we may have gotten used to 'living with the bomb', this existential threat also generated transnational political alliances that created nuclear-free zones, campaigns to end nuclear testing, and most recently, an international convention (treaty) against nuclear weapons. What the global anti-nuclear movement showed and shows is not only that the majority of the world abhors nuclear weapons: it also demonstrates that global public opinion did and will shape futures too.

Drawing from this experience, it becomes clear that what is indispensable for a less unequal future is the consolidation of a transnational political movement that disavows entirely the 'common sense' of neoliberal ideology. Neoliberalism must be replaced with a new standard, namely a people-centric vision of a sustainable economic future. The anti-nuclear movement offers hope that such an outcome is possible, even as its limits suggest this model may not be enough to ensure meaningful and universal change.

Techno-optimists

The final group of futurists are the techno-optimists. Their vision of the future is based on a Whiggish reading of the past, which sees human society as always improving due to the development and application of novel technological solutions. From Karl Marx to Elon Musk, measuring human progress by the advance of technology becomes a convincing portrayal of how crises are opportunistic triggers for new peaks of human endeavour. The march of technology, they propose, has managed to find solutions to problems ranging from food shortages to deadly diseases.

While true at one level, there are huge gaps in this seductive account. In medicine, for example, treating rare cancers takes priority over finding vaccines for malaria, while in agriculture, increasing gross output of foodgrains takes precedence over sustainable methods and the survival of small landholders. The technological fetish has, in general, led to public policies that forego addressing root causes in favour of solutions that do not question existing structures of inequality and unfairness. This leads to the reinforcement of existing social hierarchies even as the pandemic shows itself to be stunningly non-discriminatory in practice.

The power of the pandemic comes from its unequivocal demonstration that no one is beyond the reach of the virus. It does not consider national origin, class, caste, ethnicity or sexuality in its effects (gender and age appear to matter, however, with men and the elderly more likely to be affected). Even so, some social groups are more likely to be afflicted than others due to the imposition of all-too-familiar logics of difference and hierarchy. These fault lines become visible when politicians propose that the elderly should sacrifice themselves for the good of the young, when countries follow a strategy of 'herd immunity', which, in the absence of a vaccine, forgoes universal testing and treatment for the 'natural selection' of the fittest, when millions of migrant workers are sent home without protection, when people living in slums are expected to adopt social distancing, or when some regions of a country are preferred over others in the supply of necessary medical equipment. Almost everywhere, we find that the powerful and well-connected are more likely to be able to get tested and treated promptly. It is particularly telling that it is only when prominent and high-value individuals begin to get infected or die that the scale and severity of the crisis becomes apparent to all and impossible to ignore. These outcomes reflect the strength of the social divisions in our world that even a non-discriminatory virus finds hard to overturn, technological virtuosity notwithstanding.

Turning from absences to actions. Techno-optimists rightly describe the twentieth century as a series of stunning 'victories' over disease, from polio to HIV. But this account also excludes critical elements, the absence of which tells a very different story.

Consider the HIV epidemic, another zoonotic event of the recent past. First associated with a stigmatised community and their allegedly debauched lifestyle, the scope and scale of the HIV epidemic was long obscured due to a biased, uneven and haphazard public health response. It took years for the virus to be seen as a health crisis that was not restricted to gay men and to be correctly understood as a global issue. Public anger at state inaction led to radically new forms of activism, which raised public awareness of the HIV crisis through dramatic demonstrations. Social movements such as the AIDS Coalition to Unleash Power (ACT-UP) even played a part in improving the medical response by constructively breaking down the boundary of expertise, separating expert from layman and doctor from patient.

Eventually, the scale of the problem was realised, funding improved, and anti-retrovirals generated following a long and complex lab and clinical testing process. This led to an affordable drugs regimen being approved that allowed people with AIDS to survive infection and stay alive. This hugely positive outcome was far from guaranteed. It required a confrontation between Western pharmaceutical companies and national governments around the world. Indian generic drug manufacturers played an important role in making a life-saving cocktail available cheaply. South Africa and Brazil used sovereign powers to make these drugs available to their afflicted populations, overturning international norms in the process. There is, however, one more lesson to be drawn from the HIV-AIDS crisis, beyond indifference, bias, poor public health management and the value of social movements. HIV-AIDS may be under control, but it is not over.

This pandemic is likely to be like HIV in this respect. Covid-19 may come under control when a vaccine is found, but the crisis will not be over. Techno-optimists will claim the end of the pandemic with the arrival of a viable vaccine. It will not be.

Conclusions

First, in the absence of concerted social action within and across national boundaries, the likelihood of change in the direction of inclusion and fairness, however desirable and possible, is very low. Due to the power of vested interests and the social tendency to fear any alteration of the status quo, even a world-historic turning point (from the standpoint of exposing human vulnerabilities) may not change very much.

Second, what is unique about the Covid-19 pandemic is its lack of discrimination and universality of reach, joined with the absence of a distinct end-point to the crisis. What is *not* different is the unevenness of who is affected and who suffers more. This crisis is not a historic moment or 'turning point', as much as it is a historical process. The difficulty of coming to terms with this ongoing crisis in its fullness comes from the complexity of intersections of these three characteristics: universal, endless and uneven.

Reference

Klein, Naomi. 2007. *The Shock Doctrine: The Rise of Disaster Capitalism*. London: Allen Lane.

24

Seven Lessons for the Future

*For the World after Covid-19**

Prem Chandavarkar

Reflecting on the experience thus far of the Covid-19 pandemic, I propose seven lessons we must learn for the world we need to build after it is over.

Markets Cannot be the Primary Backbone

Ever since the late twentieth century, the democratic world has largely been reorganised around a set of neoliberal beliefs that posit: (i) the self-organising capability of markets is more efficient than any form of centralised control; (ii) government embodies centralised control, making it inherently inefficient; and therefore, (iii) the state must retreat into a minimal role that leaves as much as possible to markets. This logic is even extended to social goods such as health and education, and an earlier era of state responsibility for these goods is giving way to increasing reliance on the private sector. The state's primary obligation shifts from reducing uneven development by redistributing wealth to enhancing the global competitiveness of private enterprise.

The pandemic has exposed some structural fault lines in these assumptions. Markets, because of their short-term orientation and poor accounting of externalised costs (such as environmental degradation and inequality), are poorly positioned to organise and

* First published in *The India Forum*, 15 May 2020.

allocate social goods. Moreover, markets orient towards efficiency rather than resilience and are therefore powerless when things go wrong at a systemic level. A healthcare infrastructure that aims to work at close to 90 per cent efficiency (as any commercial enterprise would seek to do) contains insufficient resilience to deal with a substantive shift in healthcare needs, let alone a pandemic. The consequent helplessness of markets under current circumstances sees them desperately crying out for assistance from a state hitherto dismissed as inefficient.

This does not mean completely eschewing free markets. It is just that we need to reverse our priorities. In his classic text, *The Great Transformation* (1971), Karl Polanyi points out that while markets have existed since time immemorial, the subordination of society to markets is a relatively recent phenomenon that is not found before the industrial revolution. This privileging of markets has led to the construction of fictitious commodities, where the components of markets are treated as if that is all they are meant to be, ignoring their entanglement with social and ecological contexts that lie beyond the reach of markets.

Land gets reduced to an asset, and its links in memory, culture and environment go unrecognised by the economy. Lives get reduced to labour, and if there is no demand for labour, lives go unrecognised. Polanyi argues that this fiction of markets leading society provokes a countermovement of social protectionism that begins to dominate politics, so the claim of efficient markets remains a myth that never existed in reality. Looking ahead, we may leverage the potential energy in free markets, but we must always contextualise them so that they are subordinate to society.

We have granted this privileged position to markets invoking Adam Smith's famous metaphor of 'the invisible hand', arguing that that they are efficient because of their capacity to self-organise. But this does not mean it is markets alone that have this capacity, and the principles of self-organisation can also be effectively applied to social and political realms. The mechanisms we have needed to call on to deal with the pandemic shine light on what should be the primary backbone: (i) resilient localised infrastructures of care; (ii) high degrees of citizen engagement and participation; (iii) the foregrounding of expertise under conditions of high transparency and accountability; and (iv) the stewardship of the state where maximising public health and welfare is the primary concern. The states that have most effectively dealt with the pandemic while laying the grounds for a resilient future are the ones who have adopted these measures.

We Need an Inclusive Politics of Recognition

The pandemic has exposed another fault line in the failure by society to adequately recognise large sections of the population. These are the segment of people labelled as 'the precariat', a term that arose in the 1980s to describe those whose employment and incomes are insecure, who are dependent on daily earnings for their basic sustenance, who are not granted secure access to food, healthcare and education, and who are exposed to the greatest hardship when the economy slows down. Under neoliberalism, the precariat has been forming a larger and larger percentage of the population, especially in recent years. Their condition gets heightened in conditions like a pandemic, when their tales of hardship become visible as their collective volume becomes difficult to ignore.

The pandemic has shown that the precariat cannot be so easily disregarded behind 'does-not-affect-me' blinkers. Their manual labour is crucial to the continued operation of many businesses, public services and other sectors of work, so their presence cannot be eliminated. They often live in low-quality housing in conditions where it is difficult, if not impossible, to practise mitigating measures such as physical distancing or take sanitation precautions. This then affects the entire population given that a virus does not respect boundaries of class or geography.

Two situations observed in India show how the elite are also affected by the failure to recognise the precariat:

- Government of India imposed a nation-wide lockdown to control the spread of the novel coronavirus, but the system had neither the knowledge base nor the mindset to forecast the impact of this lockdown on wage labourers who had migrated to cities and other areas of greater prosperity and opportunity. Deprived of any social safety net where they worked, these workers had no choice but to immediately embark on long journeys to their villages where they could draw on support from local kinship structures. A lockdown meant to contain the virus by suppressing the movement of people undermined its efficacy by sparking a large-scale migration.

- Indian cities are managed by paradigms of urban planning and land markets that impose high values on all the land parcels delineated in a master plan. This sets up thresholds of affordability that disqualify half or more of the urban population who are without the means to officially locate themselves on a land-use plan. They are forced by the official paradigm of urban and economic planning to live outside it, consequently pushed into informal housing such as slums and unregulated layouts. There the insecurity of tenure forces them to continue living in low-quality built environments. Since they form a substantive percentage of the urban population, the spatial discontinuities that ensue prevent the efficient functioning of urban services such as electricity, water and traffic.

A country is able to survive with low levels of citizen recognition through one or a combination of two strategies: (i) the use of autocratic structures of repression that do not permit the unrecognised (or the non-conformist) to have a voice and/or (ii) offering consistently high rates of economic growth where the payoff, even if unequal or not immediate, is considered by all to be worthwhile.

Where only the first strategy is deployed, continuity is based on sustaining the current structures of power through tight control. History has shown that control over the long term is difficult to achieve, and once change gains a foothold, it rapidly destabilises the regime.

When both strategies are deployed in conjunction, the pandemic has introduced vulnerability by upending the expectation of consistent economic growth, at least for the next few years. It will be interesting to see what happens in those countries where the structure provides economic freedom while constraining political freedom. The genie of economic freedom cannot be put back into the bottle, and without the backing of economic growth, can a strategy of political repression survive on its own?

People may be forgiving of low levels of political recognition that are counterbalanced by high levels of economic recognition. When low GDP growth destabilises economic recognition, then marginalisation across the board is perceived, and dissatisfaction and dissent can erupt. For long-term resilience, society must achieve high degrees of recognition on all fronts.

In their book, *The Spirit Level: Why Equality is Better for Everyone* (2010), Kate Pickett and Richard Wilkinson show a strong correlation between high levels of inequality and poor scores on public health. This applies across rich and poor countries, occurring because inequality erodes social trust, increases anxiety and illness, and encourages excessive consumption. A quest for higher equality should not entail a communist mindset that seeks to reduce everyone to the same status, for there is sufficient evidence to prove that such a strategy is doomed to failure. As Amartya Sen (1999) and many other development economists have argued (Osmani 2017), policy should be driven by equality of rights and opportunity rather than equality of status. This will be possible only when governance is structured on an inclusive politics of recognition.

Local Government is the Core

The pandemic has shown that feet on the ground and on-the-spot assessment are crucial in creating resilience. This is the only means by which the situation can be dealt with, whether it is in providing healthcare or in making the assessment to classify neighbourhoods by the extent of spread of infection in order to devise appropriate containment strategies. While aggregating data on a large scale is important for discerning wider patterns, the reliability of the data and the successful implementation of any response are only possible by a close linkage between governance and citizenry at a decentralised level. The last mile problem is not confined to communication networks, it also applies to government and can be resolved only by resilient localised systems.

Decentralised governance offers greater visibility of government, promotes higher degrees of citizen participation and enables the greatest sensitivity to local nuances. A decentralised system would operate by the principle of subsidiarity that allocates subsidiary functions to the central authority. Under this principle, the local level does the maximum possible, and what cannot be achieved at its scale is delegated to the next higher level, which also operates by the same principle. This model of bottom-up delegation must replace the top-down model that prevails in most countries.

Our Relationship with Nature Must be Harmonious

Kate Raworth (2017) argues that our development model assumes an economy that must grow whether or not we thrive, whereas we need an economy that makes us thrive whether or not it grows. The problem occurs because we measure our economy narrowly by the visibility of financial and physical flows within it, rather than in broader terms of public welfare or ecological stability.

Raworth proposes the model of a doughnut as a visualisation of how we should measure our economy. A set of public welfare indicators form radial spokes in the doughnut, and each indicator is assessed on two counts: the inner ring of the doughnut that indicates a social foundation below which it must not fall and the outer ring that represents an ecological threshold it must not cross. It will be interesting to watch the city of Amsterdam and the results of its recent decision to adopt this doughnut model for its post-pandemic economy (Boffey 2020).

While the methodological protocols by which such a model could be implemented require much more thought and research, the model is important. The inner ring of social foundations is tied to the politics of recognition mentioned above. And the outer ring of an ecological threshold is linked to many ecological crises that we must face. There is the spectre of climate change that looms over us, and many of our cities are plagued by levels of pollution that damage health and shorten lives.

But it is not just climate change and pollution that are of concern; the coronavirus is also a consequence of our problematic relationship with nature. Our economic model, in its quest for unending growth, catalyses support for certain business typologies such as mining, logging, and biases the economy of meat, dairy and agricultural products toward large-scale business. This promotes substantive intrusions into the natural world, deprives many species of their natural habitats, and enforces a closer proximity between humans and wild animals, consequently creating fertile grounds for the propagation of zoonotic viruses.

SARS-CoV-2 is a zoonotic virus, and we have seen an increase in the rate of incidence of zoonotic viruses in the last few decades. It is well within the realm of possibilities that the pandemic that currently plagues us may never have occurred under an economic paradigm that was ecologically sustainable.

In a classic (yet largely neglected paper), written in 1966 and titled 'The Economics of the Coming Spaceship Earth', economist/ philosopher Kenneth E. Boulding argues that there are two kinds of economics we can practise: cowboy economics and spaceship economics. Our current economic paradigm, in its expectation of continued growth, operates on the metaphor of the cowboy who assumes he is in a vast and unlimited plain, and looks to continually expand the frontiers of his homestead on that plain.

The other kind of economics uses the metaphor of a spaceship to illuminate how, within such a closed capsule, no astronaut can embark on any action without taking into account the impact of his/her action on fellow astronauts. Boulding argues that a planet is a relatively closed system of matter, energy and information, and our choice of economic paradigm must start with acknowledging this fact. An open system can rely on measuring its performance in terms of throughput, which is why we depend on a measure of GDP in assessing our economies. This fiction of an open system fails to comprehend the limits of the system and consequently dismisses the impact that inputs and outputs have.

In our obsession with throughput, we make inadequate effort to differentiate between those inputs that are exhaustible and those that are renewable. And we fail to account for the feedback effects that outputs have on the system. In contrast, in a closed system we are acutely aware of the limits of the system. Both inputs and outputs are acknowledged as being constituents and must be evaluated in relation to the entire capital stock that constitutes the system. The focus shifts from throughput to maintaining the quantity, quality and harmony of the capital stock.

This necessarily means taking a far longer-term view than the current paradigm asks us to. Boulding admits this is challenging for it is difficult to answer the man who asks, 'What has posterity ever done for me?', and the conservationist tends to offer vague ethical responses that carry little weight in the situation. Boulding asks us to recognise that the welfare of individuals depends substantially on the extent to which they can identify with others. The most satisfactory individual identity is one that is anchored within a community, not just in space but also extending over time from the past into the future.

There is sufficient historical evidence that a society that loses its identity with posterity loses its positive image of the future, consequently losing a perspective within which present problems can be evaluated and tackled. Such a society soon falls apart. We have considerable self-interest in posterity and must therefore consider its ecological dimensions within our economic paradigm.

Local Business Must be the Foundation of Economic Policy

The vulnerability in depending on global supply chains is revealed during a pandemic. But this is far more than a matter of self-reliance. We currently have an economic paradigm that revolves around the ownership of capital. This in itself is problematic, for as Thomas Piketty (2014) has demonstrated with depth of evidence, in a system that relies on capital, the rate of return on capital tends to be higher than the rate of economic growth. This benefits the owners of capital, making the system tend towards increasing levels of inequality.

Economic policy is consequently rigged in favour of big banks and large corporates with passive shareholders. Survival is harder for small and local businesses that provide goods and services in a sustainable way with a higher percentage of the population participating in the creation of economic value. The dominance of finance encourages marketing strategies that seduce the middle class into higher levels of debt, increasing vulnerability across the system. Finally, the focus on increasing capital value starts reaching a stage where the tail begins to wag the dog. Profits are ploughed into share buybacks or dividends rather than investment in productive renewal. Management performance is judged on short-term measures of profit, share value and market share, rather than long-term sustainability.

Networks of local businesses are more tuned to the nuances of regional culture and ecology. They also circulate value within the community rather than sucking it out in the way global corporates tend to do. This is not to say that large businesses must have no place in the system, but to argue that both politics and economics must operate on the principle of subsidiarity.

In Relationships, Quantity Time is Quality Time

Shifting now to the personal front: for those of us who have the luxury of a home we can be secure within and with the financial means to survive periods of lockdown, we suddenly find more time to spend at home than we have in the past. This gives us an opportunity to reflect on the displacement of valuable relationships from our life. There is also a growing incidence of people thinking of others they have not devoted time to and reaching out over phone or video chat in order to reconnect. And those who have the company of loved ones within the home have an opportunity to feel the value of intimacy and reflection in an abundance they have not known for a long time.

When there is a pressure on time, we feel that the few moments away from work that are possible must be evaluated by the intensity of pleasure they give us. We seek refuge in entertainment, restaurants, bars and other experiences offering heightened pleasure. We situate our relationships within this quest for the adrenaline of pleasure, giving scant time to open-ended existence with others where no explicit purpose is foregrounded. But now, deprived of alternatives, we are spending that kind of time and discovering the power of serendipity.

Imagine walking through a beautiful garden. We may acknowledge its beauty in our first walk through it, but when we repeatedly walk through the same garden we start to appreciate the nuance and detail we did not see in our first stroll, and we are awestruck by the way the garden changes across the seasons. The depth of our experience increases as we invest more time in it. This happens in our relationships with people as well as in relationships with the neighbourhoods we inhabit.

In Milan Kundera's philosophical novel *Slowness* (1997), he speaks about our addiction to speed, our neglect of slowness, and cites a Czech proverb that talks about allowing for time to spend in gazing at god's windows. We must recognise that the people we live with and the places we inhabit are all forms of god's windows that would have evaded our perception if we had not invested in the quantities of slow time that gave us the opportunity to watch them with a gaze of wonder devoid of expectation or judgement.

The Priorities in Our Lives Must Begin within Us

We have become embedded in a system where our priorities are predicated either on idiosyncratic personal whim or on external rationalisations. Subjective whim does not bind us as a society. And a faith in pervasive rationality blinds us to the manner in which private claims compete to define the public interest. We consequently get seduced by political rhetoric that disconnects us from the wisdom that our bodies inherently contain.

In the book, *Walking on the Pastures of Wonder* (2015), John O'Donohue, in a series of conversations with John Quinn, talks about this inner wisdom we all possess that is revealed in everyday acts. Even the act of speech, which we habitually and unthinkingly carry out on a routine basis, shows a creative capacity where, from out of the silence within, we coax sound and meaning. All of us exhibit this creative capacity in so many other daily acts: walking, dancing, singing, laughing, cooking, thinking. This creativity is so powerful that we must dedicate effort towards acquiring the capability to harness it. When this rigour is absent, we fail to come to terms with our own inner wisdom, and our consequent existential anxiety persuades us to look elsewhere.

O'Donohue (2015: 15) observes: 'One of the sad things is that so many people are frightened by the wonder of their own presence. They are dying to tie themselves into a system, a role, an image or a predetermined identity that other people have actually settled for them.'

Our reliance on externalities shifts our focus from wisdom to knowledge, and the reductivity of this shift deeply damages and destabilises our social and ecological fabric. This predicament is captured by Julio Ollala in his book, *From Knowledge to Wisdom: Essays on the Crisis in Contemporary Learning* (2004), in a passage which says:

> Knowledge has become another possession and therefore it has also become the object of greed. Wisdom, on the contrary cannot be a possession. It cannot be traded, regulated or registered. It cannot be owned by any individual, because it lives in a territory that is not solely human, it is shared with the gods. Wisdom is not what we know about the world, it is what the world discloses for us. If knowledge can live in greed, wisdom can only live in gratitude. If knowledge belongs to thought, wisdom belongs to the soul. If knowledge creates silos and divisions, wisdom integrates. If knowledge is knowing about it, wisdom is being it ... Wisdom has a sense of timing and relevance that is mostly hidden to knowledge. Knowledge may deny meaning, wisdom is inseparable from it. Knowledge lives in the mental domain, wisdom also lives in soul and spirit.

Wisdom is an inner spirit that removes our existential anxieties by revealing our place in a world that is already enchanted with meaning. Our consciousness of it can never be adequately articulated in words or external rationalities. It can only be embodied by us, either in the bonds of affection and harmony that we continually re-enact with others and our environment, or in the arts, songs, poetry and other metaphoric forms we breathe life into.

A political economy that has no recognition of inner wisdom will always distort us into false myths that do not resonate with our inner being. If we wish to form a society that is resilient, just and fulfilling, the search must begin within.

References

Boffey, Daniel 2020. 'Amsterdam to Embrace "Doughnut" Model to Mend Post-coronavirus Economy'. *The Guardian*, 8 April. Available at https://

www.theguardian.com/world/2020/apr/08/amsterdam-doughnut-model-mend-post-coronavirus-economy (accessed 1 April 2020).

Boulding, Kenneth E. 1966. 'The Economics of the Coming Spaceship Earth'. Paper presented at the Sixth Resources for the Future Forum on Environmental Quality in a Growing Economy in Washington, D.C., 8 March. Available at http://www.zo.utexas.edu/courses/THOC/Boulding_SpaceshipEarth.pdf (accessed 1 April 2020).

Kundera, Milan. 1997. *Slowness*. London: Faber and Faber.

O'Donohue, John and John Quinn. 2015. *Walking on the Pastures of Wonder*. Dublin: Veritas.

Olalla, Julio. 2004. *From Knowledge to Wisdom: Essays on the Crisis in Contemporary Learning*. Boulder, CO: Newfield Network.

Osmani, S. R. 2017. 'The Capability Approach and Human Development: Some Reflections'. United Nations Development Programme Human Development Reports, April. Available at http://hdr.undp.org/en/content/capability-approach-and-human-development-some-reflections (accessed 1 April 2020).

Pickett, Richard and Kate Wilkinson. 2010. *The Spirit Level: Why Equality is Better for Everyone*. London: Penguin Books.

Piketty, Thomas. 2014. *Capital in the Twenty-first Century*. Cambridge, MA: Belknap Press.

Polanyi, Karl. 1971. *The Great Transformation: The Economic and Political Origins of Our Time*. Boston: Beacon Press.

Raworth, Kate. 2017. *Doughnut Economics: Seven Ways to Think Like a 21st Century Economist*. Vermont: Chelsea Green Publishing.

Sen, Amartya. 1999. *Development as Freedom*. New York: Alfred A. Knopf.

Notes on the Contributors

Itty Abraham is Professor and Head of the Department of Southeast Asian Studies, National University of Singapore.

Rosa Abraham is Research Fellow, Azim Premji University, Bengaluru.

Thomas Abraham is Adjunct Associate Professor, University of Hong Kong.

Prerna Agarwal is Teaching Fellow, Department of History, Ashoka University.

Faizi Ahmad is Assistant Editor (Digital), *The India Forum*.

Amit Basole is Associate Professor of Economics, Azim Premji University.

Pratiksha Baxi is Associate Professor, Centre for the Study of Law and Governance, Jawaharlal Nehru University.

Upendra Baxi is Emeritus Professor of Law, Universities of Warwick and Delhi.

Pratik Chakrabarti is Chair in History of Science and Medicine, and Director, Centre for the History of Science, Technology and Medicine, University of Manchester.

Gorky Chakraborty is faculty member, Institute of Development Studies Kolkata.

Prem Chandavarkar is an architect in Bangalore, writing, speaking and blogging on architecture, urbanism, philosophy, politics, education, environment and art.

C. P. Chandrasekhar retired as Professor, Centre for Economic Studies and Planning, Jawaharlal Nehru University.

Naorem Pushparani Chanu is a PhD scholar, Institute of Development Studies Kolkata.

Sheetal Chhabria is Associate Professor of History at Connecticut College, the United States.

Maitreesh Ghatak is Professor of Economics, London School of Economics.

Radhicka Kapoor is Senior Fellow, Indian Council for Research on International Economic Relations, New Delhi.

Surbhi Kesar is Research Fellow, Azim Premji University.

C. J. Kuncheria is Deputy Editor, *The India Forum*.

Rahul Lahoti is Visiting Faculty, Azim Premji University.

Nomaan Majid is a member of ILO's Decent Work Team for South Asia.

Harsh Mander is a human rights and peace worker, writer, and teacher, and works with survivors of mass violence and hunger, homeless persons and street children.

R. Nagaraj is Visiting Fellow, Centre for Development Studies, Thiruvananthapuram.

Gayatri Nair teaches Sociology at Indraprastha Institute of Information Technology, Delhi.

Harish Naraindas is Professor of Sociology, Jawaharlal Nehru University, and Honorary Professor, Alfred Deakin Institute, Deakin University.

Paaritosh Nath is Research Fellow, Azim Premji University.

Honey Oberoi Vahali is a psychoanalyst, and Professor of Psychology, School of Human Studies, Ambedkar University Delhi.

Vikram Patel is Pershing Square Professor of Global Health, Harvard Medical School.

K. Sujatha Rao retired as Health Secretary to the Government of India.

M. Govinda Rao was a member of the Fourteenth Finance Commission, and is a former Director, National Institute of Public Finance and Policy, New Delhi.

Debraj Ray is Silver Professor, Faculty of Arts and Science, and Professor of Economics, New York University, and part-time Professor, University of Warwick.

C. Rammanohar Reddy is Editor, *The India Forum*.

Ananda Lal Roy is a biomedical scientist, Bethesda, the United States.

Ramprasad Sengupta is Emeritus Professor of Economics, Jawaharlal Nehru University.

Navsharan Singh is a feminist researcher.

S. Subramanian retired as Professor, Madras Institute of Development Studies, and is a former Indian Council of Social Science Research National Fellow.

Lore Vandewalle is Associate Professor, Department of Economics, and Pictet Chair for Finance and Development, Graduate Institute, Geneva.